The British System of Government

by the same author

Federalism, Finance, and Social Legislation

Small-Town Politics

Representative and Responsible Government

Representation

Political Integration and Disintegration in the British Isles

Nationalism and National Integration

The British System of Government

ANTHONY H. BIRCH

London
UNWIN HYMAN
Boston   Sydney   Wellington

Published by the Academic Division of

Unwin Hyman Ltd
15/17 Broadwick Street, London W1V 1FP, UK

Unwin Hyman Inc.,
8 Winchester Place, Winchester, Mass. 01890, USA

Allen & Unwin (Australia) Ltd,
8 Napier Street, North Sydney, NSW 2060, Australia

Allen & Unwin (New Zealand) Ltd in association with the
Port Nicholson Press Ltd,
Compusales Building, 75 Ghuznee Street, Wellington 1, New Zealand

First published in 1967
Eighth edition 1990

British Library Cataloguing in Publication Data

Birch, A. H.
The British system of government – 7th ed.
1. Great Britain – Politics and government – 1979–
I. Title
354.41   JN231
ISBN 0 04 445256 X

Library of Congress Cataloging in Publication Data

Birch. Anthony Harold
The British system of government.
Bibliography: p.
Includes index.
1. Great Britain – Politics and government – 1945–
I. Title
JN231.B57   1986   320.941   85–22977
ISBN 0 04 445256 X

Typeset in 10 on 12 point Century by
Computape (Pickering) Ltd, North Yorkshire
and printed in Great Britain by
the University Press, Cambridge

To Peter and Tanya

Contents

Contents

Part V: The Citizen and the Government

Tables

Preface to the Eighth Edition

This book has been extensively revised for this edition, to take account of the numerous developments in British politics since the seventh edition was prepared in 1985. In addition, I have added an entirely new chapter on the conduct of British foreign policy.

For their help on particular questions I should like to thank Professors Geoffrey Alderman of the University of London and Richard Powers of the University of Victoria. I am also, as always, very grateful to my wife Dorothy for her support and assistance.

Victoria, B.C.   A. H. Birch
1989

Abbreviations

AA	Automobile Association
BBC	British Broadcasting Corporation
BMA	British Medical Association
CND	Campaign for Nuclear Disarmament
ESRC	Economic and Social Research Council
GDP	Gross domestic product
IRA	Irish Republican Army
MP	Member of Parliament
NATO	North Atlantic Treaty Organization
NCCL	National Council for Civil Liberties
NEC	National Executive Committee (Labour Party)
NFU	National Farmers' Union
NUM	National Union of Mineworkers
PC	Plaid Cymru
PLP	Parliamentary Labour Party
PPS	Parliamentary Private Secretary
PR	Proportional Representation
RAC	Royal Automobile Club
RSPCA	Royal Society for the Prevention of Cruelty to Animals
RUC	Royal Ulster Constabulary
SDLP	Social Democratic and Labour Party (Northern Ireland)
SDP	Social Democratic Party
SNP	Scottish National Party
UK	United Kingdom

Part I
The Social Basis

◇ 1 ◇

British Society and the British People

This book is concerned with the nature of British political institutions and the way in which they operate. Both the institutions and their mode of operation have been shaped to a large extent by the nature of the society in which they have developed, and they reflect and embody the habits and assumptions of the people who operate them. This is a general truth about political systems that applies not only to the government of Britain but also to the government of other nations; and not only to the government of nations but also to the government of small societies within nations. It can be seen as clearly as anywhere in the government of voluntary societies. Thus, student organizations tend to be ultra-democratic because students dislike authority, and to have elaborate rules of order because of the ingenuity with which student politicians exploit any ambiguity or loophole in the rules. Church organizations, on the other hand, tend to be dominated by a few leading personalities and to have very loose rules of procedure that reflect the belief that relations between members should be characterized by mutual trust and good faith. Nations are similar to voluntary societies in this respect; how they are governed depends to a large extent on the beliefs and habits of their citizens and the social relations between them. The most appropriate introduction to a study of British government is therefore a short discussion of some of the salient characteristics of British society and the British people.

The Component Parts of British Society

The term 'Britain' is slightly ambiguous, being used sometimes as a shorthand equivalent of the political entity called the United Kingdom of Great Britain and Northern Ireland, sometimes as a short version of the social entity called Great Britain, and frequently (by the English) as a synonym for England. As 83 per cent of the people of the United Kingdom live in England, the whole political system is heavily influenced by the charter of English society. However, as the state is, strictly speaking, multinational, it is appropriate to begin by saying a word about Ireland, Wales and Scotland.

3

Ireland is best regarded as England's oldest colony, having been invaded by the English in the twelfth century and governed in colonial fashion until 1800, with a Governor responsible to London and a local Parliament (in the eighteenth century) composed almost entirely of Anglo-Irish landowners and merchants. Between 1800 and 1922 Ireland was legally part of the United Kingdom, and subject to laws passed by the Westminster Parliament. In the latter year, after a limited but bitter campaign of guerrilla warfare, the greater part of Ireland became an independent country known first as the Irish Free State and now as the Irish Republic, leaving the six north-eastern counties as a partially self-governing province of the United Kingdom.

Irish society and Irish politics have always been very different from English society and English politics, and strictly speaking they are outside the scope of this book. However, the political violence that broke out in Northern Ireland in 1969 has been kept within bounds only by a large contingent of British troops, and since 1972 the Belfast Parliament has been suspended and the Province has been governed directly from London. In view of these developments the political character and problems of Northern Ireland will be summarized briefly in an appendix.

Wales, like Ireland, was invaded by the English in the twelfth century. It was politically integrated with England in 1536, and from then onwards the two countries were governed as one, with no significant differences between their political institutions until a measure of decentralization was introduced in 1964.

The social integration of Wales and England has inevitably been a more gradual process than their political integration. Until the nineteenth century the Welsh language was spoken by the great majority of people, although English had been the language of government since 1536 and the Welsh middle classes had adopted both the English language and many aspects of English culture. During the nineteenth century the development of coal-mining and industry in south Wales brought a large influx of English workers, while the development of state education was accompanied by an official campaign to establish English as the universal language of discourse. By 1981 only 19 per cent of the people of Wales claimed any knowledge of Welsh, and it is only in rural areas and a few small towns that the language is used. Traditional Welsh culture has declined along with the language, and it would be easy to conclude that Welsh society will be completely integrated with English society within two or three generations.

Such a conclusion may not be warranted, however. For one thing, a vigorous campaign is being promoted to revive the Welsh language and culture, and the Welsh nationalist party, Plaid Cymru, has had some significant electoral successes since 1967. As a result of its campaigns, the fourth television channel in Wales uses Welsh as its medium. Secondly, there are in fact subtle differences between Welsh and English society, quite apart from the language and the traditional culture of rural Wales. Lacking their own aristocracy, the Welsh tend to be more egalitarian than the English and are considerably more reluctant to vote Conservative. Since the franchise was extended to most working-class men in 1867, the Conservative Party has always had difficulty in winning more than a handful of the Welsh parliamentary constituencies. In the twenty-three elections held between 1900 and 1987, excluding the 'coupon election' of 1918, Conservatives gained an average of 5.9 Welsh seats out of a total that varied between 34 and 38. Until 1922 Wales was overwhelmingly Liberal in sentiment and since then it has been overwhelmingly Labour. In addition, Welsh people tend to show more emotion than the English, and this affects their political attitudes and behaviour. A leading student of Welsh politics has observed that 'Welsh political culture is . . . shot through with Welsh cultural and national values and is thus inherently conducive to anger and conflict' (Madgwick, 1977, pp. 236–7).

The position of Scotland is different again. For several centuries Scotland was an independent state, and when it joined in political union with England and Wales in 1707 it did so by agreement, not by conquest. Moreover, although the Scottish Parliament voted itself out of existence, other Scottish institutions remained intact, including a distinctive legal system, a distinctive (and rather advanced) educational system and the Presbyterian Church of Scotland. With this history, it is not surprising that the Scottish people have a secure sense of national identity, which has survived nearly three centuries of political union with England and is now the basis of a lively nationalist party that seeks to regain Scottish independence.

It follows that there is a real sense in which British society is multinational. However, the differences between England, Wales and Scotland are limited in extent. The Industrial Revolution has had a similar impact on each, and they are all highly urbanized. Engineering is the largest single industry in each. There is a high level of personal mobility between the various parts of Britain, and communication statistics reveal an exceptionally high degree of integration between England and Wales and a considerable degree between England and Scotland (see Birch, 1977, ch. 3). The centralized nature of British government has further reduced the social differences between the various parts of the country.

It is therefore reasonable, in a brief treatment, to outline the characteristics of British society as if it were one society, even though occasional reservations have to be made to allow for Welsh and Scottish differences. Table 1.1 gives some basic facts about the constituent territories, with Northern Ireland included for comparative purposes.

Some Characteristics of British Society

As the resolution of conflicts is one of the main functions of government, the nature of the divisions and cleavages in society has a major influence on the character of the political system. Cleavages vary in kind, and one of the most important lessons to be drawn from a study of politics is that conflicts deriving

Table 1.1 *The Constituent Territories of the UK*

	Population (millions)	Population %	Relative Income per head %	Roman Catholics %	Gaelic speakers %
England	47.4	83.3	102	9	—
Scotland	5.1	9.0	98	16	1.6
Wales	2.8	4.9	87	7	19.0
Northern Ireland	1.6	2.8	78	35	—
United Kingdom	56.9	100.0	100	11	1.1

from linguistic, religious, or racial cleavages are usually more difficult to resolve than conflicts deriving from economic cleavages, whether the latter be between regions of the country or classes within society. There are two reasons for this difference. The first is that people are locked into their linguistic, religious and racial groups, usually having no wish to change even if they could, whereas people can hope to escape from a depressed region or class by individual mobility. If they themselves cannot escape, they can hope that their children will do so. The second reason is that it is easier for governments to mitigate economic conflicts, by a process of incremental adjustment, than it is for them to mitigate linguistic, religious, or racial conflicts.

The contemporary world provides ample evidence for these generalizations. Linguistic conflicts have created constitutional crises in both Belgium and Canada. Religious conflicts have led to prolonged violence in Northern Ireland, Lebanon and India. Racial conflicts have led to riots in American cities and to bloodshed in many African and Asian states. Economic conflicts, though present in all countries, are normally resolved peacefully by bargaining, wage increases, price controls and adjustments to the tax system.

In this perspective, Britain can be counted as fortunate in that modern British society is relatively free from the most troublesome kinds of cleavage. There is no linguistic cleavage in Britain except in some parts of Wales, and as the Welsh-speakers comprise only 1 per cent of the British population (and can virtually all speak English as well) this does not pose a serious threat to political stability. Religious divisions are no longer of any general significance, largely because of the decline of religious conviction. Less than 3 per cent of the population attend church on a normal Sunday, and the attitude of the great majority of people towards religion is one of indifference. There are a few constituencies in and around Glasgow and Liverpool where the concentration of Roman Catholic voters is so great that the Labour Party, at least, normally nominates a Catholic candidate; but these are areas of heavy Irish immigration, so that the religious dimension to political life there can be regarded as an importation from across the water. In addition to its nominally Christian population, Britain has about 400,000 Jews, 600,000 Hindus and Sikhs and over a million Muslims. However, no statistics are available regarding attendance at synagogues, temples and mosques. The fact that a minority of the Muslims are fundamentalists raises the possibility of social conflict over religious issues, as became apparent in 1989 when the Ayatollah Khomeini of Iran called upon militant Muslims to murder the British author Salman Rushdie on account of some allegedly blasphemous passages in a novel he had written. However, it remains true that, in general, religious loyalties have little impact on British political life. The contrast with Northern Ireland is obvious and there is also a marked difference between Britain and the United States on this matter. In America politicians are apt to be judged on moralistic grounds, while the strength of religious feeling about the control of abortion was demonstrated by the bombing of twenty-eight abortion clinics by religious zealots during 1986. In Britain political and religious issues are normally kept separate and the great majority of British voters neither know nor care what religious views (if any) are held by candidates for political office.

The question of race is rather more delicate. For many centuries Britain has had a high degree of ethnic homogeneity, with immigrants arriving only in a trickle and thus easily assimilated. In the nineteenth century the arrival of large numbers of Irish settlers sometimes created tension in industrial areas, but did not lead to any permanent social problems. In the present century British society has easily absorbed several contingents of European immigrants seeking refuge from the political problems of their own countries. In round numbers, these contingents comprised 150,000 Russian Jews in the years before the First World War, 65,000 German Jews in the 1930s, 100,000 Polish ex-servicemen who stayed on in 1945, and 30,000 Hungarian refugees in 1956. In the late 1950s, however, social tensions and problems resulted from the arrival of considerable numbers of Pakistani, Indian and West Indian immigrants, who until 1962 had unrestricted right of entry to Britain as citizens of Commonwealth countries. As soon as this development came to the attention of the general public, opinion polls showed that over 80 per cent of the public were opposed to it, and in 1962 immigration of this kind was restricted by the Commonwealth Immigrants Act. Subsequent measures have tightened the controls, but by 1989 Britain had 2.4 million Commonwealth immigrants and their descendants and it is officially estimated that by the end of the century the number will be about 3.3 million.

The existence and growth of these ethnic minorities, largely concentrated in a few cities, has given rise to various types of concern. Firstly, there has been concern that the minorities may suffer from racial discrimination. The promotion of good race relations is a matter upon which all the major political parties are agreed, and overt discrimination in almost all fields of activity has been made illegal by successive pieces of legislation, but some covert discrimination in employment undoubtedly occurs. Secondly, there has been concern that the minorities might not become integrated into the British economy and British society, sharpened by the revelation that black children have (for whatever reason) done markedly less well in the British educational system than white

7

children and Asian children have. Thirdly, there have been fears that areas containing sizeable ethnic minorities might be marked by violent conflicts between races, or between minorities and the police. There have in fact been violent clashes between young black citizens and the police in Bristol, Liverpool, Birmingham and parts of London, but few direct clashes between blacks and whites. The clashes involving the police will be discussed in Chapter 17.

Economic divisions with a geographical (as distinct from a class) basis fall into two categories: divisions between urban and rural areas, and divisions between more prosperous and less prosperous regions. Divisions between urban and rural areas are relatively unimportant in Britain because the country is more urbanized than any other country in the world apart from city states like Hong Kong and Singapore. The proportion of the total male workforce engaged in agriculture was only 1.8 per cent in June 1988 (the seasonal peak) and is lower than in any other country apart from Kuwait. One of the consequences is that in British politics there is no sharp clash between representatives of urban and rural interests. The farming industry is an important pressure group, but its influence depends on the goodwill of the government and the fact that the country could not easily afford to increase its imports of food, not upon the voting power of people dependent on agriculture for their livelihood.

Regional disparities in prosperity are inevitable in any sizeable country, and in Britain they have been accentuated since the 1920s by the decline of several older staple industries such as coal-mining, shipbuilding and textiles. These industries are mainly situated in Wales, Scotland and the north of England, so that the inter-war period saw a sizeable migration of people towards the more prosperous midlands and south-east. Between 1945 and 1979 all major political parties subscribed to the view that it was the government's duty to divert industrial growth to areas of relatively high unemployment, with the object of minimizing this kind of migration. The consequence of this agreement was that regional economic differences, while having a significant effect on policy, did not lead to many overt political conflicts. Government policies in this period had a somewhat beneficial effect on the poorer industrial areas, but at a considerable cost to the areas of potentially high economic growth and undoubtedly at some cost to the British economy as a whole. Since 1979 the Conservative government has gradually abandoned these policies as part of its plan to free industry from direct political controls. A consequence is that regional economic differences are now having less influence on government policy-making but more impact on political debate, with the Conservative and Labour parties having opposing views on the issues involved.

Another factor that reduces the impact of regional issues is the centralization of the mass media. There is no other country of Britain's size in which the press is so dominated by national newspapers. The choice is wide, there being eleven national morning papers that can be delivered to the doorstep throughout Britain; but they are all edited in London. Five of these constitute the serious, 'quality' press, with a combined circulation of 2.8 million in 1989. The other six are popular tabloids, with a combined circulation of 12.0 million. It is estimated that 75 per cent of the population over the age of sixteen read one or more of these eleven national dailies. With a handful of exceptions, Welsh and provincial English papers are read in addition to national papers rather than as alternatives to them, and people tend to look to the national press for political news and to their local papers to find out what is on at the cinema. The only papers that can be regarded as alternatives to the national press are the *Yorkshire Post* (with a circulation of 92,000), the *Western Mail* (circulation 81,000), the *Liverpool Daily Post* (circulation 71,000) and the *Birmingham Post* (circulation 36,000). It will be seen that their combined circulation is insignificant compared with that of the national dailies. The Sunday press is similarly centralized, a readership survey showing that 87 per cent of the population over the age of sixteen read one or more of the eight national Sunday papers.

However, Scotland is an exception to this general rule. It has three important daily papers of its own in the *Scotsman*, the *Glasgow Herald* and the *Daily Record*, as well as several smaller independent dailies and the Scottish editions of British national papers. Statistics show that in Scotland the total circulation of the Scottish-owned daily papers is about the same as that of the London-owned papers, and the Scottish editions of the latter contain a high proportion of Scottish news even though they are now all edited in England.

It is of course, also important that the main national radio network is owned by the government and that the two main television news programmes are produced by national agencies, one by the BBC and the other by an independent organization that provides a news service for all the commercial television companies.

The consequence of all these factors is that political news is much the same all over the country. In the United States, where sectional differences are considerable, and all newspapers and radio stations are local, it often happens that at any one time people in different parts of the country are concerned with quite different political issues. In the south-western states a prominent issue might be the position of Mexican immigrants; in Texas, the politics of the oil industry; in the Midwest, the federal government's policy towards agriculture; in the North-east it might be foreign policy. As a result, in an election the fortunes of the parties may vary between regions, the Democrats gaining in one part of the country and the Republicans gaining elsewhere.

In Britain, the combined effect of the smallness of the country, the absence of marked sectional differences and the existence of national newspapers is that political localism of this American kind rarely occurs except in Scotland. Local issues do not often make newspaper or television headlines, and when they do they usually make headlines all over the country – at any rate in England and Wales. This state of affairs is partly responsible for the fact that from 1945 until the 1980s movements of political opinion were remarkably uniform over the whole of the country apart from Scotland. If the government of the day lost popularity, the general tendency was for it to lose popularity almost everywhere. If there was a swing from one main party to the other in a general election, this was reflected in all the regions of England and Wales, with minuscule variations.

Scotland followed the general trend from 1945 to 1955, but after that date it veered slowly but steadily to the left, putting the Conservative Party into the position of a permanent minority north of the border. In the 1983 election the Conservatives won only twenty-one of the seventy-two Scottish seats, despite getting a large majority in the country as a whole, while in the 1987 election they held only ten Scottish seats.

In England and Wales uniform swings continued until 1983, when the intervention of the new Social Democratic Party (SDP) made a difference. The SDP, acting in electoral alliance with the Liberal Party, took many more votes from Labour in the south of England than it did in the north. The consequence was that in most of southern England the main battle was between the Conservatives and the Liberal–SDP alliance, with Labour coming third, while elsewhere the traditional Conservative/Labour conflict continued to dominate the polls except where there were local pockets of Liberal strength. In the 1987 election the alliance gained slightly fewer votes, but regional differentiation in voting became even more marked as a consequence of the contrast between the prosperity of much of southern England and the relative poverty of the older industrial areas of northern England and Wales. The Labour Party gained votes in these areas without making any impact on the southern counties, where its record was even poorer than that of the Conservative Party in Scotland. In this way regional economic and social differences have now come to have a very significant impact on the party system.

The Class System

It has sometimes been observed that the British are more conscious of considerations of social class in their relations with one another than citizens of other western societies, and some account of the class system is essential in any discussion of the characteristics of British society. However, when people talk of a class system they do not always refer to the same phenomenon. There are in fact three quite different models of what a class system consists of. In one model the difference between classes is conceived as being a difference of power; in another it is a difference of status; and in a third it is a difference of interests.

The view of the class system in terms of power derives from the theories of Karl Marx. In the Marxist model of society the ownership of the means of production determines class identity and class relationships. In an agricultural society the owners of land dominate the landless, who are forced to work on the land for low rewards. In an industrial society the owners of capital become the dominant class, with the landowners relegated to the position of a small *rentier* class and the great majority of people forced to sell their labour to the capitalists. The majority, known to Marxists as the proletariat, are exploited by the capitalists and cannot escape from their condition of exploitation except by a revolution that would transform society by expropriating the possessions of the capitalist class and establishing a socialist form of industrial organization. Revolution will be difficult, because the dominant class in any society controls the machinery of government and can use the coercive power of the state to crush incipient revolts. Class relationships in a capitalist society are therefore relationships of conflict, with democratic institutions (if they exist) serving the pacifying function of giving the workers the illusion of popular control without actually giving them political or economic power.

Marxists would acknowledge that the class system of modern Britain is not usually viewed in this way, and is in any case much more complex than this bare model suggests. They would insist, however, that the model reveals the realities of power that underlie the day-to-day controversies and compromises that are the stuff of democratic political debate.

A second model of the class system, much favoured by social commentators and journalists, views class differences as essentially differences of status. In modern Britain, it is said, people categorize one another by a variety of indicators, such as accent, clothes, manners, type of school attended, recreations pursued and type of car driven. At an immediate practical level, this is undoubtedly a more useful model than the first one. When British people meet strangers in a pub or on a train, this is exactly how they go about classifying one another. It is in terms of this model that the British may be more conscious of class than the Germans or Dutch or Americans are. However, from the political point of view, status differences may be only a superficial guide to behaviour. People from quite different status groupings can be found sharing political ideals and interests, while people of similar status may be committed to opposing political parties. In so far as we are concerned to use the class system as an explanatory factor in understanding political behaviour, the most useful model of the class system is neither the one based on power nor the one based on status, but the one based on interests.

What is of crucial importance is that people with different sources of income and different occupations have different economic interests, and that these differing interests are reflected in the party system and the policy-making process. People who derive much of their income from rents or investments, as an example, have a long time-perspective. They have little need to worry about unemployment, unless there is a major slump, and relatively little need to worry about inflation, which will increase the value of their property and investments. Their most direct political concerns will be to minimize or avoid having a capital gains tax and to minimize or avoid having effective death duties.

Professional and business people whose income depends on their individual talents and efforts are in a different position. They characteristically own little property apart from their house, so that they will not be particularly concerned about capital gains tax but will have a direct and strong interest in the continuance of tax relief on mortgage interest payments. They will be very upset by inflation, which is apt to cut their net income because salary-earners are not so well protected against inflation as either the propertied classes or the unionized wage-earning section of the workplace. They have less direct reason than wage-earners to be worried about the level of unemployment. They are less concerned about death duties than the propertied classes but may be particularly concerned about the quality of the educational system, as they want their children to have at least as good an opportunity as they had to acquire professional qualifications. Like the propertied classes, people in this category are very much more likely to support the Conservative Party than the Labour Party, because they see the Conservatives as more likely to protect their economic interests.

The third distinctive category comprises manual workers, whose economic position has always been less secure than that of people in the two categories so far mentioned. In the nineteenth century Britain produced a large industrial proletariat whose members suffered not only from relatively low incomes but also from various kinds of insecurity and hazard. They were often hired by the day and subject to unemployment without notice. Their working conditions often posed threats to their health. Unlike most salary-earners, they were not paid when sick. They usually lived in rented housing and were thus at the mercy of possibly rapacious landlords. Having small incomes and little property, they were not worried about the level of taxation. Knowing that their incomes depended on collective action, they were concerned about the legal position of trade unions. Without superannuation schemes, and unable to save, they depended on their unions and the state for pensions in old age.

To itemize the concerns of manual workers in this way is to draw up what became the main agenda of the Liberal government of 1905–14 and the Labour Party from 1918 onwards. The Liberal government gave unions immunity from legal action in respect of industrial disputes and also authorized them to collect a political levy from their members for donation to a political party, which in practice meant the Labour Party. The Liberals also launched state insurance schemes to provide for benefits in case of sickness or unemployment and for pensions after retirement. The Labour Party promised to extend these benefits, to establish a free and universal system of health care, to provide municipal housing for workers at subsidized rents, to enact measures to cut the rate of industrial accidents, and to use the budget to tax the rich and help the poor. It therefore follows that manual workers have had good economic reasons to support the Labour party, as (until the 1980s) the majority of them have done.

In this model of the class system white-collar workers occupy an intermediate position, having better working conditions and more security of employment than manual workers but not being nearly so well off as professional people or business executives. It is therefore not surprising to find that in the elections of 1950 and 1951, the first in which voting behaviour was analysed by sample survey techniques, white-collar workers split about fifty-fifty between voting Conservative and voting Labour.

In recent years the British class system, viewed as a system of differing economic and social interests, has undergone marked changes. In the first place, economic and technological changes have led to a move from manufacturing to service trades, while within industry the growth of automation has increased the number of technicians and computer operators but brought about a reduction in the number of manual workers. The proportion of the workforce in manual occupations fell from 70 per cent in 1951 to 52 per cent in 1981 (see Halsey, 1987, p. 15) and has fallen to well under 50 per cent since 1981. Secondly, the measures of social security and industrial safety promised by the Labour Party have all been achieved and are accepted by all parties. Thirdly, the widespread (though not universal) growth of affluence has led to a reduction in the differences in living conditions that were apparent in the immediate postwar period. When people come to own their own house, to have central heating and to own a car they reach a plateau of comfort that takes the edge off the feelings of resentment that were once common. This development has been paralleled by the equalizing effects of supermarkets and television, which reduce differences in lifestyle and tastes. The spread of comprehensive schools has had a similar impact. The general trend of the past two decades has been for British society to become more egalitarian, even though the unemployed and certain other disadvantaged minorities remain trapped in poverty.

The consequence of these economic and social changes is that class consciousness has decreased. Surveys in the 1980s showed that only about half of the adult population identified themselves with a particular class. And in parallel with this decrease in class consciousness, there has been a decrease in the correlation between the occupation of voters and their behaviour at the polls. As will be shown in Chapter 6, the 1970s and 1980s have been marked by a class de-alignment in partisan allegiance and voting behaviour.

Political Attitudes and Values

The British system of government is determined not only by the history and social characteristics of the country but also by the political attitudes and values of the British people. Some of these have been mentioned already and many others will emerge during the course of the book. However, one or two of them have played such an important part in shaping political institutions that they merit a special place in this opening chapter.

The first of these is a very strong attachment to personal liberty. This is so well known that it hardly needs explanation, but a few contemporary examples may reinforce the point. The British would never accept the widespread security checks for bureaucratic posts that are taken for granted in the United States. The British would not agree to a proposal to ban extremist parties in

13

times of peace, as communist and fascist parties are banned in West Germany. If it were revealed that the British police had conducted several hundred illegal break-ins, a British Prime Minister would not feel able to tell parliament that such actions were justified in the campaign against potential terrorists and criminals, as the Canadian Prime Minister did in 1978. If any British minister were to make such a statement, it would be followed by a storm of public protest, which simply did not happen in Canada. Equally, it is inconceivable that a British government would instruct the security police to compile files on the political affiliations and activities of all candidates for political office, irrespective of party, as the Canadian government has done. Nor would British citizens accept the peacetime identity cards, and the need to register addresses with the police, that are a routine feature of life in some continental countries.

Even in minor matters of everyday life, similar contrasts can be found. British people would never accept the situation of many Canadian provinces, in which it is a legal offence to consume alcoholic beverages in the open air, and a glass of beer at a picnic can lead to prosecution. British motorists would not easily accept the low speed limit that is obeyed in docile fashion all over the United States, together with regulations making it a legal offence for a motorist to adjust the carburettor on his own car. British swimmers would hardly put up with the situation on American beaches, where the provision of life-guards is immediately followed by rules making it an offence to swim anywhere except in a small roped enclosure in front of the life-guard. British yachtsmen would be appalled by the detailed regulations about safety equipment that French yachtsmen have to cope with. In all kinds of ways Britain is still a land of freedom, and any readers who doubt this should move overseas and find out for themselves.

A second generalization that can be made about British attitudes to government is that they are endlessly pragmatic. The British do not have a written constitution and have no wish to invent one. They have no coherent theory of the state. They have inherited a set of political institutions and their instinct is to adapt and modify these rather than to replace them by new ones. One consequence of this is a rather extreme kind of institutional conservatism, which allows a medieval body like the House of Lords to survive into the present and the indefinite future. Another consequence is that British administrative arrangements are labyrinthine in character, like an old building that has been continually improved and extended.

Proposals for radical reform are sometimes made, but they are invariably blocked, diverted, or undermined by this preference for compromise and incremental adjustment. A national economic plan was commissioned in 1964 but abandoned in 1967. Radical proposals to reform the Civil Service in 1968 resulted in small piecemeal changes, leaving the structure of the service intact. The Civil Service College was established to train senior administrators, but it has turned out to be a rather small college offering very short courses. The campaign to create national assemblies for Scotland and Wales in the 1970s collapsed in the face of political resistance and public apathy. The British are no longer particularly smug about their institutions, as they were until the 1960s, but dramatic changes in structure are not to be expected.

A third and quite different generalization that can be made about British political attitudes is that the British people (like many other peoples) appreciate the appearance of strong governmental leadership. In the early years of Queen Victoria's reign Sir Robert Peel made the following comment on this topic:

> I could not admit any alteration in any of these bills. This was thought very obstinate and very presumptuous; but the fact is, people like a certain degree of obstinacy and presumption in a minister. They abuse him for dictatorship and arrogance, but they like being governed.   (Rosebery, 1899, p. 67)

That was a long time ago, but in 1967 Harold Wilson displayed a similar attitude when interviewed by a political scientist who was also a Labour MP. When presented with a list of possible cases of back-bench influence on policy, the Prime Minister did not say – as government leaders in many other democracies would have done – that he had taken account of the views of his parliamentary colleagues and the movements of public opinion they represented. On the contrary, he went through each example carefully 'to demonstrate that on no occasion was he consciously deflected from his original purpose, even over mode of presentation or timing, by any estimate of what dissident groups on his back benches might say' (Mackintosh, 1977b, p. 85).

Evidence that British voters like the appearance of firm leadership is to be found not only in scattered public opinion polls but also in the striking effect that the 1982 war in the Falkland Islands had on the popularity and esteem of Margaret Thatcher. Public assessments of her performance as a Prime Minister increased markedly during the conflict and remained at a higher level after it was concluded. She had displayed strong leadership and this commanded public admiration. Her party's continuing lead at the polls and in elections throughout the 1980s, despite the unpopularity of many of her social policies, reveals the degree to which political leadership is respected.

It does not follow from this that the British people actually experience strong government. On the contrary, compromise and concessions to pressure groups have been regular features of government policy in many areas. On the occasions when bold initiatives have been taken, governments have often had to modify or withdraw their measures in the face of opposition. In 1969 the Labour government had to abandon both its plan to reform the House of Lords and its proposal to regulate industrial relations. The Conservative government's decision in 1970 to give no more subsidies to declining industries was abandoned within two years. The 1971 Industrial Relations Act was effectively sabotaged by trade union opposition. Three plans to build a third airport for London were given up in the face of public hostility in the areas chosen for its location. The Callaghan government showed notable weakness over the issue of devolution to Scotland. Margaret Thatcher's plan to liberalize shop trading hours was rejected by the House of Commons. The Thatcher government has been more determined than any other government since 1950, but the general postwar record indicates that caution and compromise have been more common than bold initiatives and strong leadership.

Political Culture

This leads into an area of controversy about what social scientists commonly describe as the British political culture. In 1959 a survey of political attitudes in five countries revealed that the British people were generally more confident and trusting in matters political than were the citizens of the United States, Germany, Italy and Mexico. They were more certain of getting equal treatment from bureaucrats and police, more confident that their views would get consideration from bureaucrats and police and more confident than Germans, Italians and Mexicans, though not than Americans, of their ability to do something about unjust regulations imposed by local or national authorities (Almond and Verba, 1965, pp. 70, 72, 142, 181). The organizers of the survey concluded that the political culture of the British could be described as deferential and allegiant.

There has been considerable debate in recent years about how far these attitudes have changed since 1959. Before scrutinizing the evidence, it may be observed that there are two general reasons to expect that changes may have occurred. One is the development of the New Left movement in the 1960s. The issues upon which this movement revolved were mainly international rather than specifically British; they included the threat of nuclear war, the racial policies of South Africa and the American involvement in the Vietnam war. However, the movement exposed a whole generation of young Britons to radical ideas and brought many thousands of them into conflict with the police at political demonstrations. It would be surprising if it had not had some lasting effect on political attitudes.

The second development is public concern about Britain's relative economic decline. This also emerged during the 1960s and it became the dominant topic of political debate during the 1970s. There has been an inevitable tendency to seek scapegoats for this decline, and civil servants have been numbered among the candidates. Whereas they seemed immune from public criticism before the 1960s, since that decade they have come increasingly under attack for their poor record in economic forecasting and their alleged inefficiencies.

In the absence of a general survey that repeated the 1959 questions, the evidence regarding recent British attitudes is scattered. However, the available statistics give indications of a growth of scepticism. While in the 1959 survey 83 per cent of respondents said they expected equal treatment from bureaucrats, in a 1972 survey of teenagers only 18 per cent believed that 'government officials give everyone an even break' as against 55 per cent who thought that

Table 1.2 *Trust and Cynicism among Young Londoners: 1978*

	Most of the time %	Only some of the time %
How often do politicians tell the truth?	18	74
How often do national governments put the needs of the country and the people above party needs?	23	63
Do you trust the government to do what is right?	29	65

	All the people %	A few interests %
Is this country run for the benefit of all its people or for a few big interests?	32	52

	Disagree %	Agree %
Parties are only interested in people's votes, not their opinions.	14	77
MPs lose touch with the people pretty quickly.	10	81
Public officials don't care much about what people like me think.	20	72

Source: Data taken from a survey of political attitudes of young people in Hackney South and Shoreditch, reproduced here by permission of the ESRC Data Archive at the University of Essex.

'they give special favours to some' (Hart, 1978, p. 44). In 1959, 59 per cent said they expected 'serious consideration of their point of view' from bureaucrats, whereas in a 1973 national survey 65 per cent agreed with the proposition that 'Public officials don't care much about what people like me think' and only 30 per cent disagreed (Marsh, 1977, p. 118). As shown in Table 1.2, a poll of young Londoners in 1978 revealed that only 20 per cent disagreed with this last proposition.

There is also evidence of an increased readiness to resort to various forms of direct action to achieve political objectives. The evidence of a trend comes from the record of public behaviour, and confirmation that this behaviour receives a fair degree of public support is to be found in at least two surveys. The 1973 national survey revealed that 15 per cent approved of street blockades and the occupation of buildings in furtherance of a political objective, while 18 per cent thought it was 'justified to break the law' to 'combat excessive rent, tax, or price increases', 16 per cent thought this was justified to 'further strikes and oppose legal regulation of industrial relations', and 12 per cent thought it was right 'as a generalised means of furthering a legitimate cause' (Marsh, 1977, pp. 45, 53). It may be said, of course, that only a small minority approve of direct action and law-breaking for political purposes. Statistically this is true, but 15 per cent of the adult population amounts to about 6 million people, and this is a large number of potential law-breakers to be found in a liberal democracy where public attitudes have been described as deferential.

Not surprisingly, scholars have interpreted the evidence about changing attitudes in different ways. Kavanagh has concluded that the 'old restraints of hierarchy and deference' are 'waning' (Kavanagh, 1980, p. 170). Beer has suggested relationships between political attitudes and cultural changes in British society, and has written in striking terms of 'the collapse of deference' (Beer, 1982, pp. 107–48). Norton, on the other hand, has explicitly rejected Beer's analysis and has asserted that 'the political culture remains predominantly an allegiant one' (Norton, 1984, p. 34).

My own conclusion is that it is more helpful to think of the British political culture as being fragmented than it is to describe it either as having collapsed or as being substantially unchanged. Clearly the attitudes of some sections of British society are now anything but deferential. The urban riots of 1981 and the violence associated with the miners' strike of 1984–5 are sufficient evidence of that, and there is survey evidence in addition. Equally, most citizens still have a high regard for the police, most reject direct action for political objectives and most still regard public servants as honest, even if no longer as specially efficient. The break with earlier attitudes has not been a universal trend but has been concentrated in specific (though varied) groups: among students and ex-students having radical convictions; among trade unionists in certain declining industries; and among young people in inner-city areas facing poor living conditions and the probability of long-term unemployment. The figures in Table 1.2 are taken from a survey of young white people (aged 20–24, immigrants excluded) in a working-class district of inner London; they show a degree of cynicism that would not be shared by middle-aged residents in prosperous suburbs, and is highly significant even though not universal.

In interpreting these figures, it should be noted very few of the respondents were unemployed, but those who were displayed greater cynicism than the others. These data lend support to the view that the British political culture is best described as fragmented.

Further Reading

For a fuller discussion of social structure and political culture, see Moran (1985), *Politics and Society in Britain*, chs. 1 and 2.

Part II

The Constitutional Framework

◇ 2 ◇

The Nature of the Constitution

Of the 170 or more nations that at the time of writing are members of the United Nations Organization, all but one have written constitutions, which set out the nature and powers of their institutions of government. These constitutions may be short or they may be long; they may be helpful guides to the operation of the political systems concerned or they may be seriously misleading; but from the point of view of the student they at least have the advantage of serving as a point of departure and a point of reference. The only nation that does not have such a constitution is the United Kingdom.

Of course it does not follow from this either that Britain lacks a body of constitutional law or that this law is based entirely on custom and precedent. There are numerous statutes concerning the composition and powers of particular institutions. Thus, the powers of the monarchy are limited by the Bill of Rights of 1689 and the Act of Settlement of 1701; the powers of the House of Lords are defined by the Parliament Acts of 1911 and 1949; and the modern electoral system is regulated by the Representation of the People Acts of 1948 and 1949. There is no lack of statutory provisions regarding the various institutions of government, considered individually. What is lacking is a documentary and authoritative statement of the relations between these institutions.

The consequence of this lack is that when writers and speakers describe the British constitution they produce accounts that are often significantly different from one another. These differences will be explored, but before moving to this topic it is important to note that there is one feature of British constitutional arrangements about which no disagreement is possible. This feature is the limited political influence of the courts of law. They have developed Common Law over the centuries and by doing so have helped to define the liberties of the citizen. However, where statutes exist the courts have no power to question them or challenge them. Judges cannot declare statutes to be unconstitutional, as can be done in many liberal democracies, either on the grounds that the statute infringes a declaration of personal rights (as in the United States, Canada and West Germany) or on the grounds that it covers an area of activity that is outside the jurisdiction of the national legislature. In Britain Parliament is sovereign, in the sense that there are no constitutional limits to its authority. A small part of this authority has recently been handed over to the European Community, but this was a grant of power that could legally be rescinded by a future Parliament. The British constitutional system is therefore unusual among democratic systems in its absence of checks and balances.

The constitutional questions about which commentators differ relate to the balance of practical power and influence between Parliament and the administration. Granted that Parliament can, in law, do whatever it likes, the question remains of whether parliamentarians actually run the country or merely act as a rubber stamp for decisions taken by ministers and civil servants. The answer to this question, which should be determined by empirical investigation, is sometimes implied by the language in which constitutional matters are discussed. And it often seems that participants in constitutional discussions are using two quite different languages.

The Languages of the Constitution

The predominant language at the present time is best called the 'liberal language', because it embodies a number of ideals associated with the liberal reform movement of the nineteenth century. In this language the central concept is 'the sovereignty of Parliament'. It is emphasized that in the British system of government supreme power lies with Parliament, which has direct and exclusive control over legislation and indirect control over the actions of the executive and the central administration. In respect of legislation, Parliament is said to be both omnipotent and omni-competent: there is no constitutional restriction on its authority; and other law-making bodies in the country (such as local councils) exercise their powers only so long as Parliament authorizes them to do so. In respect of administration, Parliament is said to have ultimate control by virtue of the convention that ministers are responsible to parliament both for their own decisions and for all the actions of their departments. Government policy may be framed in the Cabinet, but Cabinet ministers have to answer to Parliament for all that they do and may be forced to resign by a vote of no confidence in Parliament if their actions do not meet with parliamentary approval.

It is of course accepted, and indeed emphasized, that within Parliament the House of Commons is now the centre of power, and that the members of that House have to answer to the electorate. Those points are sometimes expressed in another concept known as 'the sovereignty of the people'. It is said that while Parliament is legally sovereign the growth of representative institutions since the 1860s has transferred the ultimate power over issues of policy from Parliament to the people. Ministers have to answer to parliament between general elections, but at elections the government and all its parliamentary supporters have to answer to the electorate, who either endorse their policies by returning them to power or reject them and give a mandate to the rival party.

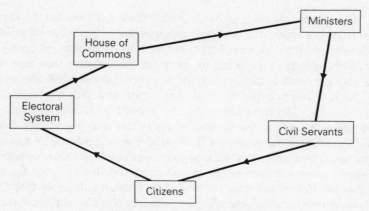

Figure 2.1 The liberal model

In this view of the constitution our political life is dominated by a chain of command that leads from the electorate to the House of Commons, from the Commons to the Cabinet and other ministers and from the ministers to the civil servants who carry out their instructions. Since civil servants have some authority over citizens, the chain of command eventually completes a circle, as is illustrated in Figure 2.1. The system is said to be democratic because it ensures that government policies reflect 'the will of the people'.

This is a crude and over-simplified version of the view of the constitution that appears to command most general acceptance and to underlie most of the comments on political affairs that are to be found in the popular press. It is by no means universally accepted, however. If the average higher civil servant were asked to comment on it, he would probably say that it gives an unrealistic picture of the flow of power. The British civil servant does not see the role of the departments as being confined to the implementation of policies that are made by politicians, bending to the will of the electorate. He knows that policy and administration are intimately related and that many, perhaps most, changes of policy are initiated in the departments as the result of memoranda written by civil servants, not by politicians. He might even suggest that the diagram would illustrate the situation more accurately if the arrows pointed in the opposite direction.

A good example to support this bureaucratic view of the constitution is afforded by the reform of the gambling laws in 1960. This major reform, which permitted the establishment of betting shops, involved issues that many people regarded as issues of moral or political principle. It was proposed immediately after a general election and had clearly been in the pipeline before the election, but the government had carefully refrained from raising it as an electoral issue. The movement for the reform was in fact generated within the administration, using this term in a wide sense to include the police.

Until 1960, the law had prohibited off-the-course betting on horse-races for cash, although this was permitted on credit. Since most manual workers were unable to secure credit, the consequences was that a large-scale illegal industry had developed, with an annual turnover of tens of millions of pounds. The unsuccessful efforts of the police to stamp out this industry took time that the police thought could better be devoted to other purposes and also tended to bring the law (and possibly the police) into disrepute with the betting public. Chief Constables had therefore frequently pointed out to officials in the Home Office that there was a case for the reform of this law, and when a reforming Home Secretary in the person of R. A. Butler was appointed he took up this suggestion. The next step was the appointment of a Royal Commission, which consulted various affected interests and mustered the evidence for reform; after that the Home Secretary persuaded his Cabinet colleagues that a reform was both administratively desirable and politically feasible; officials in the Home Office made the first draft of a new law on the subject; and then, but only then, the government informed Parliament of its intentions. It remained for ministers to persuade back-bench MPs that the reform was desirable and for the MPs to defend the proposal when it was criticized by their constituents.

It will be seen that this story puts the democratic process in a rather different light from that of the constitutional view summarized in Figure 2.1. The reform of the gambling laws was certainly a reform that met the wishes and needs of the citizens most affected by these laws, but these wishes were not expressed through the electoral system and Parliament. Instead, they were taken up by the administration, which persuaded the politicians of the case for reform. The main role of back-bench MPs in this whole story was that of fending off criticisms by citizens who disapproved on moral grounds of the liberalization of the gambling laws.

Other examples could be cited to support the view that in practice many political reforms are initiated from within the administration rather than by party politicians in Parliament, but it is unnecessary to give them because the liberal model of the constitution is in fact open to objections that are far more radical than this. The most important of these is its failure to depict the role of the Crown in the British system of government. In the liberal language there is no indication that ministers are appointed by the monarch (on the advice of the Prime Minister), and that both ministers and civil servants are servants of the Crown, not of Parliament. Nor is there any indication that the House of Commons can meet only when it is convened by the Crown (again acting on the advice of the Prime Minister). It is true that the House must be convened at least once every twelve months, but a great deal can happen in twelve months and a body that lacks the power to convene itself cannot properly be described as the centre and source of authority. In 1963, when Lord Home took office as Prime Minister, he advised the Queen to postpone the opening of Parliament until he had had time to divest himself of his title, fight a by-election, and take a seat in the House of Commons. The Opposition was annoyed by this, but had no power to do anything about it.

Equally, the liberal view of the constitution fails to take account of the independence enjoyed by the executive in the conduct of foreign policy and the making of war. There are other countries (notably the United States) in which treaties are made subject to ratification by the legislative assembly, and if the British Parliament were really as powerful as the liberal language implies it would be reasonable to assume that this situation obtained in Britain. In fact treaties are concluded by ministers in the name of Her Britannic Majesty; they are not subject to ratification by Parliament; and they cannot be disowned by Parliament. Declarations of war are made in a similar fashion, and Parliament is told that war has been declared, not asked whether war should be declared.

A further weakness of the liberal view is that it ignores or virtually ignores the position of the House of Lords in the British constitution. It is true that the power of the House of Lords has greatly diminished in recent decades, since the Parliament Act of 1911 abolished its power to veto legislation. But the House exists, its powers are not negligible and it cannot properly be ignored simply because it cannot be fitted into the chain of command that the liberal view assumes to be the central feature of the constitution.

People who are conscious of these features of the constitution, including most ministers, top civil servants and constitutional lawyers, rarely use the liberal language when discussing constitutional matters. Instead, they use a language that may for convenience be called 'the Whitehall language', both because many of those who use it are connected with the departments in Whitehall and because in this language it is Whitehall rather than Parliament that is depicted as the centre of government.

The Whitehall language emphasizes the importance of the Crown in the British constitution and the fact that ministers and civil servants are servants of the Crown, responsible for governing the country according to their view of the public interest and not obliged by law (though to some extent they are by convention) to take account of opinions expressed in Parliament. In this language Parliament appears not as a corporate entity wielding power but as a pair of debating chambers in which public opinion is aired and grievances are ventilated. It is noted that Parliament is convened and prorogued by the Queen, acting on the advice of her ministers, and it is suggested that the political process consists in part of a debate or conversation between Parliament on the one hand and the government on the other. Parliament has the right to criticize the actions of the administration, to withhold assent to legislation and in the last resort to pass a motion of no confidence in the government of the day. But it does not have the right to participate in or to control the administration. In this view of the constitution, which is illustrated in Figure 2.2, there is clearly something like a separation of powers between Parliament and the executive, and there is no chain of command except that within the administration itself. It will be seen that in this model of the constitution there are also clear places for the police, the courts of law and the armed forces, which cannot easily be fitted into the liberal model.

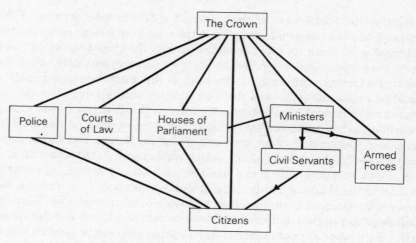

Figure 2.2 The Whitehall model

The coexistence of these different views of the constitution raises two questions that must now be answered. The first question is: should one view be regarded as right and the others as wrong, or do both views contain aspects of the truth? If the answer to this is that both views contain aspects of the truth, as will be suggested, a second question follows. This is: how can we account for the fact that an adequate explanation of the British system of government apparently requires the use of two rather different languages?

The Constitution in Practice

It is suggested that both views of the constitution embody aspects of the truth. Taking the second view first, it is certainly true, as a matter of constitutional principle, that the monarch (acting on the advice of the Prime Minister) decides when and when not to convene Parliament, that ministers are servants of the Crown, not of Parliament, and that Parliament does not have the right to control the activities or expenditures of the executive, but only the right to call ministers to account for what the executive has done.

This view of the constitution is not only correct as a matter of principle but is also a helpful guide to practice. The British administration conducts its affairs in substantial independence of Parliament, in respect of not only defence and foreign relations but also domestic matters. An example is the decision to bring about a major expansion of higher education that followed the publication of the Robbins Report in 1963. The first point to note about this is that the report was not made available to MPs until the government had considered its contents and formulated a policy in regard to its recommendations. This policy was in fact announced by the Prime Minister the day after the report was published. The second point to note is that the implication of this policy was entirely a matter for executive action. The amount of money made available for university expansion was decided by the Treasury and the ministry for higher education, with the Cabinet acting as arbiter in case of dispute. It is true that Parliament had to authorize this expenditure, but the British Parliament has no power to increase financial estimates presented to it and has never been known to decrease them. When several new universities were established in the 1960s, these universities were granted degree-giving powers by royal charter, no parliamentary action being required. By the same token, the reductions in public grants to universities between 1979 and 1984 were also decided upon within the administration, without effective control by Parliament.

In this whole process Parliament had no real function save to act as a forum for criticism and debate. Certain discussions in Parliament may have had an influence on government policy, but this influence was not necessarily any greater than that of discussions in the correspondence columns of *The Times* and was almost certainly less than that of private discussions between the universities and the departments. It would seem that Figure 2.2 gives a fairly accurate illustration of the role of Parliament in regard to policy for higher education.

On the other hand, this view of the constitution is clearly incomplete. Its most crippling omission is that it takes no account of the fact that the composition of the House of Commons determines which party or parties will form the government. In the twentieth century the normal situation has been for one party to have an absolute majority of seats in the Commons and for members of this party to fill all ministerial appointments. There were exceptions during both world wars, when coalition governments were formed for the sake of national unity even though the majority party could have kept its monopoly of ministerial posts had it chosen to do so. There were also exceptions in 1923–4, 1929–31 and 1977–9, when no single party had a majority of seats in the Commons. In these periods the country was ruled by minority Labour governments that depended for their parliamentary majorities on the support of the Liberals (and in 1977–9 on support from Scottish and Welsh nationalists also). Each of these minority governments came to a sticky end. In 1924 the Liberals withdrew their support; in 1931 the Labour government collapsed with internal divisions; and in 1979 both the Liberals and the Scottish Nationalists voted against the government on a motion of confidence. In each of the ensuing general elections the Labour Party was defeated.

A corollary of this weakness in the Whitehall view of the constitution is that no adequate account is given of the importance of elections in the British political system. A general election is not simply a way of choosing the people who will conduct debates in one of the Houses of Parliament; it is the institution that determines which party or parties will govern the country. And the prospect of the next general election is rarely far from the minds of politicians and has an influence on government policy as well as on parliamentary debates.

The other weaknesses of the Whitehall view of the constitution flow from the fact that, by focusing attention on the conduct of administration, it tends to underestimate the role of Parliament in the political life of the country. In the first place, Parliament is the training-ground for political leaders. The great majority of ministers achieve ministerial office because they have made a mark in parliamentary debates, and as a consequence of this they tend to remain parliamentarians at heart, with a special sensitivity to parliamentary criticism even though they know there is no danger of it leading to an adverse vote. Then again, the attention of the press is focused on Parliament and for this reason parliamentary criticism of the government may have an effect on public opinion that is out of proportion to the real weight of the criticism. And, even if it does not have such an effect, ministers, being human, may sometimes fear that it will do so, and may moderate their actions accordingly. The behaviour of civil servants is also affected by their wish to avoid provoking parliamentary questions about their departments.

It follows that both these views of the constitution embody aspects of the truth, and that both are necessary to a balanced account of how government is conducted in Britain. The question of why these two different views exist side by side must now be answered. This question can be dealt with very briefly, though the answer to it falls into two parts.

In the first place, each view of the constitution incorporates a set of political values. Each purports to be an objective description, but in fact each is based upon a particular way of looking at politics. The Whitehall view is based upon the values of the administrator, who sees government as a way of providing public services and promoting the public interest, and tends to regard party conflicts as a distraction that may be necessary but is somewhat irrelevant to the main business in hand. The liberal view is based on the values of the democratic theorist, who thinks that the essential criteria of good government are that all shades of opinion should be reflected in public discussion and that in the end the will of the majority should prevail. There is no necessary contradiction between these views, but they emphasize different aspects of the political process. To some extent they reflect differing values of different actors on the political stage, with back-bench champions espousing the liberal view and senior civil servants thinking in terms of the Whitehall view. But this difference in values emerges only occasionally as a conflict between groups, because most people, including most politicians, embrace both sets of values, emphasizing the one or the other according to the situation in which they find themselves. Thus any Cabinet minister is likely to think mainly in terms of the Whitehall view, knowing as he does that the Cabinet is responsible for governing the country and that Parliament is normally a place where decisions have to be justified and only occasionally a place where they are made. But a minister is also a former back-bencher and a future member of the Opposition, and in these roles he will be conscious of the importance of Parliament and the need to maintain its influence over the government of the day. So he may speak with two voices about the role of Parliament in the constitution, each voice reflecting legitimate views about what the role should be.

The other part of the answer is that each view has a basis in British history. To put the matter in its simplest form, the Whitehall view reflects those features of the constitution that have remained fairly constant from the eighteenth to the twentieth centuries while the liberal view reflects the ambitions and achievements of nineteenth-century reformers who transformed the political system from one of oligarchy to one of democracy. Both views remain valid because the reformers did not abolish institutions but merely changed their nature to a greater or lesser degree. To understand the present constitution it is therefore necessary to know something of both eighteenth-century institutions and nineteenth-century reforms, and these will be discussed in the following two chapters.

Before moving to these historical chapters it may, however, be helpful to give advance notice of the constitutional matters that are still subject to change and controversy. One of these, to be mentioned in Chapter 3 and discussed more fully in Chapter 8, is the recent decline in the effectiveness of party discipline in Parliament. This raises questions about the factors underlying party discipline and the reasons for its decline. A second issue, to be discussed in Chapter 4, is that of the powers of the monarch in regard to the appointment of the Prime Minister. It is an issue that might become critical in the event of an election in which no one party won an overall majority of seats. A third issue, also to be discussed in Chapter 4, is that of the composition and role of the House of Lords. It is by no means a new issue, having been on the agenda for most of the twentieth century, but it has become more critical now that the House has displayed a greater readiness to amend or defeat government measures and the Labour Party has promised (or threatened) to abolish the House entirely if it is returned to power. These constitutional questions are all very much alive today, and the brief account of historical developments that follows in the next two chapters will place them in perspective.

Further Reading

For a fuller discussion of alternative views of the constitution see Birch (1964), *Representative and Responsible Government*; for an examination of recent changes see Norton (1982), *The Constitution in Flux*; for an analysis of current constitutional issues see Jowell and Oliver (1985), *The Changing Constitution*.

◇ 3 ◇

The Development of Liberal Institutions

The central institutions of British government are extremely old. The monarchy has an almost unbroken history dating from before the Norman conquest, and the two Houses of Parliament both have medieval origins. The development of these and other institutions in the medieval and early modern periods is a subject for historians; the student of modern politics can safely begin at the end of the seventeenth century.

In this period three events of great importance took place in quick succession. The first was the revolution of 1688, in which a group of politicians invited William of Orange to bring an invading army to England in order to depose James II from the throne. It was a bloodless revolution because when it came to the point James's lieutenants would not fight, but it was a revolution nevertheless. The success of this venture greatly strengthened Parliament's position in relation to the monarchy, and it was immediately followed by the Bill of Rights of 1689. In this Bill it was declared, among other things, that henceforth the monarch could neither make nor suspend laws without the consent of Parliament; that he could not raise money except by parliamentary grant; that he could not maintain a standing army without parliamentary authority; and that neither he nor anyone else could restrict the right of free speech within Parliament. A few years later the Act of Settlement of 1701 decided the immediate succession to the throne, declared that no future monarch could either be or marry a member of the Roman Catholic Church and deprived the monarch of the power to dismiss judges, who henceforth could be removed from office only by a resolution of both Houses of Parliament.

The Eighteenth-Century Constitution

This Revolutionary Settlement inaugurated a period of stable government and gradual constitutional evolution that continued without any major legislative change until the great Reform Act of 1832. The eighteenth-century constitution was one in which the mass of the people had little direct influence; it was a system of government by a small ruling class. However, it was distinguished from the autocratic systems of continental Europe (and of England under the Tudors) by some vitally important features.

First, and of most importance to the ordinary person, it gave its citizens a considerable degree of liberty. True, punishments were harsh and a man could be hanged for stealing a sheep. But he could not be punished except for a clear offence against the law; he was entitled to a fair trial; and, most important of all in terms of its political effects, he was free to criticize the government as much as he pleased so long as he kept within the laws relating to libel and sedition. Only those who value political liberty but do not enjoy it can appreciate just how much it means. It is not surprising therefore that some of the most eloquent praise of the eighteenth-century British constitution came not from Britons but from foreigners who visited the country. One of these was Voltaire, who wrote in the following terms of the rights of the subject in Britain:

> To be secure on lying down that you shall rise in possession of the same property with which you retired to rest: that you shall not be torn from the arms of your wife, or from your children, in the dead of night, to be thrown into a dungeon or buried in exile in a desert; that when rising from the bed of sleep you will have the power of publishing all your thoughts; and that, if you are accused of having either acted, spoken, or written wrongly, you can be tried only according to law. These privileges attach to everyone who sets his foot on English ground.

The explanation of this liberty lay partly in the nature of British society, which was both more tolerant and less rigidly hierarchical than that of France and many other continental countries. But another French observer, Baron Montesquieu, suggested that a good part of the explanation was to be found in the structure of the central government. The basis of British liberty, he declared, was the separation and balance of powers between the executive, the legislature and the judiciary. In France the king dominated all three and the result was despotism; in Britain the executive was restricted on the one hand by the fact that it did not control Parliament and on the other by the independence of the judiciary, and the result was freedom. The same view was put forward by the English constitutional lawyer Sir William Blackstone, who made the following comment on the independence of the judiciary:

> In this distinct and separate existence of the judicial power in a peculiar body of men, nominated indeed, but not removable at pleasure, by the crown, consists one main preservation of the public liberty; which cannot subsist long in any state, unless the administration of common justice be in some degree separated both from the legislative and also from the executive power.
>
> (Blackstone, 1809, p. 268)

And elsewhere in the same teatise Blackstone noted that 'the total union' of the executive and legislature 'would be productive of tyranny' and commended the balanced nature of the British constitution, in which the executive was a part of the legislature but was not identical with it (ibid., p. 153).

At the time when Blackstone wrote, the executive consisted of the king and six or seven ministers. The ministers were chosen, and could be dismissed, by the monarch, so that he was able to exercise a good deal of influence over government policy if he chose to do so. On the other hand, neither he nor his ministers could control Parliament. They could influence its behaviour through the distribution of patronage and the formation of cliques and parties, but MPs were jealous of their independence and were not willing to be dominated by the executive. Neither the executive nor the legislature could control the actions of the courts, in which judges held office for life once they were appointed.

This system of government could be described as both constitutional and parliamentary. It was not in any sense democratic. Parliament in the eighteenth century was based on the medieval principle that consent to taxation and legislation should be given by representatives of the three 'estates of the realm', the nobility, the clergy and the commons. The nobility and clergy had their representatives in the House of Lords while the rest of the population were represented by the 'knights of the shires' and the members for 'parliamentary boroughs' who sat in the House of Commons. The House of Commons was elected on a very narrow franchise, and until the 1832 Act less than 5 per cent of the adult population enjoyed the right to vote. This franchise was based on property qualifications that varied from one area to another, and the constituencies themselves were wildly unequal in size and number of electors. There was no machinery for the redistribution of seats to take account of population movements, with the result that some constituencies retained the right to send representatives to Parliament even though their population had dwindled so that only a handful of electors lived there. These constituencies were known as 'rotten boroughs'. Such a representative system was easily manipulated by those who possessed social influence and wealth, and their task was made easier by the absence of any effective laws against bribery and other corrupt practices at elections. Wealthy landowners could put their nominees into seats that were normally uncontested, and it has been estimated that in 1793 about 150 landowners (many of whom were themselves in the House of Lords) controlled almost half the seats in the House of Commons. The Duke of Newcastle alone controlled eleven seats. Moreover, the Treasury could control up to 100 seats by the careful distribution of patronage, so that the governing group at the time of a general election was normally safe from defeat. Ministries were brought to an end as the result of intrigue among the ruling élite, intervention by the monarch, or failure to get parliamentary support for their policies, but not by the verdict of the electorate.

This system of government was democratized during the course of the nineteenth century. However, no legislative change was made in the powers of the monarch, the two Houses of Parliament and the judiciary. The representative system was transformed by successive extensions of the franchise, and the result was to transform the working of the governmental system without changing its structure, which remains today very similar to that of the eighteenth-century constitution.

The Movement for Reform

The changes brought about by the Industrial Revolution were the basis of the movement for political reform that developed in the last two decades of the eighteenth century and eventually resulted in the Reform Act of 1832 and the numerous other reforms that followed the Act. The development of industry led to the growth of classes whose fortunes depended on industry, notably mill-owners and manufacturers but also including merchants, tradesmen and skilled artisans. These groups grew in numbers, in wealth and in social influence, but the political system denied them both adequate representation in Parliament and influence over local administration. Their under-representation in the House of Commons was thrown into relief by the growth of large industrial towns that had no parliamentary representative of their own, including Manchester, Birmingham, Leeds and Sheffield.

The campaign for political reform was waged by a number of largely unrelated groups who differed in both their arguments and their methods. There were spokesmen for the industrial and commercial interests who advocated a redistribution of parliamentary seats to take account of population movements and the establishment of franchise qualifications that would be uniform over the whole country, though it was assumed that a property qualification would be retained. There were middle-class societies devoted to political reform who proposed changes of a more sweeping nature, using arguments drawn from the writings of intellectual reformers like Joseph Priestley, Richard Price and Jeremy Bentham. And there were the new political unions, composed mainly of skilled workers, who adopted the revolutionary ideas that Tom Paine had advanced in his pamphlets and in his book *Rights of Man*.

This is not the place to discuss the differences between these arguments and the relations, such as they were, between these groups. It must suffice to say that their discussions and activities were largely responsible for the generation of a reform movement that was to transform the British political system from an oligarchy to a democracy in the sixty years following 1830, and was also to professionalize the central administration and to create the modern system of local government. The intellectual leaders of this movement were the legal reformer Jeremy Bentham, his friend and associate James Mill, the latter's son, John Stuart Mill, and the great Victorian administrator, Edwin Chadwick. Their political ambitions can be sketched in a few sentences.

In the first place, they wanted the representative system to be reformed so that the House of Commons would reflect all the interests and classes of the nation. Some reformers advocated the rapid adoption of universal suffrage while others thought that a gradual extension of the franchise would be both more appropriate and more practicable. But they all insisted that Parliament should represent the nation rather than simply the upper classes. Secondly, the reformers wanted the executive to be fully accountable to Parliament. They were the first to insist (in the 1830s) that the new habit of Cabinet ministers of accepting collective responsibility for their policies should be regarded as a principle of the constitution, and a very important principle at that. Thirdly, the reformers wanted to see the administrative system organized in a more efficient and professional way, with sinecures abolished, recruitment based on merit rather than on personal connections, and each department controlled by a political head who could be held individually accountable to Parliament for its work rather than by a board that was not accountable to anyone.

The reformers won their first and most crucial victory in the passage of the Reform Act of 1832. This Act increased the electorate from 5 per cent of the adult population to 7 per cent, which in itself was hardly a revolutionary change. However, this quantitative change in the franchise was less important than two other features of the Act. One of these was that the Act abolished the system of local franchises, which varied from one constituency to the next, and replaced it by a uniform national franchise. The implication of this was that representation was being granted not to areas and municipal corporations but to individuals. The change made further demands for reform inevitable and also deprived the opponents of reform of some of their more persuasive arguments. Until 1832 they had been able to produce the familiar British argument that, although the system might not be logical, it was hallowed by tradition. It would be wrong to deprive boroughs of a right to parliamentary representation that they had long enjoyed; since nobody wanted to increase the size of the House this made it difficult to give direct representation to the new industrial towns; and in any case the residents of these towns should regard themselves as 'virtually represented' by the members for older industrial towns, which had similar interests. After 1832 these points lost all their force, and the opponents of further reform had no firm ground on which to take their stand.

The other feature of the act that was of considerable significance was the way in which it was passed. In the election of 1831 the proposed reform was the only important issue, and in constituencies up and down the country reformers demanded that the candidates pledge themselves to support it if they were returned. The result was a sweeping victory for the reformers, and the subsequent Parliament was the first one whose members could claim that they had been given a mandate by the electors to pursue a specific policy. Strengthened by this development, the Prime Minister persuaded the king to agree to create sufficient new peers to secure the passage of the Bill through the House of Lords. The threat proved sufficient and the Lords eventually let the Bill go through. The potential supremacy of the people over the Commons was thus made clear for the first time in the election of 1831, and the supremacy of the Commons over the Lords was asserted for the first time just twelve months later. It was this that led Disraeli to remark that 'the aristocratic principle has been destroyed in this country, not by the Reform Act, but by the means by which the Reform Act was passed'.

The immediate effects of the Act on the working of the political system were important even though they were not dramatic. The main consequence was that the choice of government was effectively placed in the hands of the Commons. Some discretion remained with the monarch but the limits within which it could be exercised were narrowed. When a ministry was defeated in the Commons on an issue of confidence, the Prime Minister felt obliged to resign or to ask for a dissolution. If he resigned, the monarch rarely had any choice but to offer the post to the leader of the largest opposition group. In case of a dissolution the question of who should form a government was effectively settled by the votes taken in the first few meetings of the newly elected House. In short, the convention that the government should be collectively responsible to parliament, and in particular to the House of Commons, was firmly established as a principle of the constitution.

This principle assumed considerable prominence in the middle years of the nineteenth century because the nature and distribution of party loyalties resulted in a series of government defeats. The Irish party consisted of a group of about eighty MPs on whose support no government could rely with any confidence; the Conservatives were split by the repeal of the Corn Laws in 1846 and for many years after were divided into protectionists and free traders; and the Liberal Party had Whig and Radical wings whose differences were occasionally reflected in the division lobbies. Most governments in this period had to depend on more than one group for support, and in any case the discipline within groups was very slack. The consequence was that in the thirty-five years between the first and second Reform Acts ten governments were brought to an end by defeat in the Commons and no government succeeded in staying in office for the entire life of a Parliament, from one general election to the next.

It was in this period that writers with liberal sympathies laid stress on the supremacy of Parliament in the British constitution. Gladstone described the House of Commons as 'the centre of our system' and said that the supremacy of the Commons over the administration was 'the cardinal axiom of the constitution'. Walter Bagehot described the Cabinet as 'a committee of Parliament'. The Duke of Devonshire said that Parliament 'can dismiss a ministry if it is too extravagant, or too economical; it can dismiss a ministry because its government is too stringent or too lax. It does actually and practically in every way, directly govern England, Scotland and Ireland.' Certainly it seemed in this period as if the reformers' aim of parliamentary control of the executive had been achieved. Not only were ten governments brought down in thirty-five years, but also it was established as a convention that each minister should answer to Parliament for the blunders of his department, the first ministerial resignation for this reason occurring in 1855. However, with the franchise extended to less than 10 per cent of the adult population, it could not be said that the House of

Commons yet represented anything like the whole nation. In the late 1850s and 1860s the attention of liberals was therefore focused on the need for a further reform of the electoral system.

This reform came in 1867, when Disraeli introduced an Act that almost doubled the electorate in one stroke. For a Conservative leader to seize the initiative in reform in this way was a surprise, and it was said that he 'stole the Liberals' clothes when they were bathing'. It was also an extremely shrewd and far-sighted move; Disraeli realized that the progressive extension of the franchise was inevitable, and that it would relegate his party to the position of a permanent minority unless something could be done to attract lower-class voters to the Tory banner. Few of his colleagues had much confidence in this possibility, but, as R. T. McKenzie once said, Disraeli 'saw the working-class story in the British proletariat as the sculptor sees the angel in a rough lump of stone'. History has triumphantly vindicated his judgement.

Besides extending the franchise, the 1867 Reform Act deprived the House of Commons of the right to decide on the validity of elections in cases of protest, and put questions of this kind within the jurisdiction of the courts. This was a move towards the elimination of corrupt practices in elections, which was carried a great deal further by the adoption of the secret ballot in 1872 and the establishment of effective controls on electoral expenditure, and sanctions against bribery, by the Corrupt Practices Act of 1883.

In 1884 there was yet another extension of the franchise, which increased the electorate by 67 per cent and gave the vote to the great majority of adult men. Perhaps equally important, the Redistribution Act of the following year was the first important step towards the equalization of territorial constituencies. Before this Act the electorates in the most populous constituencies in England were over forty times as big as those in the smallest constituencies; after the Act the ratio was only seven to one.

The result of this second wave of reform, when five major acts were passed in eighteen years, was an electoral system that could reasonably be called democratic. True, it was not until many decades later that the liberal reformers' objective of 'one man, one vote; one vote, one value' was finally achieved. Complete manhood suffrage did not come until 1918. Women acquired the vote in two instalments, those over thirty being grudgingly given the rights of full citizenship in 1918 and their younger sisters getting the same privilege ten years later, when it had become clear to even the most suspicious male that they were not likely to subvert the constitution. The second vote enjoyed by university graduates and some business proprietors was not abolished until 1948. But these later changes, important as they were to the groups concerned, made relatively little difference to the working of the representative system. After 1885, this system ensured that Members of Parliament, and therefore the government, had to keep the support of the greater part of the population if they wished to stay in office, just as the system before 1832 had made it necessary only for them to keep the support of the aristocracy and the country gentry. The whole transformation had occurred during the lifetime of William Gladstone and his contemporaries.

The Development of Party Management

Liberal reformers had assumed that the extension of the franchise would make the House of Commons more representative of the nation without in any way diminishing its influence over the administration. Indeed, many reformers thought that the authority and the power of the House would be enhanced if it could claim to reflect all sections of society. However, at this point there occurs a twist in the story. The assumptions of the reformers were not borne out by events, because the most significant political development in the years following the 1867 Reform Act was one that few had foreseen. This was the development of large-scale party organization and a form of party management that made it possible for the government of the day to ensure that its parliamentary supporters would toe the party line on important issues.

Up to 1867 the political parties were simply parliamentary groupings, with some organization inside Parliament but without mass memberships or branches in the constituencies. Elections were fought by individual candidates, not by a party organization. To some extent the candidates gained or lost support according to the popularity of their parties, but generally speaking the main determinants of a candidates' fortunes at the polls were his popularity in the constituency and the success of his personal campaign. It followed that party leaders had very little power over their parliamentary supporters, who could be sure of keeping their seats so long as they kept control of the situation in their constituencies. The sanctions for party discipline did not exist, and back-bench revolts were common.

This situation changed after the reforms of 1867 and 1872. The extension of the franchise meant that the more populous constituencies contained several thousand voters, too many for the personal appeal and influence of the candidate to be sufficient to carry the day. The limitations placed on electoral expenses made it impossible for candidates to go on buying large numbers of votes by bribery, lavish entertainment and free beer all round. And the adoption of the secret ballot in 1872 made even the most discreet forms of corruption less effective, since the candidate had no clear way of checking that the voters had honoured their side of the bargain.

These changes created a clear need for party organization, at any rate in the urban areas, and as it happened the move in this direction was given extra impetus by a direct consequence of the reforms that had not been foreseen. Before the redistribution the city of Birmingham had been a two-member constituency, with each elector having two votes. In 1868 its representation was increased to three members, but the electors were still limited to two votes each. The Liberals had a majority in the city, and it immediately became clear to a group of shrewd local politicians that careful organization was necessary to ensure that this majority resulted in the election of all three Liberal candidates and not just the two most popular. They thereupon created a representative organization of Birmingham Liberals with an annual subscription of a shilling, a committee in each ward, a general committee for the whole city and an executive committee to take charge of electoral tactics. This organization located Liberal voters and persuaded one-third of them to vote for each of the three possible combinations of Liberal candidates in the 1868 election. The result was entirely successful, and the Birmingham caucus (as it came to be called) was subsequently taken as a model by local party organizers up and down the country.

This development of party organization in the constituencies might have led to the growth of local party bosses, as in the United States. In fact, for a variety of reasons (of which one was that the political scene happened at that time to be dominated by the two outstanding party leaders of the century, Gladstone and Disraeli) the development led to the emergence of national party organizations in the shape of the National Liberal Federation and the National Union of Conservative Associations. These organizations came to acquire a strategic place in the political system as parliamentary candidates became increasingly dependent on organized support for their election campaigns.

The relationship between these new national party organizations and the parliamentary leaders was not immediately settled. In both parties there was an attempt by ambitious politicians (Joseph Chamberlain on the Liberal side and Lord Randolph Churchill among the Conservatives) to build up the power of the organizations in order to promote their own political aims. But both these attempts failed, and their failure settled the question in favour of the parliamentary leaders. The same period, namely the twenty years following the 1867 Reform Act, also saw the development of efficient party bureaucracies, staffed with professional organizers and propagandists and under the direct control of the parliamentary leaders. It was these bureaucracies, by name the Conservative Central Office and the Central Liberal Association, that undertook to find candidates for local party organizations in need of them, and so were able to hold out the promise of a tangible reward (in the shape of a safe seat) for the loyal party man.

These developments laid the foundation of the party loyalty that has been so conspicuous a feature of the British political scene in the twentieth century. While MPs were entirely dependent on their own efforts and popularity for re-election, they could vote against their party leaders without risking their seats. When they became dependent on organized support for re-election, and the organizations that provided this support were controlled (directly or indirectly) by the party leaders, the independence of back-benchers was sharply diminished.

As it happened, the strength of the government in relation to back-benchers in the House of Commons was also increased by the procedural reforms of the

Table 3.1 *The Growth of Party Loyalty in Parliament*

Period	Number of government defeats	Defeats per year (average)
1856–61	52	8.7
1862–7	60	10.0
1868–73	50	8.3
1874–85	70	5.8
1886–91	13	2.2
1892–7	9	1.5
1898–1903	2	0.3
1904–70	34	0.5

early 1880s, which were introduced in order to frustrate the attempts of the Irish MPs to disrupt government business. The most important of these reforms was the introduction of the Closure, which gave the government effective control over parliamentary time. All these developments, taken together, transformed the relationship between Parliament and the government in the last third of the century. The nature and extent of the transformation is indicated by Table 3.1. As can be seen, the relationship that had developed by the 1890s continued, without significant change, throughout the first seven decades of the twentieth century. However, it has to be added that in the 1970s the pattern changed again. For reasons that will be examined in Chapter 8, this decade saw a remarkable increase in the frequency of government defeats, yielding sixty-five defeats in the nine years up to the 1979 election (7.2 per year). In the 1980s the number of defeats has fallen again, with only three in the first ten years of the Thatcher government (0.3 per year), this being the result partly of larger government majorities and partly of Mrs. Thatcher's highly effective style of leadership. However, her government has had to make repeated concessions to back-benchers to keep their support, to an extent that was unknown before 1970 (see Norton, 1985, pp. 29–36). At this juncture it is difficult to say whether the Parliament of 1970–74 marked the beginning of a secular trend towards greater dissidence by back-bench MPs or whether, with a longer historical perspective, future commentators will look back on the 1970s as an exceptional decade.

Conclusion

The democratization of the House of Commons did not strengthen the position of the House in relation to the executive, as might have been expected. Instead, it was the main cause of developments in the party system that gave the executive the means of controlling the House of Commons. The executive remains responsible to Parliament, but since Parliament has become fully representative of the nation the practical significance of this has changed. The nature and significance of ministerial responsibility to Parliament in the twentieth century will be examined in later chapters, but it must not be assumed that they can be summarized in terms of the 'chain of command' implied by liberal views of the constitution.

Further Reading

For the ideas of the reformers see Birch (1964), *Representative and Responsible Government*, chs. 3–5; for an examination of the changing relationships between Commons, Lords, Cabinet and monarch see Mackintosh (1977a), *The British Cabinet*, chs. 2–9.

◇ 4 ◇

The Survival of Medieval Institutions

The development of liberal institutions changed the British political system without completely transforming it. The 'chain of command' concept of government was superimposed on the older system of balance, but the old institutions were not abolished. It is not part of the British political tradition to do away with established institutions, and the modern constitution abounds with practices and offices that have survived from medieval times. Some of these are symbolic and perhaps picturesque but have little or no practical importance; a good example is the procedure by which members of the House of Commons are summoned to the House of Lords for certain formalities by a gentleman dressed in medieval clothes who bears the title of Black Rod. It is not our purpose to discuss formal procedures of this kind, so practices and institutions that no longer play a significant role in the working system of government will be ignored in this book.

There are, however, two surviving medieval institutions that are of considerable importance in the political system. One is the House of Lords, much less powerful than it was but still playing an active part in government. The other is the monarchy, the existence of which affects the whole pattern of government even though the personal powers of the reigning monarch are a pale shadow of what they used to be. The role of these two institutions in the modern political system will now be considered.

The Monarchy

American commentators and students often think that there is something incongruous about the existence of monarchical institutions within a democratic system of government. In fact about half of the world's stable democratic systems are monarchical in form, and this is understandable both in historical and in political terms. Historically, nearly all European states were monarchies in the past and the monarchical institutions have survived where they have not been overthrown by revolutions. Politically, the convenience of a monarchical system in a democracy is that it provides a head of state who has been insulated

41

from party politics since childhood and can thus be accepted as neutral between the contending parties.

The roles of the British monarch may be categorized as symbolic, social and political. The first two need not concern us in this book. The political role of the monarch has changed dramatically since the beginning of the nineteenth century, though without any legislative measure or other overt action to which a date can be given. To explain how this change took place it will be helpful to distinguish the nature of the Royal Prerogative from the personal discretion enjoyed by the reigning monarch.

The Royal Prerogative is a term that denotes the authority resting with the Crown, as distinct from that resting with Parliament or the courts. Thus, it is within the Royal Prerogative to enter into diplomatic relations with other states and to conclude treaties with them; to command the armed forces, to declare war and to make peace, to appoint judges, to initiate criminal prosecutions and to pardon offenders; to summon, to prorogue and to dissolve Parliament; to appoint ministers, including the Prime Minister; to confer honours, to create peers and to appoint bishops of the Church of England. All these acts, and others, are acts performed in the name of the Crown, and the way in which they are performed cannot be questioned or controlled by the courts. Most of them are equally free from parliamentary control, though some of them are now subject to the influence of parliamentary opinion because ministers themselves are subject to that influence.

The extent of the Royal Prerogative has not diminished appreciably during the last 200 years. What has happened is that, whereas 200 years ago the reigning monarch performed many or most of these acts at his own discretion, today the monarch performs the acts on the advice of ministers or other persons. The acts are performed in the name of the Crown, but except in a few special cases the decision is no longer taken by the monarch. The conduct of foreign affairs is in the hands of the Prime Minister and the Cabinet, as are decisions about defence policy; judges are appointed by the monarch on the advice of the Prime Minister or the Lord Chancellor; ministers are appointed on the advice of the Prime Minister, and on that advice alone; honours are conferred and other appointments are made on the advice of a variety of persons.

These changes have not come about as the result of crises or been marked by formal declarations, but have simply emerged over the course of the years. It is not easy to give precise dates for them because the monarch's powers have not been taken away, but have merely fallen into disuse. Thus, with the advantage of hindsight we can now say that the royal power to veto Bills passed by both Houses of Parliament was last used in 1707, but in the 1720s it was not known that this power would never be used again. Equally, we can say that during the latter part of Queen Victoria's reign the monarch lost the power to exercise a positive influence on the Prime Minister's choice of ministers, but Queen Victoria would not have acknowledged that this was the case. At the present time there remain one or two powers of the Royal Prerogative of which the exercise is surrounded by a penumbra of doubt, at any rate in the popular mind, and these will be discussed in the following section.

The Powers of the Monarch Today

An understanding of the position of the monarch today may possibly be helped by drawing on the analogy of the position of a referee at a football match. In one sense the referee is in charge of the match; he tosses the coin to decide which captain shall have choice of ends, he determines the start and finish of the game and only he can declare that a goal has been scored. But the referee exercises this control within strict rules that he did not make and cannot influence. He has the power to give orders to players, but in his exercise of this and other powers he has less freedom of action than anyone else on the field. There are three indiscretions that the referee must at all costs avoid. The first is interfering with the natural course of the game, except when some rule has been violated. The second is partiality to one of the teams, or even the appearance of it. The third is involvement in disputes between players. If a referee fails to avoid these mistakes, he will find himself in difficulties, and serious failures of this kind will result in the termination of his career as a referee.

This is a crude analogy, but it may serve to focus attention on some of the difficulties of the monarch's position. She is expected to play a daily part in the government of the country without ever showing the slightest sign of partiality towards one party rather than another or one policy rather than another. Action by her is required at most crises and turning-points of politics, but must never be thought to be interfering with the natural course of political events. The task of the monarch is clearly one of extreme delicacy and it is only by the strict observance of convention that it is possible to keep the monarchy from becoming involved in political controversy. One important convention is that normally only the Prime Minister has access to the monarch, their discussions naturally being entirely secret. When a Prime Minister resigns other conventions are brought into play, which result in the appointment of a successor.

To delineate the role of the monarch more precisely it will be helpful to give examples of events in recent years that have led to public speculation about the extent of royal discretion. The powers that have been under discussion in this way in the twentieth century are the power to create large numbers of peers, the power to dissolve Parliament and the power to appoint a Prime Minister. After the questions arising from these have been dealt with it will be a fairly simple matter to outline the normal pattern of royal activities in relation to government.

The power to create sufficient new peers to change the majority in the House of Lords is one that has been used once and invoked on two other occasions. It was used in 1712 when Queen Anne created twelve Tory peers to secure a majority in the House of Lords that would support her government's proposals to end the war with France. It was next invoked in 1832, when the king agreed to accede to the Prime Minister's request to create sufficient new peers to swamp the House of Lords if that House refused to pass the Reform Bill. A similar pledge was given by the king in 1910 in connection with the proposal to restrict the powers of the upper chamber over legislation. The government of the day was successful in an election that turned on the issue and once again, as in 1832, the threat of the creation of a large number of new peers was sufficient to induce the House of Lords to pass the Bill in question.

It could be said, therefore, that there is a convention that if the government of the day asks the monarch to overcome the opposition of the Lords to a constitutional reform (or possibly to any important reform) in this way, the monarch is entitled (and perhaps ought) to insist that a general election be held to test the popularity of the government but should accede to the request if the government is successful in the election. In practice, however, this convention is unlikely to be used again. The Parliament Act of 1911 contained its own procedure for overcoming the opposition of the Lords to a legislative measure, after a delay of two years, and the Parliament Act of 1949 (passed under the provisions of the 1911 Act) reduced the period of delay to one year. It is difficult to envisage a measure that would be so urgent that it could not wait twelve months and for this reason it is now unlikely that any government will find it necessary to invoke the threat of swamping the House of Lords with new members.

The existence of the royal power to dissolve Parliament raises two possible questions: whether the monarch could dissolve against the advice of the Prime Minister and whether he could refuse to accede to a Prime Minister's request for a dissolution. The answer to the first question is, in all conceivable circumstances, in the negative. In the crisis over Home Rule for Ireland between 1912 and 1914 several Conservative leaders argued that the king had the right, and even the duty, to dissolve Parliament and call for a general election before letting the government proceed with a measure that would put some of His Majesty's loyal subjects under the rule of a government that they would regard as alien. King George V made no public comment on this suggestion, though he wrote to the Prime Minister at length about the prospect of civil war in Ireland and suggested that it would be desirable for a general election to be held before the Home Rule Bill was put through Parliament. The Prime Minister could not accept this suggestion, and it is clear from the correspondence that the king, though extremely anxious about the course of events, did not feel that he could dissolve Parliament any more than he could dismiss his ministers or refuse assent to the Home Rule Bill. If he had done any of these things, he would have provoked a constitutional crisis that would have jeopardized the position of the monarchy itself. Since it is difficult to envisage a situation in which the arguments for royal intervention would be stronger than they were in regard to Home Rule, it is reasonable to conclude that dissolution against the advice of the Prime Minister is not a practical possibility.

The question of whether a monarch can refuse to dissolve when asked to do so is slightly more complex. The key to the question lies in the need for the monarchy to retain its reputation for impartiality between the parties. If the monarch were to refuse a dissolution and the Prime Minister were to resign, it would presumably be necessary to ask the Leader of the Opposition to form a government. If this government were quickly defeated in Parliament, dissolution would be the only possible way out of the ensuing crisis. But this would mean that the monarch would be granting to one Prime Minister what had been refused to another, which would inevitably tend to damage the esteem in which the monarch was held by supporters of the original government. It follows that the practical rule is that the monarch can refuse to grant a dissolution only if it is known that a viable alternative government can be formed. This situation will obtain only when no one party has a majority in the House of Commons, so that there is the possibility of varying coalitions. If one party has an absolute majority and the leader of the party, being Prime Minister, asks for a dissolution, the most that the monarch can do is to express the opinion that the move might be unwise and ask the Prime Minister to give the proposal further consideration. If the Prime Minister adheres to the original position, the monarch has no real choice but to accede to the request.

These points were illustrated by the events of 1923 and 1924. The general election of 1922 had given the Conservative Party a parliamentary majority, and Bonar Law had become Prime Minister. In 1923 Bonar Law became ill and Stanley Baldwin, who succeeded him, wished to call a general election after only a few months in office. The king was unhappy at the prospect of an election when Parliament was only about a year old and he asked the Prime Minister if he would think about the matter further and discuss it with his colleagues. But Baldwin insisted on a dissolution, and the king therefore agreed to his request.

The result of this election was that no one party had a majority in the Commons, and a minority Labour government was formed with the support of the Liberals. Ten months later the Liberals withdrew their support and J. Ramsay MacDonald, the Prime Minister, asked the king for a dissolution. On this occasion the possibility existed of a viable alternative government being formed with Liberal and Conservative support, and the king (anticipating MacDonald's request) had consulted the Liberal and Conservative leaders to see if they would be willing to join in a coalition. As they were not so willing, MacDonald's request was accepted, but it is to be assumed that if a Liberal-Conservative government had been possible the king might have refused to dissolve Parliament and would have been entitled to do so. However, the longer the time that elapses without a monarch exercising this constitutional right, the greater is the likelihood of controversy if it were done.

The third royal power that has sometimes led to uncertainty about the role of the monarch is the power to appoint a Prime Minister. As both main parties now have settled procedures for the election of their leaders no problem can arise if the leading party has a secure majority in Parliament. If the need for a new appointment is created by the defeat of the existing government in an election, the outgoing Prime Minister would advise the Queen to appoint the leader of the victorious party. If a Prime Minister wishes to retire for personal reasons, he or she could be expected (health permitting) to announce that intention so as to give the party time to elect a successor. This was the procedure Harold Wilson followed in 1976. If a Prime Minister should die in office, the Queen would simply wait until the governing party chose its new leader, which need take only a few days. The Queen would then invite the new leader to form a government.

The only circumstance that might require a greater degree of initiative on the part of the monarch would be a general election producing no clear majority for any party. When this occurred in February 1974 the Prime Minister delayed his resignation until after he had tried, but failed, to secure a promise of support from the leader of the Liberal Party. If he had been given this, and had felt that he could also depend on support from the Ulster Unionists, he would presumably have remained in office. Upon his resignation the Queen sent for Harold Wilson, as leader of the Parliamentary Labour Party, and asked him to form a government. She took this step although Labour had thirty-four fewer seats than the other parties combined and could not be certain of getting parliamentary support. Ten days later Wilson told the leaders of the smaller parties that if they did not support his new government he would ask the Queen to dissolve Parliament again and hold another general election. This was a surprising threat for him to make, but it had the desired effect. His government survived without being defeated on a vote of confidence until it gained an overall majority in the election of October 1974.

As there is always the possibility of an indecisive general election, it is worth asking whether the precedent of February 1974 ought to be followed on future occasions. In parliamentary democracies in continental Europe where indecisive elections are the norm, it is common for the head of state to give a party leader a provisional rather than an outright mandate: to ask that leader to see if he can secure parliamentary support and to delay appointing him as Prime Minister until an affirmative answer is received. A good case can be made for saying that this is the procedure that ought to be followed if a future British election produces an indecisive result. Wilson's tactic worked well enough in 1974, but on another occasion the smaller parties might not be willing to fall into line. In that case, would the monarch be obliged to dissolve Parliament immediately? It might be thought that the monarch has a duty to the newly elected House of Commons, as well as to the person who has just been asked to form a government. If a second election also produced an indecisive result, would it be proper for the leader of the biggest party to secure yet another dissolution, with the prospect of exhausting the funds of the smaller parties and inducing their supporters to give up in despair?

It can well be argued that if an election produces a Parliament without a majority for any one party, the procedures ought to encourage the formation of a coalition government, which might take time. The appointment of a minority government endowed with the immediate power to threaten the other parties with the prospect of a repeat election does not seem, in principle, to be desirable on democratic grounds. This is a constitutional question on which the experience of other European democracies might be a better guide than the precedent of February 1974.

The Normal Role of the Monarchy in Government

The preceding section has outlined the role of the monarch at the various turning-points of politics: when a Prime Minister dies or resigns; when a dissolution of Parliament is proposed; and in cases of acute conflict between the two Houses of Parliament. In addition the monarch plays a small but continuous part in the normal process of government. She opens and closes Parliament each year and delivers the 'speech from the throne' setting out the legislative policy of the government at the beginning of each session. She assents to Bills after they have been passed by both Houses, this assent marking the formal completion of the legislative process. She receives ambassadors from foreign countries. She confers honours of varying degree. And as Head of State and Head of the Commonwealth she occasionally makes state visits to foreign or Commonwealth countries.

In none of these activities does the monarch have much personal discretion. The Prime Minister will always listen respectfully to the monarch's views, but the effective decisions are made by members of the government. The speech from the throne, for instance, is written by the Prime Minister even though it is read by the monarch. It is in this way that the ancient institution of monarchy has been adapted to meet the requirements of a democratic age.

In private discussion the monarch has an opportunity to present her views to the Prime Minister. It is the custom for the monarch to be sent copies of Cabinet papers and to have a brief weekly meeting with the Prime Minister to discuss current issues. The rights of the monarch in these discussions were summarized about a century ago by Bagehot as 'the right to be consulted, the right to encourage, and the right to warn'. But the monarch is not a politician and it should not be thought that the government of the day is likely to be deviated from its chosen course by royal influence.

It is evident that in the twentieth century the monarch is a figurehead rather than an active political force. However, it does not follow that the existence of the monarchy should be regarded as a formality that makes no difference to the political process. On the contrary, the institution of monarchy is extremely important in two different ways.

First, the existence of the Royal Prerogative gives the British government a substantial degree of independence of Parliament in some fields, without giving it so much independence that it cannot be called to account. Thus, the conclusion of international treaties is within the Royal Prerogative, and British diplomats can conduct negotiations and reach agreements without any fear that their work might be undone and their future position undermined by a refusal on the part of Parliament to ratify the agreements made. At the same time Parliament has the right to question the Foreign Secretary and the Prime Minister about their conduct of foreign policy so that these ministers have to explain and justify their actions in public – and to suffer a loss of reputation if their justifications fail to convince.

The institution of monarchy is also important in that it provides a Head of State who constitutes a symbol of the identity and unity of the nation. There is no evidence that a monarchical system of government is in any objective sense better than a republican system, but there can be no doubt that the continued existence of the British monarchy symbolizes in a direct and personal way the continuity and stability of the British political community, and by so doing acts as a focus for the loyalty of British citizens.

The House of Lords

While monarchies are still quite common in the world, the House of Lords is unique among legislative assemblies. It has approximately 1,200 members, of whom about 800 are hereditary peers, about 360 are life peers, 26 are bishops and 21 are Lords of Appeal. Members do not receive a salary, though they get an attendance allowance that was £52 a day in 1989. The average attendance is around 300. The composition, powers and activities of the House have been the subject of intermittent controversy throughout the twentieth century.

The House has been in a relatively weak position ever since the passage of the 1832 Reform Act, to which it had agreed only under duress. The fact that the House of Commons could henceforth claim to be based on a national suffrage gave it a degree of moral and political superiority over the second chamber. The convention of collective governmental responsibility to Parliament, as it developed, involved the Commons rather than the Lords. Ministers had to answer questions put to them by peers, but the government was not expected to resign if it was defeated in the Lords.

From the 1880s until the 1960s the House of Lords had a clear Conservative majority, and the use of that majority to defeat legislation promoted by Liberal and Labour governments has inevitably caused controversy. The rejection of the Liberal budget in 1909 particularly outraged the government of the day, which proposed to curtail the legislative power of the Lords and succeeded (with its Irish allies) in winning an election in which this proposal was the only important issue. There followed the Parliament Act of 1911, which abolished the rights of the Lords to hold up Finance Bills and reduced its power of delay over other Bills to a period of two years.

In 1945 the first majority Labour government took office. As the Labour Party had fundamental objections to hereditary peers wielding political power, it has to be asked why this government did not use its large majority in the Commons to abolish the House of Lords and replace it by a more representative second chamber. The answer to this question falls into three parts.

First, the Conservative leader in the Lords announced that his party would abide by a new convention when considering controversial legislation promoted by the Labour government. If the measure had been mentioned in Labour's election manifesto the Conservatives would not use their power in the Lords to obstruct the Bill. They would discuss the details and might suggest amendments, but Bills in this category would not be held up.

Secondly, the Labour Party had no agreed plan for a reformed or new second chamber, and it was clear that any proposal would be highly controversial and would take up a great deal of time. As the new government had a full programme of social and economic legislation to introduce, and it was clear that the Lords did not intend to delay measures of this kind, the government had a strong incentive to put the issue of constitutional reform on one side for the time being.

The third answer is that Labour politicians contemplating a radical reform of the Lords had to face the probability that a reformed House would have more prestige and more influence than the existing House. Since most Labour politicians felt that parliamentary power should be concentrated in the hands of the Commons, they jibbed at the prospect of creating a second chamber that might be an effective rival to the Commons. This dilemma was stated very clearly by Herbert Morrison, who was Lord President of the Council in the 1945 Labour government and had a general responsibility for steering legislation through Parliament:

> The Labour government was not anxious for the rational reform or democratisation of the second chamber, for this would have added to its authority and would have strengthened its position as against that of the House of Commons. Changes which gave the House of Lords a democratic and representative character would have been undemocratic in outcome, for they would have tended to make the Lords the equal of the Commons ... The very irrationality of the composition of the House of Lords and its quaintness are safeguards for our modern British democracy.   (Morrison, 1954, p. 194)

The Labour government of 1945–51 therefore made no attempt to change the composition of the Lords, though the 1949 Parliament Act reduced its power of delay from two years to one. It was in fact a Conservative government that made the first attempt to modernize the composition of the House, in the form of the Life Peerages Act of 1958. This measure enabled the Prime Minister to appoint persons of either sex to peerages that are not hereditary. By 1989 the House contained about 360 life peers, many of whom have enjoyed distinguished careers in other walks of life and have improved the quality of debates. As many of them are Labour supporters, Social Democrats or Social and Liberal Democrats, the party bias of the House has also been partially corrected.

Another Conservative reform that affected the composition of the House was the Peerage Act of 1963, which enables peers to disclaim their peerages and thus to stand for election to the Commons. In the autumn of 1963 this step was taken by the Earl of Home, upon his being invited to succeed Harold Macmillan as Prime Minister. He could not have accepted this invitation had it not been possible for him to renounce his earldom and acquire a seat in the Commons. In the first ten years after the passage of this Act twelve peers disclaimed their peerages. The Act also admitted women holding hereditary peerages to membership of the House.

These reforms, although welcomed by all parties, did nothing to change the central anomaly of the House, namely the right of hereditary peers to vote on legislative proposals for no better reason than that one of their ancestors had been included in a royal honours list. In 1969, however, a radical reform was proposed by the Labour government and was actually supported by the House of Lords. This Bill provided for a House that would contain 230 working members, all of whom would be appointed and paid, and for a process whereby the hereditary peers would gradually be phased out.

This scheme had been worked out in confidential talks between representatives of the main parties. However, some time before the Bill was drafted the Prime Minister had broken off these talks and in consequence the reform was sponsored by the government alone, so that, although the Conservative front bench gave it tacit support, it did not feel under any obligation to employ party discipline to assist its progress. At the Committee Stage in the Commons it ran into a determined campaign of obstruction from back-benchers on both sides of the House. Labour left-wingers like Michael Foot joined in an unprecedented alliance with Conservative right-wingers like Enoch Powell to frustrate a plan that they disliked for contrasting reasons. For ten days the business of the House was held up by protracted manoeuvres, skilfully planned and executed, until the government simply gave up in disgust and withdrew the Bill. Parliament had not seen a back-bench revolt on this scale since the turn of the century, and its success came as a shock to ministers and lobby correspondents alike. It also undermined some of the generalizations political scientists had been making about Parliament for the previous thirty years.

Since this débâcle there have been no more attempts at reform. Given the ever-increasing animosity between Conservative and Labour groups in the House of Commons, there is clearly no chance in the foreseeable future of securing agreement to another rational compromise like the 1969 proposal. The Conservative Party has its attention focused on economic and social problems and has lost interest in constitutional reform. The Labour Party has moved towards outright abolition of the House of Lords, with no plan for another second chamber to undertake some of its functions. The 1983 Labour electoral manifesto stated bluntly that a Labour government wanted to 'take action to abolish the undemocratic House of Lords as quickly as possible'. The pledge was not repeated in the 1987 manifesto, but the policy has not been formally changed. In this situation it is relevant to outline the present role of the House in government, with a view to answering the question of whether a second chamber is really necessary.

The Present Role of the Lords

The present functions of the House of Lords are of four main kinds. First, its members question ministers about the activities of the government and stage debates on general issues of national policy. The Lords can discuss issues in a broader frame of reference than is possible in the Commons and they conduct their debates in a less partisan way. As the House includes peers with a wide range of experience, the level of debate is often high. There are top surgeons and physicians to discuss health services, retired generals and admirals to discuss questions of national defence, bishops and archbishops to discuss religious affairs, senior judges to discuss legal issues. However, it is difficult to assess the extent of the practical influence of these debates.

Secondly, the House saves the time of the Commons by giving a first hearing to non-controversial Bills, which subsequently go through the Commons with a minimum of discussion. Since 1945 something like a quarter of all government Bills have had their first reading in the Lords, and in a fair number of cases this has resulted in an appreciable saving of time in the Commons. This way of routing Bills is particularly appropriate when the legislation is complex in a technical sense, such as Bills dealing with company law or the law relating to copyright.

Thirdly, the House of Lords revises the details of Bills sent to it by the Commons. This function has become increasingly important in the twentieth century as the activities of the state have been extended. Legislation has become more voluminous and more complex without any commensurate increase in the amount of time that the House of Commons can devote to it. Many Bills are necessarily pushed through the Commons with less discussion than they need. Detailed consideration of such measures by the Lords is usually welcomed by the Commons, by the government and by the various organizations representing interests likely to be affected by the legislation in question.

Sometimes the Lords make amendments that the Commons subsequently strike out or revise again, but in most cases detailed amendments in the Lords are acceptable to the government of the day and are endorsed by the Commons when the Bill is referred back. In some cases the amendments are initiated by the government, using discussions in the Lords as an opportunity to refine the original draft. It would be difficult to question the value of this work of revision.

The fourth and most controversial function of the House of Lords is that it occasionally rejects Bills sent to it by the Commons, or amends them in ways that are unacceptable to the majority in the Commons. As it happens, this has been done with increased frequency in recent years. In most cases the Commons majority has reconfirmed its original decision and the Lords have

Table 4.1 *Party Affiliations in the House of Lords*

| Party | Affiliations of members attending one-third of sittings | | |
	1967/8	1975/6	1981/2
Conservative	125	140	153
Labour	95	105	77
Liberal-SDP	19	22	44
Independent	52	63	57
Total	291	330	331

Source: Shell, 1985, p. 20.

accepted this, but there have been a number of cases since the botched attempt to reform the second chamber in 1969 when opposition in the Lords had led to the abandonment or significant modification of legislative proposals.

These cases can be divided into three categories: cases in which the original proposal was perceived to violate norms about the public interest; cases in which the proposal was thought to be excessively doctrinaire; and cases in which the Lords simply took a more liberal view of the issue than the government and the Commons had done. Before enumerating these cases it must be pointed out that the House of Lords no longer has a working majority of Conservatives. A survey conducted in 1988 indicated that the House contained approximately 525 Conservatives, 125 Labour supporters, 85 Liberals and Social Democrats, and 465 peers who described themselves as independent. D. R. Shell has produced a valuable analysis of the affiliations of those members who attended at least one-third of the sittings in recent sessions, and this is summarized in Table 4.1.

In considering these figures two points should be stressed. One is that the independents are genuinely independent, with voting behaviour that is rather unpredictable. The other is that party discipline among Conservative peers is weaker than it is among peers affiliated to the other parties, or for that matter among Conservative MPs; in all the cases mentioned below, Conservatives recorded votes on both sides of the question.

The first category comprises three proposals that were widely perceived to be outrageous, in the sense of being concerned solely to further partisan or sectional interests and being indefensible in wider terms. One of these was advanced in 1969, when the Labour government realized that the outdated system of electoral boundaries was biased in Labour's favour and promoted a Bill to release the Home Secretary from his legal obligation to present an extensive set of boundary revisions for parliamentary approval before the next election. The revisions had been drawn up by impartial commissions and this attempt was immediately perceived to be no more than a blatant move to gerrymander the electoral system. The Lords frustrated this move. In the event the government got its gerrymander anyway, because the Home

Secretary persuaded his parliamentary colleagues to reject the revisions he proposed, but at least the government's behaviour was exposed in its true colours.

The second proposal in this category was put forward in 1977, when the Labour government introduced a Bill at the behest of the Transport and General Workers' Union that would have had the effect of extending the control of the dockers' section of this union to workers engaged in packing and unpacking containers at any location within five miles of a registered dock. This was clearly an attempt to further a sectional interest at the expense of the public interest; it would never have passed the Commons on a free vote; and it was rejected by the Lords. When it was reconsidered in the Commons abstentions by Labour MPs prevented it being passed a second time.

The third proposal of this sort was put forward in 1984, in regard to the Conservative government's plan to abolish the Greater London Council and the councils of the other six metropolitan areas. This plan was mentioned in the 1983 Conservative election manifesto and it was made clear that the Lords would not oppose it. However, in 1984 the government proposed an interim measure, pending the adoption of legislation for the abolition of these authorities, whereby the elected members of their councils would be replaced by members nominated by lower-tier authorities. The effect of this proposal, in London and possibly elsewhere, would have been to replace Labour majorities by Conservative majorities without an election. This was perceived to be a partisan move with no general arguments in its favour, and the Lords rejected it. The rejection was reluctantly accepted by the government.

Between 1969 and 1989 there were six or seven other occasions on which the House of Lords successfully challenged measures that were seen as excessively doctrinaire. In 1975 it secured modifications in a measure that would extend the principle of the closed shop to the profession of journalism, for fear lest a trade union should secure influence over opinions expressed by journalists and editors. In 1980 it rejected a proposal to impose changes for the transport of children to and from school in rural areas. In 1980, and again in 1984, it prevented the sale of municipal housing that was specially designed for the elderly. In 1981 it reduced the scale of financial cuts aimed at the overseas broadcasting services of the BBC. In 1983 it prevented the privatization of the Ordnance Survey, the department responsible for producing all Britain's official maps. In 1984 it prevented the sale of municipal housing that had been specially designed or adapted for handicapped people. The fact that five of these reversals of government policy affected the Conservative government of Margaret Thatcher reflects the tendency of Conservative peers to be suspicious of the right-wing neo-liberal attitudes of this government. Not surprisingly, Conservative peers tend to be traditional Conservatives in their political orientation. (See Shell, 1985, for fuller accounts of these and other government defeats in the Lords.)

Finally, there have been several instances since 1969 when the Lords have

Table 4.2 *Preferred Policy of British Electors regarding the House of Lords: 1983*

Preferred policy	Party identification			All
	Conservatives %	Liberal-SDP %	Labour %	electors %
Remain as it is	72	55	44	57
Abolish it and replace by nothing	3	6	15	8
Replace by different body	6	12	14	10
Some other change	13	21	19	16
Don't know	6	6	8	9

Source: Jowell and Airey, 1984, p. 31.

insisted on liberalizing government measures. In 1971 they secured an amendment of a Bill on nationality so as to protect the rights of immigrants. In 1973 they insisted that free contraceptive services should be made available by the National Health Service. In 1973 they passed an amendment to protect areas of natural beauty from spoilation by reservoirs. In 1984 they secured a limitation on the right of the police to stop citizens in the street to search for incriminating evidence. In 1987 they abolished the use of corporal punishment in state schools, instead of just restricting it as the government had proposed. In 1988 they passed an amendment to the Education Reform Bill guaranteeing university teachers freedom to put forward controversial or unpopular opinions without endangering their jobs or academic privileges. These moves, like the other examples mentioned, illustrate the extent to which the House of Lords has become a moderating influence in British party politics. While the two main parties in the House of Commons have both adopted more extreme policies in recent years, the peers have moved towards the centre.

This brief account of the current role of the House of Lords indicates that the House performs valuable functions. It is only because of this that such an anomalous medieval institution has been able to retain influence and respect in the last third of the twentieth century. It would doubtless be possible to design a more modern second chamber that would perform these functions equally well, if not better, but the political obstacles to such a change were revealed in 1969. As things stand, the House of Lords works reasonably well and is reasonably popular. The views of a national sample of citizens are summarized in Table 4.2.

Further Reading

For some useful basic facts on the monarchy see Central Office of Information (1975), *The Monarchy in Britain*; for a brief analysis of the constitutional powers of the monarch see Marshall (1984), *Constitutional Conventions*, ch. 2; for a discussion of the role of the monarch in the formation of governments, with some European comparisons, see Butler (1983), *Governing without a Majority*; for a summary of relations between the monarch and the Cabinet see Mackintosh (1977a), *The British Cabinet*, ch. 9; on the House of Lords see Shell (1985), 'The House of Lords and the Thatcher government'.

Part III
The Actors and their Roles

◇ 5 ◇

Political Parties

The political actors in a democratic system of government include electors and voters, pressure group spokesmen and lobbyists, political parties, candidates and elected politicians, government ministers, civil servants and local officials. In modern Britain the political parties are so visible, and an understanding of their role is so essential for an understanding of the system, that it is appropriate to deal with the parties before discussing the various other actors.

The Nature of the Party System

The main characteristics of the party system can easily be outlined. First, it has been dominated for well over a century by two major parties (though not always the same two), with smaller parties playing only a minor role. This is partly because of the relative unimportance of social cleavages other than the horizontal cleavage of class, partly because the electoral system favours the larger parties and discriminates against the smaller ones.

Secondly, the major parties are parties of mass membership, having branches throughout the country and collecting monthly or annual subscriptions from their members. At the present time the Conservative Party has over a million members while the Labour Party has about a quarter of a million individual members together with about five million affiliated members who subscribe through their trade unions. Many members (including nearly all of Labour's affiliated members) do nothing for the party apart from subscribing; many others take part in social and fund-raising activities; and a minority are active in party organization or electoral campaigning. Local studies suggest that about 1 per cent of the electorate are willing to do voluntary work during elections, which would produce an average of about 500 workers per constituency if this were the general pattern. The number who actually turn out is probably a little less than this in most areas, but as there are no paid canvassers in British elections these party workers fulfil an important function during the campaign.

Thirdly, the parties are highly centralized in spite of their mass memberships. In the United States the real party managers operate at state and local level, the national parties being loose alliances formed for electoral purposes. But in Britain the local party branches have little real power except over the nomination of candidates. Local branches are encouraged to discuss questions of policy and they send in resolutions for debate at the annual conference, but in practice their influence on national party policy is for the most part rather slender.

Fourthly, both main parties, and some of the smaller ones too, are extremely active in publishing, producing a steady stream of policy proposals and pamphlets for discussion. In this way also they are quite unlike their American counterparts, which publish practically nothing.

Until 1918 the two main parties were the Conservative and Liberal parties, but the latter was displaced by the Labour Party shortly after that date. The rise of Labour was probably inevitable, given the extension of the franchise in 1884 and 1918 to large numbers of working-class citizens who had not formed loyalties to either of the other parties. Socialist parties have come to play a major role in all industrial democracies in the twentieth century, with the sole exceptions of the United States and Canada. However, why Labour displaced the Liberals rather than the Conservatives is a question that deserves a word of explanation.

One factor is social. Between the 1880s and 1918 the Liberals lost much of their basic constituency, the ambitious entrepreneurial class of the nineteenth century, whose members felt themselves to be relative newcomers on the social scene and who wanted reforms. They were gradually transformed into a prosperous business class, with a sense of being part of the British establishment. They transferred their allegiance to the Conservative Party, partly for social reasons and partly because the Conservatives seemed better prepared to defend business interests against the threat posed by the trade unions. Another reason is that the 1914 war deprived the Liberals of one of their policy planks; having stood for generations as the party of international peace and friendship, they had led Britain into that disastrous conflict and could no longer sustain the role.

Other factors were tactical and personal. The Liberals encouraged the infant labour movement, when their party's interests would have been better served by an attempt to throttle their rival at birth. During the war the party was badly split by a conflict between its two leading figures, Asquith and Lloyd George. By 1918 the Liberal Party was doomed to decline. That it had become a small third party by 1924, with only 40 MPs to Labour's 151, demonstrates that the British electoral system does not necessarily act as an obstacle to the re-alignment of the party system. On the contrary, the system hastened the process of transition in this period; under a system of proportional representation the Liberal Party would have retained far more seats than it did in 1924 and would have remained a force to be reckoned with right up to the present day. However, the Liberals did not become converted to the principle of proportional representation until just after they had lost the power to establish such a system – which was not just a tactical error but a major strategic blunder.

From 1924 until 1974 the party system was dominated by the Conservative and Labour parties, which are very different in their organization, membership and doctrines. Since 1974 smaller parties have become more significant, for reasons that were not anticipated but can easily be explained. In the remainder of this chapter the two main parties will be analysed in turn, followed by a discussion of the smaller parties.

The Conservative Party

The Conservative party has existed under that name since the 1830s, though it was first simply an organized group of MPs and peers and did not develop local branches until the extension of the franchise in 1867. In that year local Conservative associations were formed and a body called the National Union of Conservative Associations was established. Large numbers of supporters quickly rallied to the cause and by 1875 there were already 472 branches in the constituencies (Norton and Aughey, 1981, p. 204).

In discussing the structure and working of the party it is necessary to distinguish between the party at Westminster and the party in the country. At Westminster the party has a Central Office staffed by professional organizers, which was established in 1870, a committee of back-bench MPs that first met in 1922 and is known simply as the 1922 Committee, and the Conservative Research Department, which was formed immediately after the Second World War. In the country there are 633 constituency associations (one for each constituency in Britain, but none in Northern Ireland), with a membership that was estimated to be about 1.5 million in 1974 (Pinto-Duschinsky, 1985, p. 331) but had fallen to about 1.0 million by 1989. There are also numerous branches of the Young Conservatives, which had a membership of 157,000 in their peak year of 1949, but have declined since. In 1978 they were said to have approximately 27,500 members (Norton and Aughey, 1981, p. 213).

The income of the party comes mostly from individual members. The Conservative associations (almost entirely middle-class in their membership) are highly sociable groups, devoting much energy to weekly whist drives, occasional dances and garden parties, and innumerable coffee mornings and sherry parties in members' houses. All of these activities are so arranged that they contribute in some degree to party funds. In 1975/6 the local associations raised about £4.5 million, of which about 5 per cent came from business firms and the rest from individual subscriptions and fund-raising activities.

The national head office of the party had an income of just under £2 million in 1975/6, of which it is estimated that about two-thirds came from business firms (Norton and Aughey 1981, p. 216). Overall, business contributions in that financial year therefore amounted to between 20 and 25 per cent of total income. The smallness of this proportion is significant. Although the party tends to favour business interests as against labour interests, it has never been captured by business interests. As has often been noted, business firms need the support

61

Table 5.1 *Individual Memberships of the Major Parties: 1989*

Party	Approximate membership
Conservative	1,000,000
Labour	280,000
Social and Liberal Democrats	90,000
Social Democrats	11,000

of the Conservative Party more than the Conservative Party needs business support.

It may fairly be observed that this organization has proved itself to be very efficient. As is shown by Table 5.1, the Conservative Party has well over twice as many members as the other three national parties put together. As is shown by Table 5.2, the party also has far more professional organizers, particularly at the local level.

The leader of the party is elected by Conservative MPs. This is a relatively new procedure, as up until 1965 the leader 'emerged' as the result of discussions between a handful of senior figures in the party, who consulted wider groups only in an informal way. In 1965 Edward Heath became the first leader chosen by election. Ironically, in 1975 he also became the first leader to be overthrown by the vote of his colleagues, having put himself up for re-election to stem complaints about his leadership, only to find himself defeated by Margaret Thatcher.

The present procedure is open and democratic to a degree that is surprising in view of the élitist procedures that obtained before 1965. In part, this reflects the extent to which middle-class MPs have come to dominate the Conservative Party in the House of Commons, in place of the upper-class dominance that has prevailed in the past. There has to be a leadership election between three and six months after each general election, with provision for annual elections thereafter. If there is only one candidate, as has been the case since 1975, there is of course no contest and no need for a vote. But if a leader becomes unpopular or is thought to be unsuccessful, there is ample opportunity for a challenge to be mounted.

Policy-making within the party is formally the responsibility of the leader, who is not bound by resolutions of the annual conference and does not have to report to anything in the nature of an executive committee. The leader controls the Central Office and appoints the party chairman. On paper the powers of the leader are fomidable, and far greater than those of the leader of the Parliamentary Labour Party. In practice the Conservative leader has to be careful to retain the support of a majority within the party, and would therefore be unwise to ignore substantial currents of opinion among colleagues.

Even under the old procedure, the party had ways of putting a leader under pressure. Austen Chamberlain was effectively ditched as leader in 1922, Neville

Table 5.2 *Professional Staff of the parties: 1979*[1]

Party	Head office	Regional offices	Constituency organizers
Conservative	92	42	355
Labour	63	39	80
Liberal	15	6	15

[1] Excluding secretaries and ancillary staff.
Source: Rose, 1980a, p. 255.

Chamberlain was forced to resign from the office of Prime Minister in 1940, Eden and Macmillan had to cope with criticism, and Douglas-Home was gently persuaded to step down after agreeing to the new selection procedure in 1965. The fate that overtook Heath has driven the lesson home. The Conservative leader has enormous scope for leadership, but if it is not exercised effectively the leader will face trouble.

Conservative Doctrines

Conservative doctrines have become a topic of controversy since Margaret Thatcher became leader, as in the crucial sphere of economic policy she is taking the party along unfamiliar paths. This will become clear if I first outline the main tenets of traditional conservatism and then indicate the nature of Thatcher's departure from these tenets.

Traditional conservatism is a coherent doctrine that can be summarized under six main headings. In the first place, there is a conservative view of human nature that is best described as sceptical. Liberals have always taken an optimistic view of human nature, believing that people are naturally good and well intentioned, though often corrupted by society. Socialists dislike the whole concept, believing that human behaviour is shaped by social forces rather than by anything as intrinsic as human nature. Conservatives believe that children are naturally selfish and greedy and need to be educated out of this condition by socializing institutions and procedures. For this reason they support the nuclear family, emphasize the importance of education and stress the social role of religion. The argument is that the more people are socialized, the more co-operative they will be and the less need there will be for police, courts and prisons.

Secondly, conservatives have a view of what society is or should be like. Liberals believe that society is (or should be thought of as) a collection of individuals, each pursuing his own interests in a peaceful way. Socialists believe that under the capitalist system, society is divided into classes, with interests that necessarily conflict. Conservatives, on the other hand, believe that a society, if it operates properly, is an organic unity of people and groups who are bound together by feelings of mutual obligation. This belief leads conservatives to a constant emphasis on the importance of national unity. In the two decades following the Second World War, the theme of 'one nation' was stressed in their propaganda. In the 1983 election they used large posters depicting a black man, with the slogan 'Labour says he's black. Tories say he's British'.

Thirdly, conservatives are not egalitarians. They regard human inequality as an inescapable fact of life, and insist that those more fortunate in their birth or more successful in their careers have a social and moral obligation to help fellow-citizens who are less fortunate or less successful. This belief has led in the past to an emphasis on the duty of the upper classes to give part of their time to unpaid public service and on the duty of landowners to look after their tenants. In the modern era it has led the Conservative Party to join the other main parties in supporting social services, and to the slogan 'the ladder and the safety net'.

Fourthly, conservative theorists and leaders have a theory of political knowledge derived from the writings of Edmund Burke. In summary. they believe that individual human reason is not adequate to the task of working out a theory of good government from scratch. Instead of attempting this, people should build on the wisdom of past generations, which is embodied in the political institutions and traditions that the present generation has inherited. Burke was unusual among politicians of his day (he was an MP for many years) in supporting the revolution in the American colonies while being vehemently opposed to the French Revolution. His reason for drawing this sharp distinction was that the American colonists were defending their existing rights to legislate for themselves (particularly regarding taxation) whereas the French revolutionaries were insisting on the importance of theoretical, non-existing rights and attempting to remodel society in the light of theories devised by intellectuals. He predicted that the American revolution would succeed while the French Revolution would lead to a reaction and the restoration of the old regime.

Fifthly, and following directly from this fourth point, conservatives are opposed to radical changes in institutions and policies. It is necessary to adjust to technological and social changes, but politicians should do this in a pragmatic way. They should avoid the temptation to prepare a blueprint of the future. The government should respond to social changes and popular pressures, but should not try to impose its own vision of the future on society.

Finally, if conservatives had to define the proper role of government in a word, they would say it is protective. Political leaders should use their authority to protect the weaker members of society against exploitation. Conservative theorists point proudly to the fact that in the nineteenth century it was the Conservative Party that promoted laws protecting women and children against exploitation by industrialists, and regulating the length of the working day in factories. The Liberals of that period were representing the interests of the factory owners, while Conservatives, representing the traditional ruling classes, had attitudes that were in some respects more humane. A recent

Chairman of the Conservative Party, referring in his memoirs to the protective role of the state in society, said that Conservative attitudes 'may be stigmatized as paternal, but why not? We are, or should be, a family. I don't find paternal an offensive word' (Carrington, 1988, p. 375).

In another sense of being protective, political leaders should protect the institutions and traditions of society against groups who seek radical change. They should also, of course, protect the interests of the national society against threats from outside. Whereas nearly all Liberals and some socialists stress the ideals of international friendship and brotherhood, Conservatives stress the importance of national defence and skilled diplomacy. Labour governments reluctantly spend money on arms but Conservative governments do so gladly. The level of expenditure does not vary greatly, but the attitude tends to be different.

These beliefs have led Conservative governments in the past to accept most of the reforms introduced by previous Liberal and Labour governments, while rejecting those that seemed excessively radical or doctrinaire. When the Conservatives returned to power after the dynamic Labour government of 1945–51, they denationalized road haulage and the steel industry, ended food and petrol rationing and scrapped Labour's plans to modify the rights of landowners. However, they left four other major industries (gas, electricity, railways and coal-mining) in public ownership, accepted Labour's extensions to the social services and continued the policy of maintaining full employment by exercising control over the monetary and fiscal system. The elements of continuity were greater than the elements of change.

Among postwar leaders, Churchill, Eden, Macmillan and Douglas-Home embraced all the tenets of conservative theory outlined above. Edward Heath was slightly different, in that he adopted the role of a rational planner in several spheres of policy. Heath created the Central Policy Review Staff as a high-powered planning unit reporting directly to the Cabinet. He introduced a legal framework for the conduct of industrial relations. He modernized local government and merged traditional authorities to create larger units. He introduced a national policy for the control of wage and salary increases. Most of these innovations have since been scrapped, but they certainly mark Heath as a planner – some would say a technocrat – rather than a traditional conservative.

The decisive break came, however, with the election of Margaret Thatcher as party leader. She believes passionately that her role is to lead the country in a new direction rather than to conserve existing values and practices. The direction in which she points, both by policy and by exhortation, is towards the restoration of the entrepreneurial spirit that flourished in Britain from the beginning of the Industrial Revolution in the 1760s until its maturity in the 1880s. Thatcher is an individualist. She believes that the British people have gone soft and must be stimulated into recovering the adventurous risk-taking attitudes that the industrialists and merchants of earlier generations displayed. A necessary step in this stimulation must be to reduce the dependence of citizens on government by reducing the extent of state intervention in economic affairs. In 1977 the party published a booklet called *The Right Approach to the Economy*, which contained the following statement, signifying an attitude different from that of all previous postwar governments.

> We believe that government knows less about business than businessmen, less about investment than investors, and less about pay bargaining than trade union negotiators and employers. We think we understand the limitations on what a government alone can do.   (Quoted in Layton-Henry, 1980, p. 26)

These attitudes are those of an old-fashioned liberal rather than those of a conservative. In her economic policies Thatcher is undoubedly a neo-liberal, and in her style she is (as she herself proclaims) a radical. She has declared more than once that she is 'a conviction politician', and convictions on the part of the Prime Minister about how society should be changed are not really compatible with traditional conservative beliefs about the proper role of government. Margaret Thatcher is therefore a controversial leader whose economic policies have numerous critics among the parliamentary Conservative Party. It is significant that the event that established the clear control she now exercises over the party was the Falkland Islands war, for in this conflict she behaved exactly as Conservative leaders are expected to behave, rallying the country behind her in a powerful defence of national interests against a challenge by foreigners.

Controversial or not, Margaret Thatcher had acquired a very firm grip on the party by 1983 and she has promoted colleagues who share her views. Her economic policies, including a very extensive programme of privatization, have changed the British economy in the way that she wanted and have contributed to a period of growth that began in 1982 and continued without check throughout the 1980s. She is the only Conservative leader to have given her name to a doctrine, namely 'Thatcherism', and it is fair to conclude that she has modified the character of conservative doctrine in respect of economic issues.

Her influence on social policy is more difficult to assess. She has talked in disparaging terms of 'the nanny state', which seems to imply a less caring and protective attitude towards the social services. In practice, however, expenditure on the social services has increased in real terms during her period of office. This is even true of the health service, which is under-financed in comparison with the services in other advanced industrial societies. Britain does not spend enough or have enough doctors to provide a service equivalent to those of Canada, France, West Germany or the Scandinavian countries. The health service reforms announced in the winter of 1988–9, though described as radical by both supporters and critics, actually amounted only to administrative re-arrangements designed to give slightly better value for money. They did not provide for the massive injection of extra public funds needed to bring the service up to international standards, nor, on the other hand, did they involve any retreat from the postwar commitment by all British governments to a universal system of health care.

The educational reforms launched in 1988 were considerably more radical, involving more control of the curriculum by the national government, more variety in types of school and more parental choice regarding the schools attended by their children. However, it cannot be said that these reforms are out of line with traditional conservative views about education. As Thatcher is a whole-hearted conservative in respect of law and order, foreign affairs and defence, the overall conclusion must be that Thatcherism involves a changed emphasis in economic policy but the maintenance of traditional conservative approaches in other fields of policy.

The Labour Party

The Labour Party differs from the Conservative Party in its origins and structure as well as in its ideology. The party has its origins in the Labour Representation Committee, established in 1900 by a group of trade unions and socialist organizations to secure the election of working-class candidates to Parliament in order to protect and promote the interests of labour. The committee changed its name to the Labour Party in 1906 and adopted a constitution in 1918.

The 1918 constitution, which was hardly changed until 1981, gave the party a unique form of organization that reflected the assumptions of the trade union leaders who dominated the conference at which the constitution was drawn up. There are two types of membership in the party, individual members who join constituency branches and affiliated members who pay a political levy to their trade union, which the union then hands over (in whole or in part) to party funds. The arrangement is that the trade union members pay this levy (which is very small) automatically unless they sign a document to 'contract out' of doing so. After the 1926 General Strike the Conservative government changed these rules by legislation, to provide that the levy would be payable only if members took the intitiative to 'contract in', This reduced the number of affiliated members by over a third, and in 1946 the Labour government understandably changed the rule back again.

The Annual Conference of the party has, in principle, supreme control over policy, and it also elects the National Executive Committee, which takes policy decisions between conferences. The method of voting at the Annual Conference is by 'card vote', whereby the leader of each delegation from a party branch or a trade union has a card indicating how many members he represents and therefore how many votes he can cast. There are two controversial aspects of this procedure. One is that each local branch is credited with 1,000 members unless it claims more. As less than a hundred branches have as many as 1,000 members this rule means that there is no general relationship between size and voting power; very small branches have as many votes as relatively large ones.

The other and more important aspect of the system is that the leaders of the large trade unions have enormous power at the conference. The leader of the Transport and General Workers' Union has a card with 1,250,000 printed on it, so that his vote alone counts for more than the votes of all the 633 branches of the party put together. The five largest unions have half the votes at the conference. This arrangement is open to criticism (and has been criticized) on various grounds. One is that the number of votes given to a union corresponds not to the actual number of union members paying the political levy but to the number declared by the union to be 'affiliated members'. A government report published in 1984 showed that in 1983 the Amalgamated Union of Engineering Workers had 542,000 members paying the political levy but declared 850,000 affiliated members, presumably as a way of buying extra votes at the party conference. Other unions variously registered more or less than the true number, either to buy votes or to save money, and there is nothing in Labour Party rules to prevent this. It is not unknown for the number of members registered as affiliated to the Labour Party by a union actually to exceed the total number of members belonging to the union at the time (Ewing, 1987, p. 54).

Another ground for criticism is that the internal politics of the unions vary greatly. Some unions have democratic arrangements whereby leaders are mandated by the union conference to vote in particular ways at the party conference, while other unions leave a great deal of discretion in the hands of their leaders. Moreover, not all the union leaders give their primary loyalty to the Labour Party. Several sympathize with or belong to the Communist Party, while at least one belongs to the Social Democratic Party. This does not stop them wielding considerable power at Labour's Annual Conference. In the late 1960s 'the emergence of left-wing in place of right-wing leaders in just four unions was decisive in shifting the position of the entire party' (Crouch, 1982, p. 180).

Labour MPs belong to the Parliamentary Labour Party, which is charged with the duty of advancing party policy in Parliament. For most of the party's life the parliamentarians have elected their own leader, who becomes Prime Minister if Labour wins an election. In a formal sense, the leader's powers are much weaker than those of the Conservative leader. The Labour leader does not control the professional organization of the party, which is run by the National Executive Committee (NEC). The leader is a member of the NEC but he does not chair its meetings and does not have the power to appoint any of its members. In practice the Labour leader has usually acted in Parliament in a manner similar to that of the Conservative leader, and of course he enjoys exactly the same powers when Prime Minister. However, the structure of the Labour Party leaves room for internal arguments about who controls policy. As in 1981 such arguments led four leading party members to resign and form the Social Democratic Party, where they were quickly joined by twenty-six other MPs, it is appropriate to outline the nature of the structural problem at this point.

The central organization was modelled on that of British trade unions, in which there is always an executive committee with the responsibility for promoting the general policies laid down by the annual conference. The difference is that in the unions the executive committee has the practical power to do this, by conducting (or supervising) negotiations over pay and working conditions. In the Labour Party, in contrast, the NEC lacks the practical ability to do anything except control the professional organizing staff and prepare publicity. Labour policy is advanced by the Parliamentary Labour Party (PLP), which is jealous of its independence and does not take orders from either the NEC or the Annual Conference. Over the decades, there have been intermittent rumblings of discontent because the PLP has been perceived by some as disregarding conference policy.

Certain conference resolutions over the years have simply been ignored by parliamentarians. In 1960 a resolution was passed that had generated so much passion that it could not be ignored, namely a resolution opposing British possession of nuclear weapons. The then party leader, Hugh Gaitskell, refused to accept this as binding. He stated that he would not be content until he persuaded the party to reverse this policy, and at the 1961 conference he succeeded in doing this. However, the incident left a good deal of resentment among the left wing of the party, which surfaced again after the 1979 electoral defeat and led to a revision of the constitution in January 1981.

Under the new rules the leader of the PLP is chosen by an electoral college in which the affiliated trade unions have 40 per cent of the vote, the constituency Labour parties 30 per cent and the MPs the remaining 30 per cent. Another change was adopted providing that sitting MPs would have to submit themselves for reselection by their branch parties before each election, instead of being automatically re-nominated as had hitherto been the case. These changes were perceived by all commentators as a victory for the left (which was stronger in the unions and in the local branches than in the PLP), and they led to the resignation of the four leaders on the right of the party who established the rival Social Democratic Party. The nature of the ideological conflicts within the party will be discussed in a later section.

In the country, the local Labour Party branches perform the same functions as the Conservative associations, namely collecting subscriptions, holding meetings and social events, raising funds and providing voluntary workers in election campaigns. Their social life is not as active as that of their Conservative rivals, but they conduct lotteries as an alternative fund-raising device. However, the branches, having only about a quarter of the membership of their Conservative counterparts, naturally collect much less money.

Because of this, the Labour Party is heavily dependent on the trade unions for financial support. Whereas less than a quarter of the Conservative Party's regular income comes from business firms, over four-fifths of the Labour Party's regular income comes from trade unions. Labour's income in non-election years is only a little more than half that of the Conservative Party's income, but the unions keep vast reserves in their political funds and they provide large grants to the party for each general election campaign. The party is therefore not seriously handicapped in its campaigning by shortage of funds, though its activities are run on a tighter budget than those of the Conservatives and, as noted, it has fewer local organizers.

Two comments must be made about this situation. One is that the complete financial dependence of the party on the unions is bound to have some influence on party policy, over and above the influence exerted by way of the unions' control of the Annual Conference. There is no other socialist party in the world that is so dependent on trade unions as the Labour Party is. In some respects this is a source of strength, for the unions are very influential in British society, as well as being extremely wealthy. (They have enormous financial reserves, accumulated out of habitual caution rather than to meet any predictable need.) At the same time, this dependence makes the party vulnerable to changes within the unions. Changes in union leadership and policy may quickly affect the party, as happened rather dramatically in the late 1960s.

Labour Party Doctrines

In the realm of doctrine, it is for two reasons more difficult to set out the theoretical foundations of Labour's policies than it is to do this for the Conservative Party. One reason is that the trade unionists who have always played such a large role in the party have generally been uninterested in political theory. As Drucker has pointed out, the unions have an ethos rather than an ideology (Drucker, 1979). This ethos arose out of the experience of the working class in the industrial areas of Britain. It emphasizes the values of class solidarity, loyalty to leaders, plain living and plain speaking, and establishing a reserve fund to safeguard the group against unspecified disasters or attacks that the future may bring. It is the ethos of a group that feels itself vulnerable and exploited, is instinctively cautious and believes that its only real strength lies in the unity of its members. In terms of practical policies, this ethos has stressed the importance of legal rights for trade unions, of laws to guard against industrial accidents and of measures to protect workers against the misfortunes of unemployment, poor health and old age.

The second problem about identifying Labour doctrines is that the theoreticians of the party have differed rather widely among themselves. On a left-right dimension, they have varied from groups working for the abolition of capitalism to groups who merely want to improve the operation of the capitalist system and to provide social security for citizens. Among the moderates, some emphasize the importance of economic planning while others stress the desirability of achieving social equality. While the Conservative Party has generally (until the advent of Margaret Thatcher) been united on questions of principle, the Labour Party has always been riven by doctrinal disagreements.

What all Labour theorists and leaders have in common is agreement on three basic assumptions. First, they believe that society is divided into classes whose interests conflict. This is undesirable, but it is a fact of life. Conservative beliefs about the organic unity of society are regarded as mythical. Secondly, they are egalitarians, who constantly urge that measures should be taken to reduce the inequalities that flow from the economic system and the status system. Thirdly, they believe in programmatic politics. Government leaders should not be content just to adjust laws and administration to absorb the impact of technological and social changes. On the contrary, they should try to control the direction of change, should come to power armed with a manifesto and should use political authority to achieve predetermined objectives.

The translation of this working-class ethos and these socialist doctrines into a set of practical policies has always involved discussion and argument within the Labour movement. From the early years of the century until the late 1960s, these arguments were always won by the moderate wing of the movement. Communist and certain other Marxist organizations were proscribed (i.e. their members were ineligible for membership of the Labour Party), while non-Communist left-wingers were outvoted. Equally, the groups favouring centralized control always won over groups favouring local democracy or workers' self-government in industry.

From the late 1960s onwards, two developments have taken place. First, several of the larger unions have fallen under the control of Marxist or ex-Marxist leaders, with the result that their votes at the Labour Party Annual Conference have supported left-wing causes rather than the views of the mainly moderate parliamentary leaders. Secondly, the radical youth of the 1960s New Left movement have moved into local Labour Party branches, and have grown older and more influential with the passing of the years. In 1973 it was agreed to rescind the rule proscribing members of Marxist organizations from Labour Party membership, and since then Trotskyite groups have actively pursued a policy they describe as 'entryism'. A number of local branches, particularly the smaller ones, have consequently come under the control of extreme left-wingers.

These two groups of extremists, one in the unions and the other in the local branches, moved the political centre of gravity of the party to the left. In January 1981, against the opposition of most parliamentary leaders, they secured the organizational amendments mentioned above (see page 69). In practice, these may not make much difference to the behaviour of parliamentarians, but as they were promoted by left-wing groups whose declared intention was that the amendments should make a difference, it is not unreasonable for moderate MPs to have been upset by the development. Several, though not very many, moderate MPs have in fact been denied reselection under the new procedure.

Members of the Labour Party can now be divided into four distinct ideological categories. From right to left, the first category comprises moderates of the kind who effectively controlled the party from its inception until the 1970s. Secondly, there is a group of MPs and party members known collectively as the 'soft left'. Members of this group occupy the ideological position that was occupied by the left wing of the parliamentary party from 1945 until about 1970. They have a greater commitment than the moderates to promoting economic equality and extending public ownership. They also favour unilateral nuclear disarmament.

Thirdly, there is the 'hard left', whose leading figures have been Tony Benn and Ken Livingstone. This group has neo-syndicalist ideas about workers' control of industry; when Benn was Minister for Industry he encouraged workers' co-operatives to take over a motor-cycle works near Birmingham and a newspaper in Glasgow. The group is also strongly committed to the support of ethnic and sexual minorities; municipal councils controlled by the hard left have set up lesbian workshops and established committees to root out 'heterosexual prejudice' among municipal employees. The fourth group bears the name of 'Militant Tendency'; it is Trotskyite and frankly revolutionary in its intentions.

Until 1979 the party leaders were always drawn from the ranks of the moderates, but the leaders since then (Michael Foot and now Neil Kinnock) have been members of the soft left. The moderates (weakened by the defection of the Social Democrats) have lost control of the PLP as well as of the Annual Conference. It should also be noted that in the 1980s hard left groups gained control of several urban councils, including Manchester, Greater London and four London boroughs, while Liverpool was for a time controlled by Trotskyites. Partly in response to this, the Thatcher government has abolished the Greater London Council and somewhat curbed the powers of the others, while Kinnock has disassociated himself from the policies of the extremists and secured the exclusion from the party of several members of Militant Tendency. As we enter the 1990s the power of these left-wing groups – often described by the mass media as 'the loony left' – has been lessened, but their activities during the 1980s clearly tarnished the image of the Labour Party among the general public. The period since the 1987 election has been marked by a struggle by Kinnock and his immediate supporters to persuade the party to improve its electoral appeal by adopting more moderate policies, and in 1989 they were successful. The soft left appear to have become moderate in their policies, the consequence being a marked improvement in the party's popularity in the polls and in its electoral prospects.

The Centrist Parties

Under this heading we shall outline the roles of the Liberal Party, the Social Democratic Party and the Social and Liberal Democrats, formed in 1988 as the result of a merger between the Liberals and some of the Social Democrats.

The Liberal Party, after a long and successful history of political reform, fell to the position of a small third party between 1918 and 1924. In the years between 1951 and 1964 its parliamentary representation was reduced to six, leading journalists to suggest that its caucus meetings might be held in the back of a taxi. In view of this, the first question to be asked about the modern Liberal Party is how it has managed to survive for over sixty years with only a minimal degree of influence at the national level.

The main answer to this question is that the party has been kept going by its grass-roots members, who have rarely numbered less than 100,000 and are not primarily interested in issues of national policy. These members may be divided into three broad categories. First, there are a considerable number of older members, mainly drawn from the professional classes, who are attached to the internationalist ideals to which the party has always subscribed. They tend to run the local branches of the United Nations Association and to be active in other organizations concerned with international issues. Secondly, many Liberals are involved in what has come to be known as community politics. They are active in housing associations, groups concerned with environmental issues, committees to improve race relations and similar local good causes. If Conservative or Labour councillors propose that an unused church or church hall be demolished, it is a fair bet that Liberals will form a pressure group to demand that the building be preserved and turned into a day-care centre. Thirdly, there are the Young Liberals, not so numerous now as they were in the 1970s, but still active. They tend to be radical, concerned with such issues as the peace movement, nuclear disarmament and the movement against apartheid.

None of these groups is primarily concerned with economic affairs or even with the activities of the national government. They tend to focus on international or local issues rather than on the policies of the national state. In this respect Liberal Party members faithfully reflect the history and ideological orientation of their party. They are descendants of the politicians who campaigned against the slave trade, against slavery in the British Empire, in favour of free trade, in favour of international peace and the League of Nations. British Liberals have only sometimes had their main concerns at the level of the national state.

On the one hand, Liberals are idealists, believing in the possibility of international peace and justice. On the other hand, they are individualists, concerned with the liberties of the private citizen. Certainly Gladstone was a Liberal leader who reformed the financial arrangements of the national government, but he was also the leader who campaigned in a British general election on the issue of Bulgarian atrocities in the Balkans. It is noteworthy that it is the Liberal Party that promoted Home Rule for Ireland, that genuinely believes in the principle of devolution to Scotland and Wales and that favours decentralisation of government within England. In principle, Liberals would like to see the United Kingdom turned into a federation.

The electoral system has deprived the Liberal Party of fair representation since it became a third party. However, since 1970 the Liberals have made something of a comeback. This is not because of any change of philosophy or dramatic innovation in policy. It is partly because of effective leadership and partly because voters have shown signs of disenchantment with the two main parties. In 1974 voters turned to the Liberals in England at the same time as they turned to the nationalist parties in Wales and Scotland. In the February 1974 election the Liberals got 19 per cent of the total British vote, comprising just over six million voters. After the Social Democratic Party was formed in 1981 the two small parties established an electoral alliance, and in 1983 this alliance got 25 per cent of the vote - though winning only 3.5 per cent of the seats.

The Social Democratic Party was formally established in March 1981. In January 1981 the Labour Party held a special conference in London at which the rules were changed regarding the election of the parliamentary leader and the reselection of MPs. On the very next day four of the party's leaders announced the formation of the Council for Social Democracy, which was turned into the Social Democratic Party (SDP) two months later. The four leaders were Roy Jenkins, a former Chancellor of the Exchequer just returned to Britain from four years as President of the European Commission, David Owen, a former Foreign Secretary, William Rodgers, a former Minister of Transport and Shirley Williams, a former Minister of Education. They were supported by nine other Labour MPs.

While the immediate issue that led to this development was the change in Labour Party rules, the move had been envisaged before that and three main reasons for it were explained in the declaration made in January. One was what the four leaders called 'the drift towards extremism in the Labour Party'. Another was the belief that the increasingly adversarial character of British politics, leading to sharp changes in economic policy when the government changed hands, was bad for the economy. A third was concern lest a future Labour government should take Britain out of the European Economic Community and weaken the British ties with NATO. It was also important, and was spelled out later, that the founders of the SDP wanted a left-of-centre party that would not be shackled to the trade unions.

The SDP was an instant success. It got extensive publicity in all the mass media and it is reported that within ten days of its formation it had 43,588 paying members (Zentner, 1982, p. 10). Intellectuals, lawyers and doctors supported it in large numbers. Its leaders travelled tirelessly around the country addressing public meetings. Within a month the Gallup Poll reported that, if the SDP formed an electoral alliance with the Liberal Party, the alliance would be likely to win the next general election (Zentner, 1982, p. 14). All this happened before the SDP had a constitution, a single designated leader, or a set of specific policies. Its sudden popularity was the political sensation of 1981.

Throughout its first year the SDP gained strength. It won two important by-elections and attracted the support of several more Labour MPs together with one Conservative MP. By June 1982 it had thirty MPs and had also gained a fair number of members in the House of Lords. It had acquired about 70,000 members in the country. Its conferences drew an enthusiastic body of supporters, who were described as overwhelmingly white, male, middle-class and in their middle years (Stephenson, 1982, p. 111). It was the most fashionable party in Britain and was in some respects the most modern, staging dramatic media events and being the first party to encourage its members to pay their subscriptions by credit card.

However, when the SDP published a statement of its policies these were not particularly novel. It wanted to retain existing policies towards Europe and NATO, to maintain and improve social services, to drop some of the rather harsh financial policies of the Thatcher government and to try once more to eatablish a government incomes policy in spite of the failures of both Conservative and Labour governments in this field in the 1970s. The *Economist* immediately offered the new party an electoral slogan, namely 'The SDP promises you a better yesterday'.

In September 1981 the SDP and the Liberal Party established an electoral alliance, which their respective leaders had favoured for some months but which had to wait until the proposal was endorsed by the annual Liberal Assembly. According to the polls, the alliance was likely to carry the parties into power at the next general election. It therefore offered the prospect of early triumph for the SDP and the longed-for revival, after almost sixty years, of the Liberal Party as a party of government. However, the alliance was not without internal tensions and problems.

One of the problems was a difference in long-term aims and, along with that, a difference in preferences about what strategy the alliance should follow if it came to hold the balance of power in Parliament. The aim of the Liberals was simply to strengthen their position as a central party whereas the aim of most SDP members was to replace the Labour Party as the main party of reform. Liberals, having tended for over a century to regard the Conservatives as their main enemy, were inclined to form a coalition with the Labour Party rather than with the Conservatives if they had that choice after a general election had produced an indecisive result. Social Democrats, having broken with the Labour Party and wanting to replace it, were logically inclined to prefer a coalition with the Conservatives. In both the 1983 and 1987 elections the alliance leaders covered this difference by refusing to say what they would do in the event of a hung Parliament.

Another policy difference that emerged in the run-up to the 1987 election was over nuclear arms. The SDP leader, David Owen, favoured the government's plan to buy the Trident missile system while the Liberals opposed this and were divided over the whole issue of nuclear weapons. Owen and his Liberal counterpart, David Steel, patched up a compromise whereby they agreed to favour co-operation with France on a European nuclear deterrent, but this was disowned by the grass-roots Liberals, who favoured nuclear disarmament. This episode led Owen to say later that it was usless to strike a bargain with Liberal leaders because it might always be rejected by the Liberal rank-and-file.

Yet another point of tension in the alliance was the division of parliamentary constituencies between the two parties. The SDP leaders felt that they were in a strong position because their party had the more experienced leaders, had more money to contribute to the campaign, and had more support in public opinion polls than the Liberals. They argued that if the alliance were to achieve an electoral breakthrough, it would be mainly because of the SDP. On the other hand, the Liberals had more voluntary workers and had long-established constituency branches, whereas the SDP had opted for area branches, each including several constituencies. There were many constituencies where Liberals had done relatively well in earlier elections and were unwilling to see their candidate step down in favour of a newcomer from the SDP. The Liberal branches could not be told by the party leaders who should be nominated, whereas in the SDP the area branches could be given instructions. Liberal negotiators were therefore in a position to tell SDP negotiators that if they agreed to certain SDP proposals the local Liberals might refuse to honour the agreement. In the event the Liberals got much the better of the bargaining about constituencies, both in 1983 and in 1987. They kept the fifty or so constituencies in which their chances seemed strongest.

The elections themselves were a disappointment for the Liberals and a disaster for the SDP. Although the alliance candidates won over 25 per cent of the vote in 1983 and 23 per cent in 1987, they won only twenty-three seats in the earlier election and twenty-two in the later one. The Liberals won seventeen seats each time, with the SDP taking the remainder. This meant that of the twenty-eight MPs who crossed the floor of the House to join the SDP in its early days, twenty-two lost their seats in the ensuing election. This was a chilling lesson to other MPs who might have considered following their example.

Three days after the 1987 election, the Liberal leader, David Steel, sprang an astonishing surprise on his allies (and on the nation). He proposed that the two parties should merge and a new leader should be chosen by a vote of the combined rank-and-file members. As the Liberals had about twice as many members as the SDP, this meant that the new leader would almost certainly be a Liberal. The proposal immediately divided the SDP leaders. Roy Jenkins and Shirley Williams, who had both lost their parliamentary seats, came out in support of a merger, while David Owen was vehemently against it. The five MPs divided, with the two from Scotland favouring the merger and the three from southern England opposing it. After much anguished debate, the issue was put to a postal ballot of SDP members, of whom 78 per cent responded and who voted to support the merger by a majority of 57 per cent to 43 per cent. At this point the SDP split down the middle, with both halves claiming the party's name.

There followed several months of negotiation between the Liberals and the pro-merger half of the SDP. One result of these negotiations was agreement upon a title for the new merged party, which now calls itself the Social and Liberal Democrats. Another result was agreement on a fairly ambitious statement of policy objectives, but this was immediately repudiated by rank-and-file

Liberals and several Liberal MPs. A third result was the resignation of David Steel, who has been replaced by Paddy Ashdown.

The effect of these developments on public opinion has been disastrous for the centrist parties. Whereas they got 23 per cent of the vote at the 1987 election, and have previously tended to show higher figures in polls taken between general elections, their combined support fell during 1988 to about 12 per cent, splitting in the proportions of 7 to 8 per cent for the Social and Liberal Democrats and 4 to 5 per cent for the rump of the SDP. Both parties have suffered a substantial loss of members and their electoral fortunes have not been helped by their practice of putting up rival candidates to fight for the smaller centrist vote. In the European elections of 1989 the two parties actually got fewer votes than the previously miniscule Green Party.

The overall result of Steel's proposal for a merger has therefore been a resounding failure. The Liberal Party has lost its name, with all the proud historical memories that this conjured up; has lost its programme; has lost many of its members; and has lost most of its public support. The SDP has been split asunder and the only clear beneficiary of the move has been the Labour Party, which has been given the chance to recapture some of the central ground in British politics with more moderate policies.

The Smaller Parties

The most important of the smaller parties are the nationalist parties in Scotland, Wales and Northern Ireland. The Scottish National Party (SNP) represents a nationalist movement with a long history, but the party did not make a serious impact on a general election until 1970. Its rapid growth in the early 1970s reflected widespread disenchantment with the handling of British economic policy by successive Conservative and Labour governments, leading to the claim that Scotland could do better if it had its own independent government. This claim was greatly strengthened by the discovery of a large oilfield off the Scottish coast in the North Sea. If an independent Scotland were to control North Sea oil, it would clearly be a wealthy state.

In 1970 the SNP gained more than twice as many votes as in any previous election and won a seat in Parliament. In the election of February 1974 its proportion of Scottish votes rose to 21 per cent and the number of seats won rose to seven. In the election of October 1974 the proportion of votes went up to 30 per cent and the number of seats won to eleven.

This rapid growth of public support for the SNP threatened to undermine the position of the Labour Party in Scotland. Largely for this reason, the Labour government of 1974–9 prepared an elaborate scheme for the devolution of government, under which Scotland would be given a National Assembly with legislative powers in many fields, though without the power to levy taxes. While this proposal fell far short of nationalist demands opinion polls indicated that it would satisfy the apparently large number of Scottish people who had some sympathy for the nationalist cause without endorsing the demand for full independence.

Legislation to establish a Scottish Assembly was passed by the British Parliament, but its implementation was made conditional upon its securing the support of at least 40 per cent of Scottish electors in a referendum. This referendum was held in March 1979 and, to the surprise of virtually all commentators, it resulted in an affirmative vote of only 33 per cent of the electors. In consequence, the legislation was repealed. This was a devastating blow to the SNP, which secured only 19 per cent of the votes in the general election of May 1979 and saw its parliamentary representation fall from eleven to two MPs.

There followed a period of internecine conflict within the party and in the 1983 and 1987 elections its share of the Scottish vote fell to 12 per cent and 14 per cent respectively, securing first two and then three seats. This episode in Scottish nationalism is therefore a story of rise and decline within little more than a decade, but the SNP should not be written off as a failure. There is a strong undercurrent of nationalist sentiment in Scotland and another turn of historic events might see the SNP become a significant force quite quickly again.

In Wales Plaid Cymru (the Welsh Party) has a basis that is different from that of the SNP. Plaid Cymru is more concerned with the preservation of the Welsh language and culture than with the management of the economy, and its leaders want a large measure of cultural and political autonomy for Wales rather than full independence as a national state. Like the SNP, Plaid Cymru gained support in the early 1970s but suffered a severe reverse in the referendum of 1979. The proposal for a Welsh Assembly was accepted by only 12 per cent of Welsh electors. However, because the party's support is based on an enduring concern for the Welsh culture – a concern that has no significant Scottish equivalent – its rise and decline have both been less dramatic than the rise and decline of the SNP.

In the two elections of 1974 Plaid Cymru secured 10 and 11 per cent of the Welsh vote, winning two and three seats respectively. In 1979 the proportion of votes declined to 9 per cent and by 1987 it was reduced to 7 per cent, but the party still won three seats.

In Northern Ireland the position is different again. The majority of parliamentary seats in Northern Ireland have always been won by the Ulster Unionist Party, which stands for the continuation of the union with Great Britain and for a policy of keeping the social services in parity with British social services. In a real sense, this can be regarded as a nationalist party for the Protestant majority in the province. The Catholic community have supported various opposition parties, such as Sinn Fein, the Republican Party and the Social Democratic and Labour Party. The British parties are not organized in Northern Ireland and do not compete in elections there.

From 1922 until 1972 the Ulster Unionists had an informal alliance at

Westminster with the British Conservative Party, and because of this their MPs were usually counted as Conservatives when a tally was made of the results of each general election. In 1972 this alliance was broken off by the Unionists when the Conservative government abruptly suspended the Northern Ireland Parliament, which had certain devolved powers of legislation in the Province. The Conservatives paid a heavy price for this action at the next general election. In February 1974 they secured more votes than the Labour Party but four fewer seats. Had the alliance still been affective, the ten Ulster Unionist MPs would have been counted in with the Conservatives and the latter would have been declared the election winners. As it was, they emerged as losers and had to give way to a minority Labour government.

In the 1987 general election the Ulster unionists – divided by then into two wings – won fourteen of the Irish seats, while Sinn Fein secured one and the Social Democratic and Labour Party won two.

In Britain there are also several fringe parties, none of which gets more than a very small share of the votes. Chief among these are the Communist Party, the Trotskyite Workers' Revolutionary Party, and the idealistic Green Party. All the candidates for these parties lost their deposits in 1987 because of the smallness of their votes, which totalled less than 0.5 per cent of the votes cast in the election.

Further Reading

The recent book on the party system is Ingle (1987), *The British Party System*; on the Conservative Party see Norton and Aughey (1981), *Conservatives and Conservatism*; on the Labour Party see Drucker (1979), *Doctrine and Ethos in the Labour Party*, and Kavanagh (1982), *The Politics of the Labour Party*; on the Liberal Party see Bogdanor (1983), *Liberal Party Politics*; on the SDP see Zentner (1982), *Social Democracy in Britain*, and Kennet (1982), *The Rebirth of Britain*; on the Scottish and Welsh nationalists see Birch (1977), *Political Integration and Disintegration in the British Isles*.

Electors and Voters

In a liberal democracy decisions about which political party or parties shall govern the country are made by electors, casting votes in free elections. The object in this chapter is to outline the nature of the British electoral system, to discuss contemporary criticisms of it and arguments for reform and to provide a brief guide to British voting behaviour.

The Electoral System

The way in which an electoral system works depends partly upon the methods adopted of dealing with certain practical problems of electoral organization that arise in every democratic country. These include the compilation of a register of qualified electors, the delimitation of constituency boundaries, the nomination of candidates, the control of expenses and the method of translating votes cast into seats won. These problems, and the British ways of dealing with them, will now be outlined.

(1) The first problem is that of compiling an electoral register. The main question here is whether the initiative and responsibility should rest with individual citizens or with the government. If individual citizens are made responsible, and they have to register to vote in advance, those people who are apathetic, ignorant, forgetful or sick will find themselves unable to vote on polling day, when their interest might have been awakened by the campaign or they themselves might be in better health. If the government is made responsible, it is essential to ensure that the opposition parties have no reason to think that the politicians in power are taking more care over the registration of their own supporters than they take over the registration of their opponents.

In Britain this problem is dealt with by placing the responsibility for compiling the register on permanent municipal officials, who are not political appointees. In each county or borough the clerk to the council has the duty of ensuring that all adult citizens are registered. This is done by sending a registration form to each householder for completion, followed by a door-to-door canvas of those who do not return the form promptly. The register is compiled afresh each autumn and is a record of those qualified to vote on 10 October. It is published by January and comes into force on 16 February for a period of twelve months. This means that the register may be as much as sixteen months old when the election is held, but the effects of this are mitigated in two ways: persons within eight months of their eighteenth birthday on registration day are placed on the register even though they are not allowed to vote until they reach 18; and persons moving out of the constituency can vote by post (as can invalids).

(2)   The second problem is that of dividing the country into constituencies. This caused a good deal of controversy in Britain from the early part of the nineteenth century until 1944, when an attempt was made to take the matter out of politics by establishing permanent Electoral Boundary Commissions. Until that time boundaries were revised only by occasional Acts of Parliament, each one the focal point of a great deal of political bargaining. Inequalities in the size of constituencies were drastically reduced by each Act, but movements of population tended constantly to reverse this effect. Thus, after the 1918 Act the largest of the normal constituencies (i.e. excluding the outer islands) had about three times as many electors as the smallest, but by 1944 the proportion had grown to about twelve to one. The Boundary Commissions that were set up in that year (one each for England, Wales, Scotland and Northern Ireland) have the task of surveying the country as a whole at periodic intervals and of making reports and recommendations to the House of Commons. The first reports of the commissions were adopted (with some amendments) in 1948 and changed the boundaries of over 80 per cent of the constituencies.

The impartiality of the Boundary Commissions has never been questioned. They are instructed to take into account a number of social and geographical factors, including the desirability of making constituency boundaries co-terminous with local authority boundaries wherever possible. But they take no account of political factors and their proposals tend to irritate members of all parties. This was certainly the case in 1954, when the commissions published their second reports and recommended that about a third of all constituencies should suffer further alterations to their boundaries before the next election. The proposals were adopted, but the reaction from all sides was so vigorous that amending legislation was subsequently passed (in 1958) to lengthen the periods between review. Whereas the commissions had been obliged by the 1944 legislation to make national surveys at intervals of between three and seven years, the new rule is that the intervals should be not less than ten or more than fifteen years. This neatly illustrates one of the inherent difficulties in adjusting constituency boundaries: a system of infrequent changes is convenient for politicians and administrators but results in inequalities of size that grossly violate the principle of 'one vote, one value'; on the other hand, a system of constant adjustment would be highly inconvenient to all concerned. The art here, as so often in politics, is to find the most appropriate compromise.

The third report of the Boundary Commissions was due to be published and implemented at some time between 1964 and 1969. However, after the report was published it gradually became clear that the Labour government was unwilling to implement it. The reason for this was the simple one that the

changes would benefit the Conservative Party. The main movement of population since 1954 had been from the centres of large cities to the outskirts, so
that the population of largely Labour seats in the city centres had fallen below
the electoral quota while the population of largely Conservative seats on the
outskirts had grown above the quota. It was estimated at the time that the
boundary changes recommended to correct this state of affairs would have
helped the Conservatives to the tune of between five and twenty seats.

Some government action was essential since the Home Secretary was legally
obliged to 'lay the report before Parliament together with the draft of an Order in
Council for giving effect whether with or without modifications to the recommendations contained in the report'. The government met this by introducing a Bill that would free the Home Secretary from this obligation until after the
next election. This Bill was totally unacceptable to the Opposition and it was
rejected by the House of Lords. Amid mounting uproar, the Home Secretary
then resorted to the device of laying the commissions' proposals before
Parliament in the form of draft Orders but announcing that he would advise all his
Labour colleagues to vote against them. The Orders were duly rejected, and the
1970 election was fought in outdated constituencies that varied in size from
Birmingham Ladywood with 18,309 electors and Manchester Exchange with
18,643 to Billericay with 113,452. The Boundary Commissions' proposals were
adopted in full after the election.

During the 1970s two fresh concerns about constituency boundaries were
manifested. One was concern among English commentators about the deliberate over-representation of Scotland and Wales that was written into the 1944
Act. The official explanation of this is that these territories have a lower density
of population than England, but this cannot justify the extent of the over-
representation, which results in cities like Glasgow and Cardiff getting more
parliamentary seats than cities of the same size in England. The situation is
clearly anomalous, but in view of the lively activities of the Scottish and Welsh
nationalist parties (and the failure of the plans to establish Scottish and Welsh
assemblies) it seems unlikely that changes will be made.

The other concern related to the disparity in constituency sizes even within
England, which was so great that in the United States the courts would have
declared them to be in violation of the constitutional right of citizens to equal
representation. These disparities resulted not from partisan bias but from the
intense local pressures put upon Boundary Commissioners to respect municipal
boundaries when drawing up their plans.

When the commissions reported in 1982 it was clear that they had made a
considerable effort to meet this last criticism. However, this did not stop the
Labour Party from challenging the plans in court on the ground that unnecessary
variations in constituency population in the London area would operate to the
disadvantage of Labour. The court rejected this appeal. If the appeal had been
accepted, this might have delayed the implementation of the plans so that the
government would have had either to postpone the next general election or to

fight it on the basis of the 1970 constituency boundaries (which would have helped Labour in view of the movements of population that had occurred since 1970). However this may be, it seems clear that in terms of a democratic principle of 'one vote, one value' there is a good case for a revision of the instructions given to the Boundary Commissions so as to place less emphasis on respect for municipal boundaries and more emphasis on equality of population in constituencies.

(3)   The third problem is that of establishing a procedure for the nomination of candidates. In some countries where the names of the parties are printed on the ballot papers, it has become necessary to pass legislation defining what constitutes a political party and establishing rules for the resolution of conflicts between rival candidates, each claiming to be the official candidate of the same party. In the United States the need to resolve disputes of this kind has led the state governments to lay down procedures for the nomination of candidates by parties and thus to pass legislation regulating the internal organization of the parties.

In Britain these legal complications have been avoided, by the wish of all concerned. Candidates stand as individuals, simply requiring the support of ten local citizens to be nominated. There is therefore no need for rules about the internal procedures of parties. Until 1969 there was no provision for the names of parties to be printed on the ballot paper. In response to a demand that more information be permitted, Parliament then agreed to a new rule that gives candidates permision to add any slogan of their choice after their names, provided it does not exceed six words. This enables a candidate to give the name of his party while preserving the principle that each candidate stands as an individual. In practice there has been no problem about two candidates claiming to represent the same party.

The other problem about nominations is to prevent the ballot paper being extended by a long list of frivolous candidates. In some American states candidates have to be supported by a petition signed by a large number of electors unless they are nominated by parties that were included on the ballot in the previous election. That kind of arrangement is both administratively complicated (because signatures can be forged) and open to political objections (in that it may be a difficult hurdle for new parties or independent candidates to surmount).

In Britain the rule is that candidates must pay a deposit, which is forfeited if the candidate fails to secure a certain proportion of the votes cast. The size of the deposit was unchanged at £150 from 1918 until 1985, and because of inflation the effectiveness of the deposit as a deterrent steadily decreased. In the seven inter-war elections an average of 36 candidates lost their deposits; in the elections between 1945 and 1959 the average was 71; in the elections of the 1960s the average was 121; in those of the 1970s the average was 438; and in 1983 the number was 739. In 1984 an Act was passed raising the deposit to £500, while simultaneously lowering the threshold for saving the deposit from one-eighth of the votes cast to one-twentieth. The object of this change was to deter frivolous candidates and those from small extremist groups, while bearing less hardly on the smaller parties than the previous rule. In the 1987 election 290 candidates lost their deposits.

(4) The fourth problem is that of establishing control over electoral expenses, with the dual objects of preventing corruption and keeping wealthy candidates or parties from having an untoward advantage over others. In Britain electoral expenses were first regulated in 1883 and control was tightened in the early part of the twentieth century.

The controls operate at the local rather than at the national level and they depend on a simple but extremely effective device. Each candidate is required to appoint an official election agent; all expenditure designed to promote the interests of the candidate during the campaign has to be authorized by the agent; and at the end of the campaign the agent has to submit a statement of account showing how the money was spent and also showing that the total sum expended did not exceed the permitted maximum. The maximum allowed is determined by a formula and in 1987 it worked out at between £5,000 and £6,000 per candidate. This is a very small sum compared with election expenditures in North America, but British election campaigns are short, candidates get one free postal delivery to each elector, and in practice most candidates spend appreciably less than the maximum. In 1987 the average Conservative candidate spent about £4,400, the average Labour candidate spent about £3,900 and the average candidate for the Liberal/SDP alliance spent about £3,400 (Butler and Kavanagh, 1988, p. 236).

The central expenses of the parties are not controlled, but they are minimal compared with the equivalent expenditures in the United States and Canada. One reason for this is the shortness of the campaign period – normally between three and four weeks. The other main reason is that the parties cannot buy advertising time on television or radio. They get a certain number of free broadcasts each and a great deal of free news coverage, which has to be balanced and impartial between the main parties. Central publicity is therefore confined to press advertising, posters and pamphlets, and to personal appearances and news conferences by party leaders.

In the 1987 election the Conservatives spent £9.0 million centrally (two and a half times as much as in 1983) compared with £2.8 million locally, while Labour spent £4.2 million centrally (almost twice the 1983 total) compared with £2.5 million locally (Butler and Kavanagh, 1988, p. 235). Central expenditure therefore rose sharply, in part because both parties employed expensive public relations firms. However, these sums are still fairly modest by international standards, and the general conclusion of nearly all commentators is that money has only a marginal impact on election results in Britain.

(5) The fifth problem, which is currently the most contentious in Britain, is that of the method of converting votes cast into seats won. The British system, like the American and Canadian systems, is that of simple plurality in single-

Table 6.1 *General Election Results: 1974–87*

Date	Party	Number of votes (millions)	Number of seats won	Percentage of votes	Percentage of seats won
Feb.	Conservative	11.9	297	37.9	46.8
1974	Labour	11.6	301	37.1	47.4
	Liberal	6.1	14	19.3	2.2
	Others	1.8	23	5.6	3.6
Oct.	Conservative	10.5	277	35.8	43.6
1974	Labour	11.5	319	39.2	50.2
	Liberal	5.3	13	18.3	2.1
	Others	1.9	26	6.6	4.2
1979	Conservative	13.7	339	43.9	53.4
	Labour	11.5	268	36.9	42.2
	Liberal	4.3	11	13.8	1.7
	Others	1.7	17	5.5	2.7
1983	Conservative	13.0	397	42.4	61.1
	Labour	8.5	209	27.6	32.2
	Liberal–SDP	7.8	23	25.4	3.5
	Others	1.4	21	4.6	3.2
1987	Conservative	13.7	376	42.2	57.8
	Labour	10.0	229	30.8	35.2
	Liberal–SDP	7.3	22	22.6	3.4
	Others	1.4	23	4.4	3.5

member constituencies. It is sometimes called a 'first past the post' system. This system helps the two main parties and particularly helps the most successful party. It bears hardly on the smaller ones, though the extent to which smaller parties suffer from the system depends on how far their support is geographically concentrated. The nationalist parties in Scotland, Wales and Northern Ireland do not come off too badly, but the Liberals and the Social Democrats are seriously affected because their supporters are dispersed around the country. The extent of their disadvantage is indicated by Table 6.1. It is clear that in recent elections most Liberal and Social Democratic votes have been wasted because of the way the electoral system works.

The Question of Proportional Representation

Ever since 1922, the Liberals have favoured replacing the simple plurality system by a system of proportional representation. Most European democracies have proportional representation (PR) in one form or another. With the revision of the French electoral system in 1985, Britain became the solitary member of the twelve-nation European Community not to have PR. However, for several reasons the British have declined to change their system. For one thing, the British have a general suspicion of coalition government, which is the usual corollary of PR and would almost certainly be the norm if this system were adopted in Britain. The tendency of the British system to exaggerate the majority of the most successful party is widely thought to be a virtue rather than a defect, and is always so regarded by the government in power. The case for PR has been thought to be a lost cause, rather like the Liberal Party itself.

There was some movement of opinion after the 1974 elections, when a few prominent members of the Conservative Party came out in favour of PR. The rise of the SDP since 1981 has naturally won further adherents to the cause of electoral reform. The SDP is committted to PR, and the result of the 1983 election (giving the Liberal–SDP alliance 3.5 per cent of the seats in return for 25 per cent of the votes) was so obviously unfair that it has affected public opinion. Several polls since 1983 have shown that a majority of British electors believe that PR would be a fairer system. In view of this the case for and against PR deserves careful examination.

There are two general arguments commonly advanced in favour of PR and two other arguments commonly advanced against it. The first argument in favour is simply fairness. If democracy implies not only 'one person, one vote' but also 'one vote, one value', it is manifestly undemocratic for the supporters of smaller parties to be effectively denied fair representation in the legislature by the workings of the electoral system. The most vehement opponents of PR cannot deny this; they merely say that other factors make a degree of unfairness acceptable.

The second general argument is that a non-proportional system like that of simple plurality creates an adversarial style of politics between the two main parties. This is said to lead these parties to more extreme positions than most electors favour. S. E. Finer and his associates have further argued that in Britain the alternation of power between Conservative and Labour parties has led to sharp oscillations of policy that have had a deleterious effect on the British economy (Finer, 1975). This argument is, however, much more dubious than the one about fairness. The adversarial character of political debate is apt to conceal a fair degree of consensus on policy issues. Most analyses of postwar economic policy reveal a substantial consensus between the main parties from 1945 until the mid-seventies. Many commentators, on both left and right, believe that the economy needed more decisive management than it got in those years, not more compromises.

The main general argument against PR is that it leads to a reduction in the accountability of governments to the electorate and a loss of control by the electors over the composition of the next government. If government is in the hands of a single majority party that party cannot escape responsibility for what has gone wrong during its term of office. In contrast, parties in a coalition government can always try to lay the blame on their partners.

Equally, under a simple plurality system the party with the largest number of votes normally has the power to form a government, whereas under PR the composition of a coalition government after the first election is apt to be determined by a process of bargaining between party leaders from which the electorate is excluded. Moreover, one coalition government may be replaced by another during the life of a Parliament with no opportunity for the electors to be consulted in the matter. A clear example occurred in West Germany in 1982, when the Free Democrats broke their long-standing alliance with the Social Democrats in order to form a new governing coalition with the Christian Democrats. This argument about accountability and control cannot be refuted.

Another common argument against PR, frequently deployed in Britain, is that the establishment of multi-member constituencies would deprive voters of the close ties with their elected representatives that they can enjoy in single-member constituencies. However, the validity of this argument depends on which of the various possible systems of PR is adopted. It is not essential to have multi-member constituencies under PR. In the West German system half the members are elected in single-member constituencies while the other half, so composed as to give a proportional balance to the total, are elected on a regional basis. In the Irish system, which does depend on multi-member constituencies, there is no lack of closeness in the relations between constituents and representatives. As candidates within each party have to be placed in order of preference by the voters, the system produces a positive incentive for candidates to cultivate the constituency and maintain close relations with local voters after they are elected.

It may be concluded that in general a system of PR scores in terms of fair representation but is open to criticism on the ground of accountability. In the specific circumstances of contemporary Britain the question of electoral reform poses a particularly intractable dilemma. If the present system is retained, the centrist parties will continue to be seriously under-represented in Parliament. However, if a system of PR were adopted this would probably put them into a no-lose position, as in any foreseeable voting result they would hold the balance of power between the Conservative and Labour parties.

In view of this situation, it is fair to conclude that neither the Conservative Party nor the Labour Party is likely to agree to electoral reform unless it is forced into this position by a much larger contingent of centrist MPs than now exists. However, the question remains on the agenda.

The Campaign

Election campaigns in Britain are short in comparison with campaigns in most other democratic countries. Polling takes place only seventeen working days after the Proclamation summoning a new Parliament, which is made by the monarch on the advice of the Prime Minister. It is usual for the Prime Minister to announce the date of the election about a month before polling day. The approximate date of the election may be guessed some time in advance of this if a Parliament is permitted to enjoy something approaching its maximum life of five years, as were the Parliaments of 1945–50, 1959–64 and 1974–9. But this is not usually the case. The government of the day has some tactical advantage in being able to fix the date of the election, and it is normal practice for a government to make the most of this by calling the election at fairly short notice some time before the end of Parliament's term.

The development of public opinion polls has increased the importance of this advantage, but the polls are not an infallible guide. In 1970 the Conservatives won the election even though the pollsters had predicted a few weeks earlier that Labour would win. In 1974 the Conservatives were trapped into calling a snap election when the polls showed a swing in their favour that turned out to be transitory, the advantage being lost during the campaign.

The shortness of the campaign period stands in sharp contrast to the very long campaigns that are conducted in the United States. This brevity is uncontroversial because a British election campaign is not generally regarded as an occasion for interest groups to press their views on politicians, for parties and leaders to formulate attitudes and policies, and for candidates to meet the people and subject themselves to cross-examination regarding their records and ambitions. Instead, it is regarded as essentially an occasion when the parties should be given a fair and equal opportunity to rally their followers and persuade them to go to the polls, it being assumed that both the policies of the parties and the allegiance of most of the electors are established before the campaign opens.

These assumptions are largely valid. Whatever the character of the party programmes – and they may range from a generalized promise to continue on the lines that have already been followed to a detailed plan of proposed reforms – the programmes are generally prepared well in advance of the campaign and are rarely changed during it. And the surveys that have been made of voting intentions and behaviour show that most voters also make up their minds in advance of the campaign.

The voting behaviour of the minority who are uncertain may of course be of crucial importance. If it were possible for the parties to design policies and propaganda specially calculated to influence these 'floating voters', this would almost certainly be done. If the floating voters were mainly women, or pensioners, or the unemployed, the campaign might be dominated by propaganda directed particularly at these groups. This has not been the case in postwar British elections, however. Surveys in the 1950s and 1960s showed that, broadly speaking, floating voters were a cross-section of the electorate, not distinguished from their fellow-citizens by any particular social characteristics. The parties had, therefore, to aim their appeals at the whole electorate. More recently, as will be explained later in this chapter, the opinions and loyalties of the electorate have become more volatile. This has opened up the possibility of selective appeals to target groups. In the 1979 election campaign the Conservative Party made a considerable effort to win support from manual workers, with 'specific commitments to abandon wage controls, further restrict immigration, and oblige local authorities to offer to sell council houses at favourable terms to their tenants' (Sarlvik and Crewe, 1983, p. 49). This policy met with some success, as the swing to the Conservatives was greater among manual workers, at 9 per cent, than among non-manual workers, at 5.5 per cent (ibid., p. 83). Further efforts to cater for the assumed interests of particular groups can be expected in future elections, but it must be emphasized that this has not become a major feature of British campaigns, as it has of American campaigns. British electors are not so ready as many Americans are to change their votes on the basis of a single issue, and it is to be expected that British parties will continue to place most emphasis on appeals directed to a wide cross-section of the community.

At the local level the main object of party organizers is to make sure that as many as possible of the party's supporters turn out to vote. Canvassers concentrate almost entirely on supporters and try to avoid being drawn into argument by opponents. Supporters who have not gone to the polls by early evening on polling day will be called for, sometimes with a car.

Candidates are expected to make numerous personal appearances at meetings, but the personality and political views of the candidate rarely have more than a marginal effect on the result, except sometimes in the case of smaller parties. The attitude of most voters was neatly summarized by an elector in Birmingham who said: 'I'd vote for a pig if my party put one up.' It remains true that a good candidate may advance his cause by promoting the growth of a large and active local party, and this is particularly true of the smaller parties. However, this is work that has to be done between campaigns rather than during the campaign itself.

At the national level the campaign is increasingly dominated by television. Each party is allocated a few free broadcasts, being five each for the main parties and the alliance and one or two for the others in 1987. However, what is undoubtedly more important is that the whole campaign gets a great deal of news coverage, with the broadcasting authorities carefully respecting their legal obligation to provide a fair balance between the parties. Each of the national party leaders normally gives a news conference in London every morning, and these conferences are the opportunity for a running debate between the parties on policy issues. Because of this, there is no need and no demand for a direct confrontation between party leaders on television, as is staged in American and Canadian elections.

British election campaigns, though short and inexpensive by international standards, are relatively effective at getting out the vote. The turn-out at general elections comprises about 75 per cent of the electorate. It does not vary much between elections, or for that matter between constituencies in any one election. This turn-out figure is slightly lower than the norm in most other European democracies, but appreciably higher than the norm in American elections.

Voting Behaviour

To explain British voting behaviour two questions have to be asked, as follows. First, how is voting behaviour influenced by social factors such as sex, religion and occupation? Secondly, how is voting behaviour influenced by individual values and attitudes to political issues raised during the campaign? The answers to each question have to be couched partly in historical terms, for it would be a mistake to slip into the assumption that voting behaviour is determined by timeless and immutable laws.

The significance of sex and religion for voting can be dealt with briefly. In the early postwar surveys it was reported that women favoured the Conservative Party in slightly larger numbers than men. However, by 1979 this statistical tendency had virtually disappeared. Its significance for an understanding of voting was in any case never very clear. Women have different opportunities in the labour market, are more likely to be non-employed and have a more direct interest in certain social issues like abortion. There is every reason to expect that particular categories of women, having to cope with particular social situations and problems, may have distinctive political attitudes not shared by so many men. These are the proper subject of detailed inquiries (see Dunleavy and Husbands, 1984). But there is no obvious reason why women, taken as a whole, should be more right-wing or more left-wing or more centrist than men in their political sympathies.

The political significance of religion is somewhat greater, though it is declining. At the beginning of the twentieth century there was a clear and important relationship between religious affiliation and voting, with Anglicans tending to support the Conservative Party and members of other churches supporting the Liberal Party. This relationship has gradually lost its significance, partly because of the disappearance of religious issues in politics and partly because of the decline in religious faith and observance. In the 1960s it was still true that Anglicans who claimed to attend church once a month or more were significantly more likely to vote Conservative than other citizens, but only 16 per cent of nominal Anglicans made this claim (Butler and Stokes, 1974, p. 157). Moreover, most of these practising Anglicans had middle-class occupations, which also inclined them towards Conservatism. The statistical relationship is evidence of a syndrome rather than of a causal relationship between religion and voting.

The other relationships between religion and voting that emerge from some of the surveys are essentially relationships between ethnicity and voting. Thus, Irish voters (of whom there are over a million) are nearly all Catholics and mostly Labour, but the basic reason for this is that the Irish dislike the Conservative Party for historical reasons. Welsh rural voters are mostly Methodists and mostly anti-Conservative (being Liberal, Labour or Plaid Cymru), but this is also for historical and social rather than for purely religious reasons. Most Muslim and Hindu voters support Labour, but this is because of

Table 6.2 *Occupation and Voting in Britain: 1951*

Occupational group	Number of Conservative voters (millions)	Number of Labour voters (millions)	Conservative percentage of two-party vote
Business and professional	4.6	1.0	82
White-collar and intermediate	2.6	1.6	62
Manual	6.2	11.3	35
Total	13.4	13.9	49

Source: Bonham, 1954.

the assumption (not necessarily correct) that a Labour government might be more generous than the Conservative government has been about the immigration of relatives from Pakistan and India.

The relationship between occupation and party preference has been much more significant in postwar elections, though its importance has diminished recently. The relationship is not surprising since categorizing voters according to the type of occupation they follow is broadly equivalent to categorizing them according to their life experiences in material terms. Some people are fortunate or successful in their encounters with the educational system, are able to find interesting and secure employment and earn enough to satisfy their material expectations. Others are inadequately educated, face insecurity in their employment and find that their lives are dominated by a struggle to maintain acceptable living conditions for themselves and their families.

It is not surprising to learn that members of the first category have tended to favour the Conservative Party, while members of the second category have tended to favour the Labour Party. The general image of the Conservatives has always depicted them as in favour of maintaining the existing pattern of economic and social relationships, while the general image of Labour depicts it as favouring measures designed to increase the security and welfare of the less fortunate members of the community. The figures in Table 6.2 shows the relationship between occupation and voting in the 1951 election, this election being chosen because the relationship was stronger in the 1950s and early 1960s than before or since, and the 1951 election was one in which the two main parties were evenly balanced.

These figures establish a broad relationship between type of occupation and voting, as shown in the final column. However, they also indicate two other points of interest. One is that the relationship in 1951 was much stronger among business and professional people than among the remainder of the voters. Business and professional people were pro-Conservative in the ratio of 4.6 to 1. Manual workers were pro-Labour in the ratio of only 1.8 to 1. The other point is that, while the Labour Party got 81 per cent of its support from manual workers (and their wives, who were categorized according to their husbands' occupations in this study), the Conservative Party got only 34 per cent of its support from business and professional people and only 54 per cent of its support from non-manual workers of all types.

What general interpretation should be given to these figures? A widespread tendency among social scientists in the 1950s and 1960s was to interpret them in terms of a class-conflict model of politics. The middle classes, it was suggested, would naturally vote Conservative to protect their economic interests, while the working classes would naturally vote Labour to advance their very different economic interests.

A great deal of intellectual energy was then devoted to explaining the behaviour of the working-class Conservative voters, who were cast in the role of deviant cases. It was said that they were in the grip of deferential attitudes, misguidedly voting Conservative because they liked to see the government of the country in the hands of the traditional ruling classes. Another explanation stressed the relative youth of the Labour Party, suggesting that voters supported the Conservatives partly because they retained an allegiance they (or their parents) had acquired before Labour was a credible alternative. Yet another line of argument invoked the residual influence of religion on party preference. The implication of all these explanations was that working-class Conservatism could be expected to fade away with the passage of time.

There are several difficulties about this interpretation. For one thing, it implies that political behaviour is determined (or ought to be determined) by occupational status, which makes it difficult not only to account for the working-class Conservatives but also to explain why there are so many floating voters, who change parties between elections or are undecided until the campaign. On this determinist view, it is hard to understand why voting behaviour varies so much from one election to the next.

Secondly, there are simply too many working-class Conservatives for it to be reasonable to regard them as deviants. There is something wrong with a generalization that has to account for 6 million deviant cases. Thirdly, the relationship between occupation and voting has not become stronger with the passage of time but less pronounced. From 1966 onwards there has been a process of de-alignment in British politics, with the relationship between type of occupation (or class) and partisan support becoming weaker and more complex. The statistical basis for this assertion is outlined in Tables 6.3 and 6.4

These figures indicate that the class alignment in British politics, never so clear as was frequently asserted, has been withering away. In 1979 the prediction that working-class voters would support Labour was just as likely to be wrong as right. If the two Labour victories of 1966 and October 1974 are compared, it is plain that Labour lost about a sixth of its support among manual workers over the period, but won the latter election nevertheless because the Labour vote among non-manual workers held steady in spite of the increased popularity of the Liberal Party. If the two Conservatives victories of 1970 and

Table 6.3 *Division of the Vote among Manual Workers*

Vote	1966 %	1970 %	February 1974 %	October 1974 %	1979 %
Conservative	25	33	24	24	35
Liberal or minor party	6	9	19	20	15
Labour	69	58	57	57	50
Total	100	100	100	100	100

Source: Sarlvik and Crewe, 1983, p. 87.

Table 6.4 *Division of the Vote among Non-Manual Workers*

Vote	1966 %	1970 %	February 1974 %	October 1974 %	1979 %
Conservative	60	64	53	51	60
Liberal or minor party	14	11	25	24	17
Labour	26	25	22	25	23
Total	100	100	100	100	100

Source: Sarlvik and Crewe, 1983, p. 87.

1979 are compared, it emerges that the Conservatives did better in 1979 because, relative to Labour, they got a higher share of the votes cast by manual workers despite getting a smaller share of the vote cast by non-manual workers.

A study by Anthony Heath and his colleagues has cast doubt on this analysis, arguing that if voters are categorized in a more refined way it appears that occupational class is still the main determinant of voting behaviour. In this study foremen and technicians are separated from other manual workers and defined as not being working class, while women are classified under their own occupations (if they are working) instead of under their husbands' occupations. Both of these steps have the effect of reducing the number of voters classified as working class.

However, while this may be an improved form of social classification, using it in respect of 1983 voting figures suggests that it makes little difference to the conclusions that can be drawn. Heath *et al.* show that in 1983 voters in their more narrowly defined working class divided in the following proportions: 49 per cent Labour, 30 per cent Conservative, 20 per cent for the Liberal–SDP Alliance, 1 per cent for other candidates (Heath, Jowell and Curtice, 1985, p. 20). If we allow for the emergence of the SDP in 1981, these figures are not significantly different from the figures for the voting behaviour of manual workers in 1979, as given in Table 6.3. Both sets of data show that only half the working-class voters supported the Labour Party, whereas two-thirds of them had done so in the 1950s and early 1960s. The Heath, Jowell and Curtice figures also show that only 54 per cent of voters classified as members of the 'salariat' supported the Conservative Party in 1983. Without going into the niceties of classification, it is clear that this is a smaller proportion than the proportion of middle-class voters supporting the Conservatives in 1951 (see Table 6.2) and 1970 (see Table 6.4), all these being years of Conservative victory. While class is still an important influence on voting behaviour, the evidence for a process of class de-alignment over the years is beyond reasonable dispute.

This trend is not in the least surprising in view of the changing character of British society outlined in Chapter 1 of this book. Apart from the unemployed, almost everyone in Britain has become a good deal more prosperous since the 1960s. Most people have achieved lifestyles that were previously enjoyed only by a privileged minority. The equalizing effects of television, supermarkets and car ownership have been very marked. At the same time as this process of levelling up has taken place, there has been an interesting movement of a quite different kind. This is the growth of trade union membership among white-collar and professional workers, with bank clerks, nurses, hospital doctors and senior civil servants threatening to strike in support of their pay claims. The sense of distance between manual workers who strike and middle-class people who would not consider such a degrading tactic has been somewhat eroded by this development. The result of these and similar changes, as noted in Chapter 1, has been a marked decline in class consciousness. It is entirely logical that this should have been accompanied by a weakening of the relationship between class membership and voting behaviour.

While this relationship has declined, another relationship has become increasingly important in the 1980s. This is the relationship between area of residence and voting behaviour. It has always been true that area of residence had some influence, with white-collar workers, for instance, tending to be more pro-Labour in industrial areas than workers in similar occupations in rural or suburban areas. There is a long-standing tendency for electors without firm partisan allegiances to conform to the majority viewpoint in their area. In the 1980s, however, Britain experienced a period of continuous economic growth in the southern half of England combined with virtual stagnation in many of the older industrial areas of northern England and western Scotland. This was partly a result of the Conservative government's economic policies, which will be discussed in Chapter 11, and it is not at all surprising that the political consequence of it has been an increasing gap between the pro-Conservative tendencies of the southern counties and the pro-Labour tendencies of the northern industrial areas. In 1987 Glasgow and the seven largest cities in northern England returned 43 Members of Parliament of whom 39 were Labour, 3 Conservative and 1 Liberal in affiliation. In contrast, London returned 58 Conservatives to 23 Labour MPs, 1 Liberal and 2 Social Democrats. As will be seen in Figure 6.1, the rest of southern England was overwhelmingly pro-Conservative. In the 1987 election, the Conservatives gained 3 seats in southern England while losing 24 in the rest of the country.

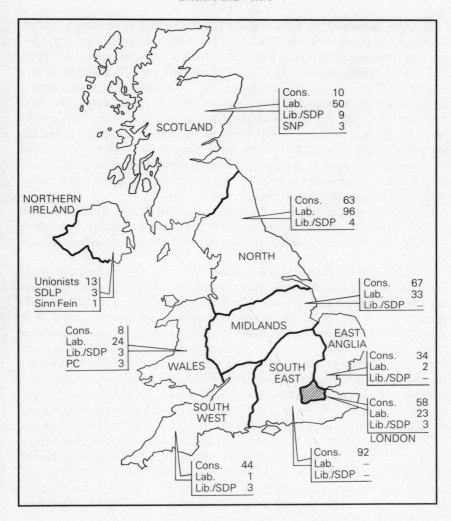

Figure 6.1 General election results by region: 1987

In addition to these social changes, there have also been some attitudinal changes. There is scattered but persuasive evidence (some of it quoted in Chapter 1) that British electors have become more sceptical about the performance of their governments. Successive failures by both Conservative and Labour governments to stop the decline (relative to other nations) of the British economy have undermined the confidence people once felt in their chosen party. Surveys have shown that feelings of loyalty towards both main parties have weakened. Voters have become more detached, more fickle in their political sympathies and more volatile in their voting behaviour.

All these developments have tended to make electors more likely to pursue individual – as opposed to collective – interests when they participate in politics, and also more sensitive to particular issues of policy. Surveys show that in 1979, and again in 1983, Labour did poorly (by its own earlier standards) among manual workers as a whole, but nevertheless maintained its support among workers in public enterprises. The reason is that Labour is seen as the party that supports public enterprises and is willing to subsidize them from general revenue, whereas the Conservative Party wants them to pay their way and has a policy of selling them back to private ownership where possible. White-collar workers and managers in the public sector were much more inclined to vote Labour than their equivalents in the private sector, for exactly the same reason (see Dunleavy and Husbands, 1984, p. 14).

Equally, Labour has held its vote among municipal tenants, because Labour favours generous subsidies for municipal housing whereas the Conservatives are inclined to raise rents. Individual self-interest is clearly a determining factor here.

In regard to the influence of policy issues on voting, we are fortunate that a study has been published revealing the political attitudes of a panel of Londoners who were interviewed repeatedly, and in depth, between 1951 and 1974 (Himmelweit *et al.*, 1981). The information made available by this study is far richer than the information gathered by the ordinary single-interview or double-interview surveys, with interviews conducted on the doorstep. The study suggests that individual values and attitudes to political issues have had a greater influence on voting behaviour than has commonly been believed, and that this kind of influence has been of growing importance in recent years. The sample of electors interviewed in this study was small, but doubts on this score about the reliability of the results have been largely resolved by the statistical analysis made by Rose and McAllister and published under the title *Voters Begin to Choose*. These authors draw their data from several national surveys based on large samples and they show that voters have indeed become more volatile in the last two decades, more likely to be influenced by attitudes to particular policies and more likely to be influenced by the campaign (Rose and McAllister, 1986, *passim*).

Himmelweit and her colleagues believe that British voting behaviour is better explained by a model depicting electors as consumers than by the more familiar model of class conflict. In the Himmelweit view electors are individually motivated, spending time to gain information about what the parties have to offer and 'buying' whichever package appears to them to be most advantageous. This implies that the 'floating voter', who seriously considers changing his votes (or abstentions) between one election and another, should be regarded as normal rather than as a deviation from the assumed norm of partisan loyalty.

The statistics derived from the study support this model. Only 30 per cent of the respondents made the same voting decision in all the six elections covered by the study (ibid., p. 34). A fair number changed more than once. They confirmed the findings of one of the earlier studies, namely that many of the floaters are keenly interested in politics, and the floaters as a category should not be regarded as apathetic (see Benewick *et al.*, 1969; Himmelweit *et al.*, 1981, p. 239). They showed that the floaters were significantly more likely than the consistent voters to be undecided at the beginning of the election campaign and that many of them made up their minds only in the last few days (Himmelweit *et al.*, 1981, pp. 47, 241). They also showed that electoral volatility and indecisiveness increased over the period covered by the study, with a third of the sample in 1974 undecided at the beginning of the election campaign (ibid., p. 193).

This increase in volatility was associated with the increased support for the Liberal Party (though not *only* associated with this). It appears that this support has been surprisingly lacking in constancy. There have been few faithful Liberal voters. Even in the two elections of 1974, separated by only eight months, there was an astonishing degree of movement into and out of the Liberal camp. Sarlvik and Crewe report that 48 per cent of the Liberal supporters in February 1974 – about 3 million voters – had defected by October, but over 2 million new voters had been attracted (Sarlvik and Crewe, 1983, p. 46).

What attracted voters to the Liberals? The conclusion of the Himmelweit study is that this is the wrong question to ask. The Liberal Party got most of its support from voters who were disenchanted with the party they previously supported but not ready to go over to the other main party. 'The Liberal vote is a vote of disaffection; it represents movement away from a party rather than movement to the party; it is a vote signifying departure rather than arrival' (Himmelweit *et al.*, 1981, p. 159). In view of this we should not be surprised that Liberal voters have been so inconstant, apt to move on to the other main party or back to their former love after dallying with the Liberals.

A detailed examination of the attitudes of the Himmelweit panel to political issues revealed that these attitudes did indeed prove to be good predictors of voting at the next election, as the consumer model of voting implies (ibid., p. 83). It was also shown that there is 'a causal chain from attitude to vote and from attitude shift to vote defection' (ibid., p. 101). It seems that there is a kind of political market-place in which party propagandists and other moulders of opinion try to shape popular attitudes to issues of the day, while electors weigh these messages against their own perception of what would be good for them and what would be good for the country as a whole.

What are the most important issues? There are several more or less permanent issues on which the Conservative Party has an advantage, in the sense that it is viewed by most electors as having the better record and/or the better policies. These are foreign affairs, defence, the protection of law and order, and the control of prices and inflation. Equally, there are several more or less permanent issues on which the Labour Party has an advantage. These are the delivery of social services, municipal housing and the control of unemployment.

There are also issues on which a party can only lose. One is the nationalization of industry, to which the great majority of electors have always been hostile. This issue has repeatedly lost votes for Labour and may do so again if a future Labour manifesto proposes more nationalization. Another losing issue is industrial relations, associated with the prevalence of strikes and the power of trade unions. This hindered the Conservatives in 1974 and Labour in 1979, both parties being blamed for the strikes that occurred while they were in power.

Issues rise and fall in their significance for the electorate, partly because of events but also because of deliberate efforts by party leaders to promote them or neutralize them. The control of immigration became an important and emotional issue in the 1960s, but is no longer significant. The introduction of comprehensive schools became salient in the 1970s, but is now a *fait accompli*. In the 1979 election the Conservatives successfully promoted the reduction of taxation as an issue. The Falkland Islands war of 1982 promoted defence to the forefront of public attention, and as this was to the advantage of the Conservatives it was exploited accordingly.

An interesting example of issue manipulatiuon is provided by policy towards municipal housing. As the Labour Party supports extensive housing provision with subsidized rents, and over a quarter of the electorate live in this type of accommodation, this is one of Labour's better issues. When Conservative governments made legislative changes to housing policy in 1957 and 1972, they incurred widespread unpopularity on each occasion. A poll taken in 1983 indicated that only 19 per cent of municipal tenants supported the Conservative Party (*Guardian*, 13 June 1983). In the face of this, the Thatcher government has promoted a new and ingenious policy. Local authorities have been compelled to offer their houses for sale to tenants at advantageous prices. As nobody is compelled to buy, tenants' interests are not infringed. However, those who take up the option are thereby transformed from tenants into owner-occupiers, and lose their interest in maintaining rent subsidies. Surveys indicate that most owner-occupiers vote Conservative.

The whole field of voting behaviour has therefore to be regarded as a field of tactical and strategic operations, in which political leaders and news editors have the initiative but the electors decide the outcome of the battle. In doing this they are influenced partly by their personal and family situations; partly by their economic interests; partly by their political and social values; and partly by their perception of current political issues, as these are presented to them through the mass media.

The Elections of the 1980s and the Future

The 1983 election was not an exciting contest, because the victory of the Conservative Party was a foregone conclusion from the beginning of the campaign. It was, however, a very interesting event. It was interesting, in the first place, because the Conservatives won in spite of having presided over the greatest growth of unemployment since the slump of the early 1930s. The Conservatives did not pretend to have a remedy for this development; on the contrary, they predicted that mass unemployment would remain for the foreseeable future. Their strategy was to disown responsibility for unemployment, saying on the one hand that it was produced by international economic forces that had affected other countries equally; and on the other that the situation would be improved only if the British people became (under Conservative guidance) more enterprising and the British economy more competitive. The message was stern rather than optimistic.

The election was also interesting because it was the first to be fought by the Liberal–SDP alliance. In a three-party situation, with the present British electoral system, the chances are that a party gaining less than 33 per cent of the votes will lose badly unless its support is geographically concentrated. Support for the alliance was spread with remarkable evenness over the whole country, and it gained just under 26 per cent of the votes. Therefore it lost badly. The Labour Party did relatively well with only 28 per cent of the votes because its support was much more concentrated. Labour had a large number of safe seats, while the alliance had hardly any.

The 1987 election had fewer novel features. Unemployment was much reduced and weighed seriously against the government only in the older industrial areas of the north, which were in any case overwhelmingly pro-Labour. The Conservatives were able to claim that their economic strategy had been successful and made much of the fact that in 1986 the British economic growth rate was actually higher than that of France (for the first time since 1958) and that of West Germany (for the first time since 1945). Both main parties put more emphasis than in previous campaigns on their leaders, the Conservatives focusing on the remarkable Margaret Thatcher and the Labour Party using modern publicity techniques to advertise the attractive personalities of Neil Kinnock and his wife. The Labour Party claimed that under the Conservative government the rich had got richer while the poor had got poorer. This was true, though not more than about 5 per cent of the electors could reasonably be described as rich and not more than about 20 per cent could actually have suffered a reduction in their standard of living, with the remaining three-quarters of the electors having become modestly more prosperous. The Conservatives produced the time-worn argument that Labour campaign promises implied more public expenditure than the country could afford. The Liberals and Social Democrats tried to hide their disagreements. The result of the election was never in doubt, with Thatcher achieving her third successive victory and saying that she intended 'to go on and on'.

Whether the next election will give her a fourth victory can only be a matter of speculation. The Conservatives have such a large majority in Parliament that this result is statistically probable. On the other hand, her government's politics since the 1987 election have certainly not been calculated to win votes. The bold reforms in education seem likely to be quite popular. However, a MORI survey for the *Sunday Times* in November 1988 showed that 75 per cent of the electors were opposed to the government's plans to privatize the water authorities, 69 per cent disliked the plan to privatize the electricity industry, 61 per cent were opposed to the plan to replace the property tax as a source of local government revenue by a fixed 'community charge' to be paid by every adult (the poll tax, in popular parlance), and 60 per cent were against the idea of replacing grants to university students by loans. By pushing ahead with these plans, the government is clearly taking a risk.

At the same time, the decline in support for the two centrist parties seems fairly certain to help Labour, while the Labour Party itself is making a remarkable effort to improve its electoral chances by dropping its more unpopular policies. Neil Kinnock has abandoned a lifelong commitment to unilateral nuclear disarmament and has persuaded Labour's National Executive Committee to remove this and several other radical proposals from the party's programme. As these changes have been endorsed by the 1989 Annual Conference the Labour Party will be able to enter the next election with a set of policies that have much more electoral appeal. The result of that election is therefore very difficult to predict at the time of writing.

Further Reading

After each general election David Butler and a colleague publish a valuable analysis of the issues, the campaign and the results, the most recent of which is Butler and Kavanagh (1988), *The British General Election of 1987*; for discussions of the case for electoral reform see Finer (1975), *Adversary Politics and Electoral Reform*, and Jowell and Oliver (1985), *The Changing Constitution*, chs. 4 and 13; for analyses of voting behaviour see Butler and Stokes (1974), *Political Change in Britain*, Sarlvik and Crewe (1983), *Decade of Dealignment*, Himmelweit *et al.*, (1981), *How Voters Decide*, and Heath, Jowell and Curtice (1985), *How Britain Votes*.

◇ 7 ◇

Pressure Groups

Seen in the light of democratic theory, the citizen is first and foremost an elector, having general views about government and expressing preferences between one political party and another. Seen in another light, the citizen is not so much a whole political individual as a bundle of specific interests and values, having definite views about particular issues of policy. A citizen with children will be concerned about education and the maintenance of child allowances; one with a widowed mother will be worried about the level of widows' pensions; sportsmen will want more playing fields; trade unionists will have views about the law relating to trade unions; animal lovers will be concerned about animal welfare. The list could be extended almost indefinitely.

While some citizens are active in political parties that embody general attitudes to government, others are active in defence of their particular interests and values. The British political scene is populated by a vast number of pressure groups, whose spokesmen are engaged in the business of exerting influence on government policies. Pressure groups are highly varied in character but they can be usefully categorized into three broad types. As so often in political science, the categories are not watertight compartments and a few groups straddle two of the categories. But this fact does not destroy the utility of the classification.

Types of Pressure Group

In the first place, there are innumerable permanent associations that are concerned to defend and promote the interests of their members. Trade unions and trade associations are the most obvious of these, but the category also includes groups concerned with religion, sports, motoring and other activities. Nobody has ever taken a census of interest groups, and their multiplicity and variety are perhaps best illustrated by a random selection of titles, as follows:

The Small Pig Keepers' Council
The National Union of Railwaymen
The Society of Authors
The Bookmakers' Protection Association
The Royal Yachting Association

The National Union of Students
The Free Church Federal Council
The Take Away Fast Food Federation
The Royal Automobile Club
The British Limbless Ex-Servicemen's Association
The British Insurance Brokers' Association
The National Federation of Pakistani Associations

Very few of these organizations are concerned exclusively with political
action. The majority of them provide services of various kinds for their
members and many of them regard this as their main function, turning to politics
only when the interests of their members are threatened by government action
or by the activities of other groups in a way that can be prevented only by
government action. But the range of government activities is now so great that
most interest groups take on a political role from time to time, acting in ways
that will be discussed in a later section.

The second category comprises organizations that are concerned not with the
protection of their members' interests but with the promotion of some kind of
social, moral, or political cause. Groups of this kind are best called promotional
groups, and a complete list of the promotional groups that play a role in the
British political process would be just as varied, though not so long, as a
complete list of interest groups. Some examples follow:

The Royal Society for the Prevention of Cruelty to Animals
The Lord's Day Observance Society
The Council for the Preservation of Rural England
The Campaign for Nuclear Disarmament
The Noise Abatement Society
The Organization Against Sexism in Software
The Howard League for Penal Reform
The Friends of the Earth
The Anti-Apartheid Movement

Promotional groups tend to have smaller memberships than interest groups
and, unlike the latter, to draw their members very largely from the upper and
middle classes. Some promotional groups are well financed – there really are
people who leave their money to animal welfare societies – while others have to
spend a good deal of energy trying to raise funds. But the success of promotional
groups in their political activities does not depend either on their ability to claim a
mass membership or on their ability to mount an expensive campaign; it
depends rather on the quality of their arguments, the energy they put into their
activities and the existence or otherwise of a group opposed to the cause they
are supporting.

A third category consists of groups that spring into existence to fight a
particular proposal and are wound up after the issue has been decided.
Government authorities propose to build a new highway, power station, or

airport; local residents feel that their interests are threatened by the proposal and hold a meeting to protest against it; and within days or weeks a new pressure group is in business. S. E. Finer called such groups 'fire-brigade groups', which is self-explanatory (Finer, 1966). A more neutral way of describing the members of this category would be to call them temporary defence groups. They have become increasingly prominent in recent years, partly because of the power of example; the news that a spontaneous association of citizens has wrecked the plans of a county council or government department spreads quickly, and encourages the formation of groups in other parts of the country with similar objectives.

Pressure Groups and the Administration

Group spokesmen engage in politics in various ways. They write to newspapers; they organize public demonstrations; they speak in Parliament; they sit on government advisory committees; they negotiate directly with government departments. As a broad generalization it is probably true that the more conspicuous their activities are, the less influence they are likely to exert. Public demonstrations are rarely effective; speeches in Parliament are only occasionally effective; while representation on official committees is always helpful, and informal negotiations with government departments pay more dividends than any other form of activity. It is a generalization to which exceptions can be found, particularly in the realm of moral issues. But the point is true enough for it to be sensible to pay most attention in this chapter to the relations of group spokesmen to government departments.

It would be a complete mistake to assume that there is anything sinister about the influence of group spokesmen in Whitehall or to imagine that they usually have difficulty in gaining a hearing. On the contrary, government departments think it both proper and necessary to consult the 'affected interests' in the normal process of administration. They think it proper because the affected interests, broadly defined, will include nearly all those likely to have an informed opinion on any issue that may be in question. They will know best how the existing arrangements work and what their shortcomings are; they are in the best position to judge how effective any proposed changes are likely to be; they can draw attention to the particular difficulties involved in the introduction of reforms. Of course, the responsibility for government policy rests with the minister, and he should not allow himself to be 'captured' by the affected interests, but in the British political tradition it is thought entirely proper that he and his permanent staff should consult fully with these interests before notifying Parliament of any modifications in policy that he proposes to introduce.

The tradition of constant consultation with the affected interests is strengthened by two further considerations. One is that, as will emerge in Chapter 10, British civil servants are not specialists. They are intelligent people with a good education who acquire a facility for familiarizing themselves with specific problems, but they need advice on technical matters and they often find that they can get it most conveniently by consulting the spokesman for the industry or activity with which they are concerned. The other consideration is that government departments need the co-operation of the relevant sections of the public if administration is to be efficient and government policies are to be successful. No government could be happy with a situation in which it had constantly to rely on its powers of coercion. Economic policies need the co-operation of both sides of industry if they are to succeed; educational policies need the co-operation of teachers and local authorities; health policies need the co-operation of the medical profession. Consultation does not guarantee co-operation but its absence would almost certainly cause resentment; it is a necessary even though not a sufficient condition of successful administration.

Not all group spokesmen are consulted by government departments because not all groups are recognized as having a legitimate interest in the matters at stake. The Ministry of Defence does not consult pacifist groups, who have to resort to other means of bringing their views to the attention of those in authority. But government departments are generally liberal in their attitudes to this matter, and many promotional groups enjoy fairly close contacts with the relevant departments. Certainly this is true of the groups concerned with social welfare and with penal reform.

There are some groups that are thought so useful by the government that their position has been strengthened by financial support from public funds, or even by legislation requiring certain categories of persons or firms to join them. One is the Cotton Board, established by statute to act as an intermediary between the various branches of the cotton industry and the government. Another is the Pharmaceutical Society of Great Britain, charged with certain regulatory powers and duties. Others include the National Council of Social Service, the Royal Society for the Prevention of Accidents and the Central Council of Physical Recreation.

The complexity of the consultative process varies from one field of activity to another and depends largely on the number of interest groups involved. In most aspects of economic and industrial policy, the government department concerned will have to balance conflicting pressures from the trade associations on one hand and the trade unions on the other. In regard to agricultural policy, the situation was for many years more straightforward because the National Farmers' Union (NFU) was the only group involved. From 1947 until 1972, the level of government support for agriculture was determined by lengthy negotiations between officials of the NFU and officials of the Ministry of Agriculture and Fisheries, which resulted in a 'global award' for the industry. Although the NFU was not always happy with the size of the award, it was rarely willing to jeopardize its good relations with the civil servants involved by attacking the ministry in public. A somewhat cosy relationship therefore developed, which was transformed in January 1973 by Britain's membership of

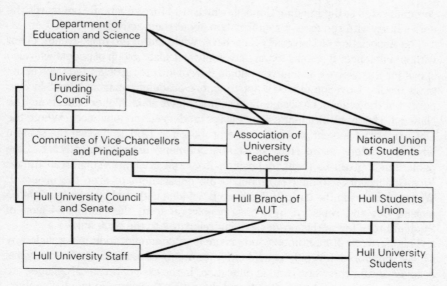

Figure 7.1   The university network

the European Economic Community. Since then, the most important decisions regarding British agriculture have been taken in Brussels, and the relationship between group spokesmen and decision-makers has become more complex.

For some years, the British Medical Association (BMA) enjoyed a relationship with the Ministry of Health that was rather similar to that between the NFU and the Ministry of Agriculture and Fisheries. However, this relationship also has become more complex recently, primarily because other spokesmen for groups within the National Health Service have challenged the virtual monopoly of the BMA. Some of the general practitioners are now represented by another organization and some of the junior hospital doctors have formed a third organized group. Moreover, the nursing profession has become unionized and hospital porters have attempted to influence government policy through the National Union of Public Employees.

The situation regarding universities has always been rather complex. In Britain higher education is largely financed by the government but funds are distributed by the University Funding Council, a body whose members are drawn largely from the academic profession. The network of organizations dealing with the government of universities is illustrated in Figure 7.1, in which the writer's former university is taken as an example.

Messages, inquiries and proposals flow constantly in all directions along the line of communication indicated in this diagram. The universities are engaged in what seems to be an almost continuous process of framing and revising plans for the future. Such plans have financial implications and have therefore to be communicated to the Funding Council, which in its turn constantly bombards the universities with requests for information about their activities.

The Association of University Teachers, while out of the mainstream, is not without influence. It speaks for an extremely articulate group of people who also speak for themselves, in a never-ending flow of letters, articles and talks in the mass media. Governments are apt to ignore academic opinions about foreign policy but they cannot easily ignore academic views about higher education. The National Union of Students also enjoys a degree of influence. When the Department of Education and Science proposed in 1971 to abolish the system whereby student unions enjoy substantial autonomy in their expenditure of the public funds given to them, opposition from the students (supported by the Vice-Chancellors' Committee) induced the department to drop the proposal. When ministers in the early 1980s floated the idea that student grants might be phased out and replaced by loans, opposition from the National Union of Students resulted in this proposal being relegated to the back burner.

This network of institutions and channels of communication is paralleled by similar networks for polytechnics, for colleges of education, for technical colleges and for the world of adult education. In the case of technical colleges the local authorities are also involved, and they have their own influential spokesmen in bodies like the County Councils Association. Those responsible for higher education in the ministry have to deal with all these numerous spokesmen, on whom, indeed, they rely for information and for guidance about what is feasible. Since higher education cannot be entirely separated from secondary education, they have also to consider the views of the various and influential spokesmen for both state and private schools.

It follows that civil servants in the ministry dealing with education have to deal with a great variety of spokesmen for the various sections of the educational world, who are usually in disagreement with one another. Partly because of this, the ministers responsible for education are given to appointing advisory committees that will hear evidence from all interested groups and contain representatives of many of them, in the hope that the committee will relieve the minister of the difficult task of balancing rival claims and assessing conflicting proposals.

Action through Parliament

Parliament is somewhat less important than the administration as a focus for group pressures in most fields. As the great majority of Bills are drafted by civil servants and sponsored by the government of the day, it is clearly better to apply pressure while the legislation is being planned than to wait until after the Bills are published. Governments dislike major amendments to their legislative proposals and can usually rely on party discipline to prevent such amendments being passed. For this reason, Parliament is less important as a channel of group pressures than is the United States Congress.

It is also noteworthy that in Parliament there is nothing like the level of lobbying on foreign affairs that is accepted as normal in Congress. In 1974, for instance, the Greek-American lobby, representing only a very small proportion of the population, was powerful enough to secure an arms embargo on Turkey following the fighting in Cyprus – a decision that weakened the entire Western alliance and caused anxiety in the State Department, the Pentagon and the White House. It is inconceivable that any pressure group could have this kind of impact on defence or foreign policy in Britain.

However, Congress is exceptional among legislative assemblies in its constitutional separation from the executive and in the weakness of party discipline within it. Pressure groups are highly active in the British parliamentary process even though they are less successful than their American equivalents.

In the first place, a large number of MPs are sponsored by pressure groups. During the last three decades, between 40 and 50 per cent of Labour MPs have been sponsored by trade unions, which pay most of their electoral expenses and may also pay the MPs a retainer. In 1966, when Labour had a comfortable majority, 150 out of 365 Labour MPs were sponsored by unions. In 1979, when Labour lost, the proportion of union MPs was higher, with a total of 133 out of 269. This arrangement serves the function of keeping manual workers in Parliament, for the great majority of the other Labour MPs come from middle-class backgrounds. In this sense it can be claimed that sponsorship makes the House of Commons more representative of the electorate; it certainly ensures that union interests are adequately expressed.

The other parties do not have sponsorship arrangements in the same formal way, and do not permit outside bodies to pay the election expenses of their candidates. However, many individual MPs in all parties act as consultants or advisers to pressure groups and some get a retainer or honorarium for doing so. Business groups and farmers have Conservative MPs active on their behalf. The National Union of Teachers always has at least one Conservative MP acting for it as well as two or more Labour MPs.

It is not thought in any way wrong (as it would be in Congress) for MPs to accept financial help in these ways. Nor is it clear that MPs getting financial assistance from pressure groups are more vigorous in furthering the interests or causes of the groups than are other MPs who act without payment for groups with which they sympathize. As has been remarked: 'Increasingly parliamentary spokesmanship is thought of as a role all private Members may undertake more or less regularly on behalf of the interests and causes to which they are attached. No MP or peer is so characterless as to fail to have a few such attachments' (Potter, 1961, p. 276).

The ways in which MPs can help a group are many and varied. They may ask questions in Parliament on the group's behalf. They may take up particular matters with the minister concerned. They may speak on behalf of the group at party meetings, particularly at meetings of specialized groups of back-benchers.

They may sign motions calling upon the government to modify its policies in this way or that; for instance, on one occasion lobbyists from the theatrical world persuaded over half the Members of Parliament to sign a motion asking the government to abolish entertainment tax on the theatre. Governments are naturally concerned to keep in favour with back-bench MPs when this is possible, and these activities are not without influence on policy.

In the legislative field, MPs may introduce Private Members' Bills that have been drafted by, or in consultation with, particular pressure groups. The animal welfare groups are particularly successful in promoting legislation, partly because there are no countervailing groups arguing the opposite case. The Royal Society for the Prevention of Cruelty to Animals has a Parliamentary Department that advises friendly MPs and provides them with draft legislation. Smaller groups may employ one of the several firms of parliamentary agents to draft legislative proposals.

Moral issues provide good opportunities for MPs acting on behalf of pressure groups, because governments are reluctant to insist on party discipline in such matters. The death penalty was abolished by a Private Member's Bill promoted by the National Campaign for the Abolition of Capital Punishment. The law relating to abortion was liberalized as a result of the activities of the Abortion Law Reform Association. The Society of Authors (which is neither powerful nor wealthy) was instrumental in securing the passage of the Obscene Publications Act which makes literary merit a defence against censorship and gives literary critics the status of expert witnesses if legal cases arise. These and other reforms show that in some areas of legislation Parliament is very amenable to influence by a well-organized and determined group of reformers.

The Committee Stage of legislation provides another opportunity for pressure groups to exert influence. Sympathetic MPs get a daily briefing from groups during this stage, and it is easier to get a minor amendment accepted here, or to persuade the government to modify a clause, than it is to secure amendments on the floor of the House.

Public Campaigns

It has often been said that public campaigns by a pressure group are a sign of weakness, indicating that the group has failed to secure acceptance by the appropriate government department as an affected interest (or a body with useful information), and cannot achieve its aims by parliamentary action. There is clearly some truth in this generalization, which was exemplified by the activities of the Campaign for Nuclear Disarmament (CND) in the late 1950s and early 1960s. The CND was not regarded by the government as representing an affected interest and it had no specialized information not possessed by the Ministry of Defence. It therefore had no direct access to the administration and it could not hope to win parliamentary votes since party discipline on this subject was strict. A public campaign was the only alternative, and the CND was able to get the support of tens of thousands in massive demonstrations and marches. However, there is no evidence that this campaign advanced the cause of nuclear disarmament. It certainly increased public awareness of the issue, but polls suggested that the number of converts made by the CND was smaller than the number of previously apathetic citizens who were activated into opposition to the aims of the movement.

Nevertheless, it would be wrong to conclude that public campaigns are usually a waste of time. On the one hand, they may have an educative effect on public opinion that pays dividends in the long run. On the other, they can be very successful, when waged by 'fire-brigade' groups, in preventing developments that are promoted by governmental authorities but are unpopular with citizens.

Alderman has given several examples of the educative effect, notably the success of the Homosexual Law Reform Society in liberalizing public attitudes between 1958 and 1967 and the success of the Abortion Law Reform Association in accomplishing the same task between 1963 and 1967 (Alderman, 1984, pp. 104–6). Both these campaigns led to legislative reform in the latter year. Other examples include the campaign against bad housing and the campaign to secure government aid to disabled people (ibid., pp. 107–8). It can also be said that the cause of nuclear disarmament (promoted by variously named organizations) eventually achieved some success, as it was adopted in 1979 as the official policy of the Labour Party.

There are numerous examples of local campaigns to stop proposed construction projects or divert them to other locations. The most dramatic was the intense campaign waged by local citizens to overturn the government's decision in 1964 to build a third London airport at Stansted, some thirty miles to the north-east of the city. The noise and the destruction of historic buildings were the reasons for the objection, which was supported by over a hundred organizations and rapidly formed community groups. After over three years of controversy, the government agreed to appoint a commission to inquire into the costs and benefits of various alternative sites. The popular favourite was Foulness, a marshy island near the mouth of the Thames where aircraft noise would disturb relatively few people. After the most extensive cost-benefit analysis ever undertaken anywhere, the commission rejected this alternative and proposed another inland site at Cublington, to the north-west of London. There followed another dramatic campaign by local residents, which eventually led the government to capitulate and agree (in 1971) to build the airport at Foulness. Ironically, it was decided in 1974 that a new airport was not really needed in view of the move to larger (and therefore fewer) aircraft, so that popular resistance not only spared the residents of Stansted and Cublington from disturbance but also spared the taxpayer from unnecessary expense. In the 1980s the issue was re-opened, the upshot being that the small airport at Stansted is being enlarged gradually.

Other campaigns have been waged to change the planned location of new highways and power stations. If sufficient local residents object to such a plan, the government is obliged to conduct a public inquiry at which evidence can be heard. At one stage in the 1970s it was found that if objectors made so much noise at the inquiry that the witnesses could not be heard, the plan had to be deferred. Several projects were defeated, or had to be modified, as a result of this kind of tactic. The government now goes to great trouble to ensure that all critics are seen to be given a fair hearing; thus, a 1984 inquiry into a proposed nuclear power station on the east coast lasted just over twelve months.

Public campaigns of this local kind illustrate how much political influence can be exerted by groups of citizens, having very little money and no professional staff, if they feel strongly about an issue. This sort of popular influence on government has tended to increase over the past two decades, both because environmental concerns have increased and because campaigners have learned by example. It follows that public campaigns are almost as important as parliamentary campaigns as a means of securing changes in policy.

Pressure Groups and Democracy

It is possible to doubt whether the influence of pressure groups in the process of government is entirely compatible with the traditional democratic view that policy ought to reflect the wishes of the electorate, as expressed through their representatives in Parliament. It can be argued that sectional interests or groups of enthusiasts have shown themselves able to frustrate or distort the will of the majority, either through the use of superior resources or because they acquire a privileged position in the system. There is a general argument about resources, and there are also two arguments about the roles played by spokesmen for industry and the trade unions in the formulation of economic policy.

The concern that is occasionally voiced about the resources of pressure groups seems to have little foundation in Britain. There is as much freedom to organize pressure groups as there is to contest elections or form political parties. Wealth is not necessary to success and can never guarantee it. Money is always useful, but as a resource for a pressure group it appears to be less valuable than specialized information, enthusiasm, good contacts, the ability to get favourable publicity and the power to hinder the administrative process by obstruction of one kind or another. There is no money in penal reform, but the Howard League has exercised a good deal of influence over the years. The weekend walkers who formed the Friends of the Lake District have fought successful battles against the Central Electricity Generating Board. The spokesmen for Welsh dinghy sailors took on the Standard Oil Company, with the result that the company modified its plans to build a harbour and oil refinery at Milford Haven so as to preserve sailing facilities in the estuary. The campaigns on moral issues mentioned above have succeeded by virtue of the intellectual arguments and convictions of their leaders.

One concern about economic policy has taken the form of worry lest Britain develop what is commonly known as a 'corporatist' system. By this is meant a system in which major decisions about economic strategy are made by agreement between representatives of government, industrial management and the trade unions. The fear of some liberal commentators has been that Parliament might be bypassed by such an arrangement. The institution that provoked this debate was the National Economic Development Council, created in 1962 to conduct tripartite discussions of the kind mentioned but now abolished by the Thatcher government.

In practice, this council was ineffectual. Management and union spokesmen rarely agreed on important issues. Even if they did agree, there was always the chance that they would be disowned or ignored by the organizations whom they purport to represent. The Confederation of British Industry and the Trades Union Congress are loosely organized associations, with virtually no power to commit their members to a particular policy or ensure compliance with it. Government representatives were not able to impose policies on the council. For nearly two decades, those concerned with industrial affairs showed themselves incapable of a policy of 'concertation', to use the term applied to the rather successful arrangements of this kind in West Germany. The British economy might well be in better shape if they had had this ability. However, at least there is no need to worry on liberal grounds about a loss of parliamentary sovereignty.

Though there is little need for concern about the possibility that wealth might be able to buy political influence, it certainly does not follow that group pressures are perfectly balanced. The postwar period in Britain has been marked by a general tendency for producers' groups to be more influential than consumers' groups. Beer has argued persuasively that the national interest has been harmed by the 'scramble for subsidies' engaged in by industrial groups and the 'scramble for pay' engaged in by trade unions (Beer, 1982, pp. 48–76). The Thatcher government has tried hard to check this scramble, but it is not certain that its successes will be permanent. Many of these groups, along with several professional associations, have also shown hostility to radical innovations and have thus strengthened the forces of inertia in British society. But in doing this they have, for better or worse, performed a function that most British people seem to approve of.

Further Reading

The best introduction to this topic is Alderman (1984), *Pressure Groups and Government in Great Britain*; for more extended treatments students should consult Potter (1961), *Organized Groups in British National Politics*, or (more discursive but also more up to date) Wootton (1978), *Pressure Groups in Contemporary Britain*; and there are numerous case studies, such as Kogan, (1975) *Educational Policy-Making*, Buchanan (1981), *No Way to the Airport*, and Marsh and Chambers (1981), *Abortion Politics*.

◇ 8 ◇

Politicians and Leaders

The process of government is a complex activity in which the participants fill a variety of roles, including those of elector, party worker, group spokesman, legislator, administrator and minister of the Crown. All are engaged in political activity, but in a democratic system the term 'politician' is normally reserved for those who compete for public office: councillors and aldermen in local government and MPs and ministers in national government. This book is concerned mainly with national government, and the purpose of this chapter is to examine the recruitment and characteristics of Members of Parliament, their role in parliamentary politics, and the way in which some of them emerge as ministers and national leaders.

The Recruitment of Politicians

The first point to be made on this topic is a negative one. Britain does not have a locality rule of the kind that exists in the United States, and prospective Members of Parliament do not follow such a standardized route to political success as prospective Congressmen. In the United States there is a firm convention (to some extent backed by law) that candidates for political office should be residents – and usually long-standing residents – of the area in which they are nominated. A person who tries to ignore this convention is known as a 'carpet-bagger', and his chances of electoral success are much less than they would be if he were a local person. Partly because of this, the aspiring politician normally has to work his way up a well-established ladder in which he is first active in local political clubs, then runs as a candidate for local or state office, and after some success in these endeavours is able to secure his party's nomination for a congressional election. It follows that the great majority of members of the US Congress serve an apprenticeship in local or state politics before going to Washington. In most European democracies there is also a strong tendency for representatives to have roots in their constituencies; in some (such as France and Belgium) it is common for people to retain a municipal office even while serving in the national legislature.

In Britain candidates for parliamentary elections are selected by local party branches, who in this matter are virtually (though not completely) autonomous.

But, except in a few areas, local parties do not have any particular preference for local people. Candidates may indeed have served in municipal or county governments, but this service is as likely to have been in another locality as in the area where they secure a parliamentary nomination. Local selection committees want the best candidate they can get, and by and large they do not much mind where this candidate comes from. Most candidates have weak points as well as strong ones, and a local person labours under the disadvantage that his weaknesses may be known to the selection committee. Moreover, if there are two local contenders it may be difficult for the committee to choose between them and less divisive to pass over both in favour of an outsider (see Ranney, 1965, p. 110). Nor as a general rule does place of origin have any perceptible effect on the support given to candidates by voters; they vote for the party, not for the person, and are rarely interested in the personal characteristics of the candidate nominated by the party they support. Very few candidates make any claims to local residence or activities in their election addresses.

The only important qualification that has to be made to these generalizations is that most candidates in Scotland are Scots, in Wales Welsh and in Northern Ireland Irish. But candidates are not tied to any particular area within these countries, and ethnic identity is not an essential characteristic. Thus, James Callaghan is an Englishman (albeit with an Irish name) who represented a Welsh constituency for many years, while Roy Jenkins is a Welshman who lives near London and represented a constituency in Glasgow.

How are people recruited to a career in national politics? What kind of previous experience is common among candidates? One kind of experience that is fairly common is service in municipal or county government. In recent elections something like a third of the candidates had at some time in their careers been elected to a local council. It should not be thought that all these candidates had fixed their eyes on a parliamentary career and had become active in local government as a step towards this goal. This happens in some cases, but for most people in this category recruitment to national politics is a discontinuous three-stage process. First they become active in a local party branch; then they volunteer or are persuaded to stand for the local council; and later they decide to seek a parliamentary nomination. Entering national politics by this route has always been common among Labour MPs but has only recently become common among Conservatives. In postwar Parliaments between 39 and 47 per cent of Labour MPs have had local government experience, with an average per Parliament of 45 per cent. Among Conservatives only 14 per cent had had local government experiences in the Parliament of 1945–50, but the proportion rose steadily to 38 per cent in the Parliament of 1974–9 (Burch and Moran, 1985).

Another established ladder to a career in national politics is through the trade unions, which, as noted in Chapter 7, sponsor and finance many Labour candidates. These candidates, like those from local government, are usually recruited by a three-stage process. First, they are active in union affairs in their place of work; then they often become branch officers or full-time union organizers; later they are chosen by the union as prospective parliamentary candidates. One or two unions choose people when they are young and consciously attempt to prepare them for a political career, either by asking them to study the social sciences or by getting them nominated to fight elections in hopeless seats, or by a combination of these methods. But most sponsored candidates are in their middle years when they first stand, and the union concerned normally finds them a safe seat. A union like the National Union of Mineworkers is able to do this because it controls the constituency branches of the Labour Party in many mining areas. Other unions get safe seats for their nominees by offering substantial contributions to local party funds and campaign expenses. Since 1950 between 40 and 50 per cent of the Labour Members in each Parliament have been sponsored in this way. Many of them have served in local government, so there is a considerable overlap between this group and the group described above.

The only other source of parliamentary candidates that can be readily identified is the small group of political families whose sons are brought up to think in terms of a political career. The Churchills and the Cecils have played leading roles in British politics for several generations. Other families that have contributed politicians over at least two generations in this century include the Chamberlains, the Hoggs and the Woods (the family name of Lord Halifax) on the Conservative side, the Bonham Carters and the Lloyd George family among the Liberals, the Greenwoods and the Wedgwood Benns on the Labour side. The actual number of MPs recruited from this source is very small, but they are important because they have so often achieved positions of leadership.

Taken together, local government, the trade unions and the political families produce between 50 and 60 per cent of British MPs. The remainder cannot easily by 'typed'. They first make their appearance on the political scene when they apply for inclusion in the parliamentary panel of one of the three main parties, or when they apply directly for selection in a constituency. It may be appropriate to describe them as 'self-starters', since they embark on a political career without the pressures that impel members of the other three groups towards this objective.

The self-starters are on average younger than the local government candidates and the trade unionists when they first enter national politics, though older than the 'political heirs'. As a group they are better educated than the local government candidates and the trade unionists, and almost as well educated as the political heirs. It is quite common for them to have made their start in politics by achieving prominence in a political or debating club while at university. Edward Heath was President of the Oxford Union while Margaret Thatcher was President of the Oxford University Conservative Association. They are more likely than recruits from any of the other three sources to give up after an unsuccessful election campaign, or to withdraw from Parliament after only a few years. But if they stay on they are sometimes very successful; most of the country's top political leaders are drawn from the self-starters, not from the other three groups.

The Selection of Candidates

In all three parties the main responsibility for selecting candidates rests with the local party branches. When a branch decides to adopt a prospective candidate a selection committee is appointed and applications are invited. Usually at least one person will have had his eye on the constituency and will have tried to cultivate good relations with the branch chairman. Sometimes members of the selection committee invite people to apply. If the seat is safe for the party, a hundred or more applications are likely to be received, many of them from people who have no connections with the constituency and may never have been near it. If the seat is hopeless, on the other hand, the committee may have to search around for suitable applicants.

After the last date for applications the committee prepares a short list, usually of between two and six people. These applicants are then interviewed, the common procedure being for each to be asked to address the committee for twenty minutes or so, after which he is questioned for a rather longer period. At the end of the interviews the members of the committee are usually able to agree on a candidate.

The head offices of the parties are involved in this process in two ways. First, each has a panel of approved applicants and on request head office will suggest names from this panel to local parties. Sometimes head office has favoured applicants for whom it wishes to find safe seats, and the names of these applicants may be suggested time and time again. But the choice rests with the local parties and they cannot be forced to accept someone they do not like. This has been made abundantly clear when senior party members have failed to get themselves accepted for new constituencies after their old ones have been abolished by boundary changes. A slightly different example occurred in 1959, when the General Secretary of the Labour Party, having decided to enter Parliament, was unable to find a party branch willing to nominate him.

The head offices are also involved in that in each party, apart from the Liberal Party, they reserve the right to veto the selection of candidates whom they consider undesirable. This right is very rarely used but when it is the local party has little choice but to accept the decision and choose another candidate. If the local party refuses to toe the line, the normal practice is for head office to sponsor its own candidate, who is advertised as the official party candidate. Since British voters are generally loyal to the national party rather than to the local branch, the normal (though not invariable) consequence of this conflict is that the head office candidate gets the majority of the votes cast by party supporters.

When a local party has to choose a candidate, what considerations are apt to influence the selection committee? The most obvious and openly acknowledged considerations are purely personal: whether the applicant writes a good letter of application, his career outside politics, the impression he makes when interviewed, whether he has any experience of electioneering and, if so, whether he did well in his previous campaigns. In the Labour Party union membership is regarded as almost essential. In the Conservative Party some preference is given to candidates who have served as officers in the regular armed forces; between 1945 and 1975, 12 per cent of all Conservative MPs had a service background, mostly as army officers (Mellors, 1978, p. 99). Conservative selection committees attach considerable importance to success in a career outside politics, and they also like candidates to have suitable wives, who are vetted at the time of their husbands' interviews.

All the parties now stress the desirability of recruiting women candidates, but none of them has been very successful in doing this. Relatively few women put themselves forward for nomination. Of those who do put themselves forward, few get accepted for winnable seats. The development of the women's liberation movement of the 1970s made no immediate difference to this, the number of women elected in 1983 (twenty-three) being no greater than the number elected in 1945 (twenty-four). However, in the 1987 election there was a sudden breakthrough, with forty-one women being elected. These included 17 Conservatives, 21 Labour MPs, 1 Liberal, 1 Social Democrat and 1 Scottish Nationalist.

Attitudes to political issues and doctrines have not generally been stressed by the local selection committees, but they have become increasingly important in recent years in the case of the Labour Party. As noted in Chapter 5, some local party branches have been captured by militant left-wingers, who tried to replace moderate MPs by militant candidates in the run-up to the 1983 election. Their successes were not as numerous as many moderates feared would be the case, but there were some bitter battles. In the event, six moderate MPs were 'de-selected' and replaced by left-wingers, while another six left-wingers replaced moderate MPs whose constituencies were carved up by the English Boundary Commission. All these twelve victories for the extreme left were in large cities, namely London, Birmingham, Liverpool, Sheffield, Leeds and Bradford (see Butler and Kavanagh, 1984, pp. 220–5).

The Characteristics of MPs

In terms of the occupations from which they are drawn, most MPs are from the professional and business classes. This has been so for much of the twentieth century, and the proportion has increased steadily as the proportions of landowners on the one hand and manual workers on the other have decreased. In the postwar period, the number of former manual workers in the House of Commons has gone down from 108 in the Parliament of 1945–50 to 40 in the

Table 8.1 *Occupational Background of MPs*

Type of Occupation	Conservative	Labour	Others	Total
Lawyer	61	37	9	107
Lecturer, teacher, or journalist	26	102	8	136
Other profession	34	30	6	70
Business	131	25	7	163
Farmer or landowner	28	1	5	34
White-collar worker	–	22	–	22
Trade union official	–	32	1	33
Manual worker	1	37	1	39
Other	16	15	–	31
Total	297	301	37	635

Source: Mellors, 1978, pp. 64–5.

Table 8.2 *Educational Background of MPs*

Education	Elected in 1945		Elected in 1983	
	Conservative %	Labour %	Conservative %	Labour %
Public schools	83	19	64	13
Oxford or Cambridge	53	15	46	14
Other universities	12	19	26	40
All universities	65	34	72	54

Source: Burch and Moran, 1985, pp. 13–14.

Parliament of 1974–9. The category that has seen an increase over this period comprises what are often called 'the talking and writing professions', namely lecturers, schoolteachers and journalists. The number of MPs drawn from these professions rose from 104 in the Parliament of 1945–50 to 151 in that of 1974–9 (Mellors, 1978, pp. 62–6).

Table 8.1 gives a detailed breakdown of the occupational background of the MPs elected in February 1974, this election being chosen because it was the last in which the representation of the two main parties was approximately equal. The difference between the main parties emerges clearly.

Some figures regarding the educational background of MPs are given in Table 8.2. For simplicity, only the two main parties are included. These figures, like those for occupational background, show a marked contrast between the parties. The contrast is not quite so stark as it was forty years ago, but the degree of convergence (which has often been remarked upon) is really quite modest. In the Parliament of 1983 two-thirds of Conservative MPs were educated at public schools compared with one-eighth of Labour MPs. In considering these figures it should be born in mind that the public schools are attended by no more than 2 per cent of the population. Among Conservative university graduates, almost two-thirds had studied at Oxford or Cambridge, while only a quarter of Labour graduates had done so.

The contrast in educational background is even more marked among Cabinet ministers. Only three of the twenty-one members of the Labour Cabinet appointed in 1974 had attended public schools, compared with eighteen of the twenty-one members of the preceding Conservative Cabinet and eighteen of the twenty members of Thatcher's first Cabinet. Moreover, the three Labour ministers had all attended public schools in inner London, where pupils are more affected by the pressures of modern life than in the typical British public school located in the countryside. The 1979 Conservative Cabinet contained two grammar-school products (one of them being the Prime Minister), two from public schools in inner London and sixteen from public schools in rural areas.

The Work of MPs

The basic duties of an MP are easily enumerated. First, he is expected to look after the interests of his constituents, taking up their grievances with the relevant minister when he thinks this appropriate. The best approach is by a personal letter to the minister, but if this does not get results the MP can raise the matter in Parliament. If this still fails, and the MP believes that officials in the ministry have been guilty of maladministration, the matter can be referred by the MP to the Parliamentary Commissioner for Administration, who can conduct a detailed inquiry. Work of this kind takes up a good deal of time, and the majority of Members not only correspond with constituents but also make themselves available for consultation in the constituency on a regular basis.

The second main task of MPs is to conduct debates on public policy and to hold the government of the day accountable for its decisions and behaviour. This will be discussed in Chapter 12. The third main task, to be discussed in Chapter 13, is to consider legislative proposals brought before Parliament by ministers or, with less chance of success, by back-bench Members.

According to the British understanding of parliamentary democracy, MPs should act as trustees for the national interest when they carry out the second and third types of duty, not as delegates from the area in which they were elected. Since the last third of the nineteenth century, it has become normal for Members to assume that the nature of the national interest is best interpreted by their party. They naturally have some say in the determination of party policy; but as the political process has become essentially one of party government, individual MPs are expected to conform to the party line in parliamentary votes and they rarely depart from it unless they have strong beliefs or commitments regarding the issue in question.

Party management in the House of Commons is the responsibility of a small group of Members known as Whips. The Chief Whip in each party draws the attention of his colleagues to forthcoming debates by circulating notes, also (rather confusingly) known as whips, which indicate the importance of the occasion by variations in the degree of underlining. A debate underlined once is one in which no division is expected; one underlined twice is one in which there will be a division, and which MPs are expected to attend unless they have arranged to 'pair' with a Member of the other main party; a three-line whip means that the division is deemed to be of vital importance and all Members are required to attend unless the Whips have arranged a pair for them, which they will do only in cases of serious illness or absence overseas on official business.

In addition, the Whips have other important functions. They make themselves responsible for lining up speakers so as to keep each debate running smoothly, and they act as a channel of communication between back-benchers and party leaders. The Chief Whip of the governing party normally attends Cabinet meetings so that he can inform the Cabinet of the state of feeling of back-bench Members.

The arrangements for party management are therefore rather elaborate. On most occasions they operate effectively and the first seven decades of the twentieth century were marked by a very high degree of party discipline in the House of Commons. Since 1970, however, there have been numerous issues on which back-bench MPs have broken with the official party line. One reason for this development is the emergence of important issues that cut across the left-right division of view that separates the two main parties.

The British application to join the European Economic Community was one such issue, on which back-benchers on both sides of the House were willing to defy their Whips because they could not accept their party's interpretation of the national interest. When the Parliamentary Labour Party issued a three-line whip instructing Labour MPs to oppose British entry into the Community, sixty-nine Labour MPs voted in favour of entry and another twenty abstained. Another constitutional issue that produced dissidents on both sides was the proposal to create national assemblies for Scotland and Wales; the first government Bill on this subject had to be withdrawn for lack of support and subsequent Bills were amended in important ways by amendments passed in opposition to government wishes.

A second reason for the increase in dissent is the growth of ideological discord within the two main parties. And on top of these specific causal factors, there has been a general change of attitude among younger MPs, who are just not so willing to toe the party line as their predecessors were. Moreover, defying the Whips tends to be a progressive process. A back-bencher who has done so once finds it easier to do so a second time. Other back-benchers take note of the trend and assert their own independence. In the Parliament of 1974–9, 89 per cent of Conservative MPs and 81 per cent of Labour MPs voted against the Whips' instructions at least once, while 33 per cent of Labour MPs did so twenty times or more (Rose, 1983, p. 289). In the 1987–8 session, 121 Conservative MPs defied the Conservative whip on legislative issues. As about 100 of the 373

Conservative MPs had government posts of one kind or another, this means that about 44 per cent of government back-benchers voted to amend or reject a government Bill at least once, while 31 of them, or 11 per cent, did so five times or more. It is still the case that a government with a majority in the House of Commons can be sure of avoiding defeat on a vote of confidence, and can expect to get most of its legislation passed without critical amendment. But defeats on legislative matters have become more common than they were, and party managers now have to accept that a proportion of government Bills will be revised against the wishes of the government, with outright rejection also being a possibility.

The Way to the Top

It is impossible to give an exact figure for the proportion of MPs who hope to acquire ministerial office, but it seems reasonable to assume that more than half harbour this ambition. Most of these are disappointed. Of over two thousand MPs who served in Parliament between 1918 and 1955, 74 per cent failed to get any kind of ministerial appointment. A further 10 per cent achieved only the humble and unpaid office of Parliamentary Private Secretary (PPS), 9 per cent became junior ministers and only 7 per cent became full ministers (Buck, 1963, p. 47). Members may reach Parliament without having served in any other political post, but they then face a hard struggle to secure further advancement. With very few exceptions, the way to the top in British politics is through a successful performance in Parliament, first as a back-bencher attracting favourable comment by speeches and questions, then as a PPS or junior minister and finally, for the few, as a minister.

Since recommendations for ministerial posts are made to the Prime Minister by the Chief Whip, party loyalty is generally an advantage in gaining such a recommendation. Knowledge of this is one of the factors that keeps party discipline as effective as it is. However, it should not be thought that disloyalty always acts as a disqualification. Prime Ministers are looking for talent when they make appointments; evidence of independence raises questions but is not necessarily a bar. Of the nine postwar Prime Ministers, four (Churchill, Eden, Macmillan and Wilson) had been rebels at some stage in their careers. And with the recent growth of independence, it would be unrealistic for Whips or party leaders to insist upon complete loyalty as a condition of promotion. Only 93 of the 596 Labour and Conservative MPs in the Parliament of 1974-9 failed to vote against the instructions of the Whips at least once (Rose, 1983, p. 289).

A study has been made of the careers of the 282 ministers first appointed to Cabinet posts in the ninety years following 1868, the best date to mark the beginning of the modern system of disciplined parties (Wilson, 1959). This shows that 214 were drawn from the House of Commons, 24 were former MPs who had gone to the Lords, 15 had acquired their parliamentary experience entirely in the Lords and the other 29 were unorthodox appointments in the sense that they could not be described as career politicians. Most of the unorthodox appointments were made as a direct result of one or other of the two world wars. The 238 who had come up in the normal way through the House of Commons had on average spent fourteen years in that House before reaching the Cabinet. A check on the careers of members of Thatcher's Cabinet after the 1983 election shows that – apart from two peers – they had on average spent thirteen years in the House of Commons before achieving Cabinet office. It follows that Cabinet ministers are experienced parliamentarians holding positions in the government that are certain to be temporary, and they are likely to be struggling again in the Commons when their term of office comes to an end. It is important to remember this when considering the view that the Cabinet has 'usurped' Parliament's position as the centre of political power.

A small minority of ministers reach one of the top posts, to become Foreign Secretary, Chancellor of the Exchequer, or Prime Minister. Since the last war thirty-five politicians have filled these posts. An examination of their careers reveals only one way (apart from their success) in which they have differed from MPs as a whole. This is that more of them were 'self-starters', as defined above: 80 per cent compared with between 40 and 50 per cent of all MPs. Of the others, Churchill came from a political family, Bevin and Brown were trade unionists, and Attlee, Morrison, Amory and Pym reached Parliament after serving in local government.

It is difficult to make any generalizations about what distinguishes those among the top leaders who reach the office of Prime Minister, as luck plays such a large part in this. Of the nine postwar Prime Ministers, Churchill would never have made it had it not been for the war, Douglas-Home's appointment was a surprise to all commentators, and Wilson owed his leadership to Gaitskell's unexpected and premature death. Margaret Thatcher got to the top by seizing a sudden opportunity. Many Conservative MPs were discontented with Heath's leadership after he had called a snap election for political advantage and then failed to win. Heath put himself up for re-election to quell criticism; most of his critics were unwilling to take the chance of spoiling their careers by competing against him unsuccessfully; Thatcher accepted the risk and triumphed.

It may also be observed that party leaders often have to face attacks from critics within their own party. An American President is secure in office for four years and can normally be sure of re-nomination if he wants a second term. A British Prime Minister is apt to be less secure. Eden would have faced an attack on his leadership had bad health not forced him to resign, after only twenty months in office. Macmillan faced mounting criticism during his last year as Prime Minister. Douglas-Home would have had to cope with pressures to resign had he not stepped down after only twenty-one months as party leader. Heath was effectively pushed out of the leadership. Thatcher has had to cope not only with constant criticism from Heath but also with attacks on her policies by an organized group of more than thirty Conservative MPs, formed in 1985 by her former Cabinet colleague, Francis Pym. These examples are all from the Conservative side of the House because Labour critics are apt to focus on ideological issues rather than on the personal position of their leader, but Wilson is an example of a Labour leader who had to spend much of his energy holding the party together. The lesson is that political leadership is a challenging and difficult activity, which requires both dedication and courage from those who practise it.

Further Reading

For a general account of the recruitment and selection of parliamentary candidates see Ranney (1965), *Pathways to Parliament*; for a short but lively picture of how one candidate was selected see Lees and Kimber (1972), *Political Parties in Modern Britain*; for statistical data on MPs see Mellors (1978), *The British MP*; for an account of the activities of back-bench MPs see Richards (1972), *The Backbenchers*.

◇ 9 ◇

Government and Opposition

As we have seen, the leaders of the two main parties are now chosen by their parliamentary colleagues. Each can claim, in Disraeli's celebrated phrase, that he has 'reached the top of the greasy pole'. But which of them becomes Prime Minister depends on the electorate, and in a closely fought election it is not until nearly all the returns are in that one leader knows he will spend the duration of the next Parliament in 10 Downing Street and the other knows that his role is to be Leader of the Opposition. For one, the following days will be crowded with activity as he picks the members of his government; the other will be faced with the less rewarding task of conducting a post-mortem on his party's defeat.

The Choice of Ministers

Commentators have vacillated in their accounts of the relations between the Prime Minister and his senior colleagues. It used to be fashionable to describe him as 'first among equals', a description that is clearly inaccurate in view of the fact that he, and he alone, has the power to appoint them to and dismiss them from ministerial office. Recently the pendulum has swung to the other extreme and it has become fashionable to liken the powers of the Prime Minister to those of the United States President. That this is also misleading can be demonstrated by citing one simple example. When John F. Kennedy was elected to the presidency in 1960 he did not give one of the three top posts in his Cabinet to leading members of his party: the Republican Secretary of the Treasury was kept on in that office; the chief executive of the Ford Motor Company (also a Republican) was appointed Secretary of Defense; and the post of Secretary of State went to a man active in the management of a charitable foundation who had not previously held political office. No British Prime Minister has anything like this degree of freedom; in peacetime his choice is almost entirely limited to leading members of his party whose parliamentary careers have put them in the running for ministerial appointments.

Some members of the party have such status that their inclusion is almost automatic. Thus, Harold Macmillan had to give senior posts to R. A. Butler and Selwyn Lloyd; Harold Wilson had to appoint George Brown and James Callaghan; Margaret Thatcher had to appoint William Whitelaw, Geoffrey

Howe, James Prior and Peter Walker. On the other hand, even the most senior people cannot choose which posts they will have, for getting the right balance of people and posts in the Cabinet is a tricky matter that must be left to the Prime Minister. For instance, in 1945 Hugh Dalton wanted to be Foreign Secretary and was told that there was a good prospect of this; at noon on the crucial day Attlee phoned him and said he would know for certain by tea time; but at 4 p.m. Dalton was told that he was to be Chancellor of the Exchequer instead. The apparent reason for this change of plan is also interesting. It had been thought that Ernest Bevin would be Chancellor and Herbert Morrison would be put in general charge of home affairs, but relations between the two men were so bad that at the last moment the Prime Minister decided to reduce their points of contact by asking Bevin to go to the Foreign Office. Further examples of the inability of politicians to choose their ministry are the appointment of an apparently reluctant Herbert Morrison to the Foreign Office in 1950 (after Bevin died) and, conversely, the fact that Butler could have had any ministry except the Foreign Office (the one he wanted) in 1957.

The Prime Minister has to bear various considerations in mind when making appointments. He (or she) must get a team who will work together in the senior posts. He must consider the balance of power in the party and appoint people who represent the various viewpoints within it. He must get a balance of ages in his administration and encourage young colleagues of ability. He may have to consider sectional interests; every Cabinet must now contain at least one Scottish and, if possible, one Welsh member, while a Labour Prime Minister will also have to appoint an appropriate number of trade unionists. He has a large number of posts to distribute and he can find room to take account of all these factors, but much energy and thought must be spent in getting the right combination for effective government.

One of the problems that most Prime Ministers have to face is the existence of senior colleagues whose views on policy differ from their own. Experience shows that it is much wiser for a Prime Minister to include such critics in the government than to leave them out, for if they are included they will be forced to support government policy in public, no matter how many private reservations they may have. In extreme cases their reservations may be obvious, as exemplified by the *Guardian*'s comment on Tony Benn's position between 1974 and 1979; 'For much of the last Parliament, Mr Tony Benn occupied a position of almost total isolation within the Cabinet, acquiescing in its collective decision while frantically signalling to the party outside that it hurt him grievously to do so' (*Manchester Guardian Weekly*, 20 May 1979). But, even so, it was safer for Wilson and Callaghan to have the party's leading radical partially muzzled than to have him leading an open revolt against their policies. Heath's decision to exclude Enoch Powell from his government confirms this general rule, for although it may have been almost inevitable in the circumstances it is nevertheless the case that Powell's subsequent attacks on the government weakened it and may have contributed to its defeat in 1974.

Normally ministers are drawn from the two Houses of Parliament, the great majority being MPs who have climbed the political ladder rung by rung in the way described in the previous chapter. As noted there, outsiders are occasionally brought in to strengthen the team, and two at least of these unorthodox appointees proved to be superb politicans who have left their mark on British history and British government. One was Ernest Bevin, who as General Secretary of the Transport and General Workers' Union was invited to become Minister of Labour and National Service in 1940, largely because it was thought desirable to have a leading trade unionist to deal with the delicate problems posed by conscription and direction of labour. He subsequently became a Foreign Secretary of great distinction. The other was Lord Woolton, who as a chairman of a chain of department stores was asked to become Minister of Food during the war, and who played a leading role in the reform and revitalization of the Conservative Party after its defeat in 1945.

Unorthodox appointments of this kind are exceptions to the general rule that Prime Ministers must select their ministers from the two Houses of Parliament. In peacetime it remains true that nine out of ten senior ministers (as well as all junior ministers) are parliamentarians before they are appointed. It should be added that when a non-parliamentarian is appointed he must (by convention) be either given a peerage or found a seat in the Commons within a matter of weeks, but there is rarely any problem about this as it is not difficult to persuade a back-bencher of long service to retire to the Lords so as to enable the new minister to compete for his seat in the ensuing by-election.

The Ministerial Hierarchy

At the beginning of this century there were no more than fifteen departments of state, each one of them headed by a minister who was automatically a member of the Cabinet. The great expansion of governmental activities since that time has changed the picture. There are more departments and since 1964 at least nine of them have had a second full minister (usually known as a minister of state) while one or two have had three, four or even five ministers. As there are also the Law Officers and the holders of non-departmental appointments like the Lord Privy Seal, the result is that in recent years there have been at least forty ministerial appointments. Not all of their holders can be in the Cabinet, since by general agreement a Cabinet of more than about twenty members would be too large for effective discussion. It follows that the ministerial hierarchy is more complex than it used to be. There are now: (1) Cabinet ministers; (2) ministers holding offices that might but do not at the moment entitle them to a place in the Cabinet; (3) other full ministers (e.g. ministers of state); and (4) junior ministers (i.e. under secretaries and parliamentary secretaries).

In times of peace the Cabinet normally has about twenty members; since 1946 the minimum has been sixteen and the maximum twenty-three. By convention, the holders of the following offices are always members of the Cabinet:

Lord Chancellor
Lord President of the Council
Lord Privy Seal
Home Secretary
Foreign Secretary
Chancellor of the Exchequer
Secretary of State for Defence
Secretary of State for Trade and Industry
Secretary of State for Employment
Secretary of State for Social Services
Secretary of State for the Environment
Secretary of State for Scotland
Secretary of State for Wales
Secretary of State for Northern Ireland

The other departments represented in the Cabinet vary from year to year, depending partly on the personal status of the ministers concerned and partly on which issues are thought likely to cause most controversy. Thus, the ministers in charge of education and transport were included in the Cabinet formed after the 1983 election, but are not automatically given that position.

Resignation and Dismissal of Ministers

As a class, ministers have less security of tenure than members of any other profession, with the possible exception of football managers. Their appointments are the fruits of a long struggle and confer high status upon them, yet within a year of two they may be wondering how long they will survive. Junior ministers – that is, parliamentary secretaries and under secretaries – know they are on probation and that if they are not promoted within four or five years they will soon find themselves back-benchers again. They also know that the odds are against them. The minority who are promoted can look forward to only a few years as full ministers, unless they are exceptionally talented and also blessed with a modicum of good fortune. Thus, when the Conservative government took office in 1951 thirty-eight ministers and thirty-six junior ministers were appointed. Ten years later only ten of the ministers and six of the junior ministers were still in office (Blondel, 1963, pp. 157–7). Many of the others had retired or abandoned political life for a career that offered them greater security; some had been asked to resign or openly dismissed from office.

It cannot be easy for a Prime Minister to dismiss one of his colleagues but all Prime Ministers who hold office for any time find that it is an inescapable duty.

Sometimes it becomes clear that a minister is unsuited to his post; sometimes there are disagreements over policy; and sometimes a Prime Minister finds it necessary to rejuvenate a government that is beginning to look (or to get) a little stale. Prime Ministers are quite frank about this. Churchill has said that a Prime Minister must be 'a good butcher'. Attlee has stated that a Prime Minister should always warn his ministers that 'if you don't turn out all right I shall sack you', adding: 'It's awkward to have to sack a man and tell him he doesn't make the grade. But I always think it's best to tell him so frankly' (Williams, 1961, pp. 84–6). Macmillan dismissed seven of his senior colleagues in one fell swoop in 1962. Harold Wilson announced within a few days of accepting office that he would not hesitate to reshuffle his administration when this proved necessary. Margaret Thatcher has been more ruthless than any of them, dismissing twenty-one Cabinet ministers in her first ten years.

When ministers resign or are dismissed, they may be offered a seat in the House of Lords, which is a gracious way of compensating a politician who has given many years of his life to public service. They may return to business or the Bar, where the financial rewards are higher than they are in politics. Or they may simply return to the back benches in the hope that hard work or good fortune will carry them into office again a year or so later, as sometimes happens.

The Prime Minister and the Cabinet

The Prime Minister is chairman of the Cabinet and wields a good deal of authority over it. He (or she) determines the agenda, guides discussion and declares the sense of the meeting. He derives a great deal of power from the fact that ministers owe their appointments to him and knows that he can without notice either dismiss them or promote them to posts that are higher in the ministerial hierarchy. And since the Cabinet is not only an administrative body but also a committee of party politicians, the position of the Prime Minister is further strengthened by the fact that he is the chosen leader of the governing party, bearing more responsibility than anyone else for its success in the previous election and its fortunes in the next.

This does not mean that he can act as a dictator. The tradition is that the Cabinet reaches agreement on matters of policy, not that the Cabinet acts as a rubber stamp to policies enunciated by its chairman. The convention of collective responsibility means that Cabinet members have to be prepared to defend Cabinet decisions in public once they are reached, and if a minister is not prepared to do this the alternative is for him to resign. Naturally ministers do not want to resign, and this strengthens the hand of a Prime Minister who is trying to get his colleagues to agree to his proposals. But it is equally true that a series of resignations would weaken the position of the Prime Minister, and this strengthens the hand of his critics. Moreover politicians do not forget that at least one Prime Minister (Asquith, in 1917) was forced to resign because his Cabinet colleagues were dissatisfied with his conduct of affairs. It is the only clear example in the twentieth century, but as was said of Admiral Byng when he was shot in front of his fellow-officers, 'it encourages the others'.

Relationships within the Cabinet depend on a variety of personal and political factors and vary from one Prime Minister to another. Wilson was a very different leader from Heath, and Thatcher is different from them both. Moreover, in all governments there is a handful of senior ministers whose support is much more crucial for the Prime Minister than that of the lesser ministers. The formal meetings of the Cabinet are supplemented by informal discussions between the Prime Minister and these senior colleagues (some-times known as the 'inner Cabinet') and if they all agree on a policy it is pretty certain to be accepted by other ministers.

In Cabinet meetings the Prime Minister has to ensure that disagreements between ministers are resolved and to see that policies advocated by particular ministers for their departments are understood and supported by their col-leagues. He also has to guide the Cabinet in its discussions of broad issues of policy and to persuade them into supporting his own views on questions of political strategy. On occasions he may find that the weight of opinion is against him and yield to the majority view. In exceptional circumstances he may act in a more authoritative way, two outstanding postwar examples being the Suez crisis of 1956, when the Cabinet was not told of the ultimatum to Egypt until after it had been sent, and the decision to manufacture a British atomic bomb, which Attlee took after consulting only a small group of colleagues. In normal circumstances a Prime Minister would not act without Cabinet authorization, but his ability to control the agenda gives him a great deal of power provided he has the support of the departmental minister or ministers most involved. Margaret Thatcher has used her power to control the agenda and her power to create Cabinet committees in a fashion that has enabled her to dominate her Cabinet more than any other peacetime Prime Minister has done in the twentieth century. In her first two years, knowing that she could not get the majority of Cabinet ministers to support her chosen economic policies, she put economic affairs under the control of a small committee of supporters, with herself as chairman. The committee took decisions and economic policy was kept off the agenda of the Cabinet itself for twenty-five months. In 1981 she encouraged her Chancellor to prepare a very harsh budget which she knew would be opposed by several Cabinet ministers. The budget was presented to the Cabinet on the day it was also presented to Parliament, with no advance leaks or discussions, thus giving the dissenting ministers only a few hours in which to decide whether to accept the budget or resign. They all decided to stay.

A further power that can be exercised by the Prime Minister is that of controlling the information that goes to Cabinet. During discussions on Britain's application to join the European Community the President of the Board of Trade

(Douglas Jay) produced a paper prepared by his department on the industrial and commercial consequences of entry that was much more pessimistic than the view taken by Harold Wilson and the other ministers. To deal with this, 'The Prime Minister evoked the rule that the Cabinet will consider only opinions and not disagreements on matters of fact and Mr Jay's paper therefore was not circulated, though his continual efforts to reopen the issue finally led to his dismissal in August 1967' (Mackintosh, 1977b, p. 70). But Prime Ministers do not behave in this way unless they have very clear preferences themselves, and there are many issues on which they are open-minded and willing to let all points of view be aired in Cabinet.

The style that a Prime Minister adopts naturally affects the character of Cabinet meetings. In this respect, Prime Ministers can be divided into three broad categories, which can be labelled brokers, helmsmen and programme setters respectively. The Prime Minister who is primarily a broker sees his role as that of keeping the party together, minimizing damage from crises and building support for the next election. His own policy objectives will be defined, if at all, only in very vague terms. Of Britain's nine postwar Prime Ministers, Douglas-Home, Wilson and Callaghan may be placed in this category. It is true that Wilson had ambitions to be more than a broker, particularly in his first years of power when his self-proclaimed objective was to modernize the British economy. But he was not able to pursue this objective for long; he had to abandon his plan to reform the system of industrial relations because of opposition from within his party; and he was forced to make repeated somersaults in regard to British membership of the European community. In 1962 he was against Macmillan's plan to join; in 1967 he supported a British application; in 1972 he opposed Heath's bid for membership; and in 1975, while back in power and in favour of membership, he was forced to permit Cabinet members to speak publicly against his own policy. These are the actions of a leader acting as broker.

Prime Ministers who adopt the role of helmsmen play a more positive part in the proceedings of the government. They will be steering the ship of state towards some objective, as generally agreed by the top leaders of the party. They will assume leadership of the crew and will not hesitate to throw weak crew members overboard. Among postwar leaders, Attlee, Eden and Macmillan fall into this category.

The third category, that of programme setters, is reserved for those Prime Ministers who set their own objectives for the government and inspire their colleagues to pursue these objectives. Churchill filled this role superbly during the war, when he dominated his Cabinet and directed the British war effort. When he returned to power in 1951, however, he acted as a helmsman rather than a programme setter. Heath is another member of the category, coming to power as he did with the three objectives of taking Britain into the European Community, transforming the system of industrial relations and pursing a policy of economic expansion notwithstanding the risk of inflation. He succeeded in only the first of these aims, but he certainly tried all three and was unlucky in that the 1973 oil crisis (and the consequent quadrupling of oil prices) sabotaged his plans for expansion. The third member of the category is Margaret Thatcher.

Further reference to the role of the Cabinet in administration will be made in Chapter 11. But before we turn to the role of the Opposition, it is worth stressing that the Cabinet is as much a political as an administrative institution. It is a committee of party leaders, and as such its concerns are to plan the strategy of the ruling party in Parliament, to keep the public image of the governments as favourable as possible and to conduct its affairs in such a way that the party will keep or increase its majority in the next election.

The Role of the Opposition

Throughout this century Parliament has normally been dominated by the conflict between two main parties, and the smaller of these parties is officially recognized as Her Majesty's Opposition. There is no parallel to this situation in the United States, where party discipline is weak and the support given to the President in Congress may cut across party lines and may vary from one issue to another. No American politician could be given the official status and salary that are now enjoyed by the Leader of Her Majesty's Opposition.

Although in this sense the Opposition has a privileged position in Britain, the very fact of party discipline that gives it that position also denies it much influence over the activities of the government. In normal circumstances the government has a clear majority; party loyalty and party discipline ensure that this is reflected in parliamentary divisions, and the Opposition has no chance of defeating the government on an issue of substantial importance. This means that the Opposition has no hope of coming to power until the next general election is called, at a time chosen by the Prime Minister. The Opposition is almost as impotent in respect of legislation. There is no filibuster in Britain, and the government has complete control over the parliamentary timetable, subject to various conventions that are respected by the leaders of both parties. The result is that the Opposition cannot prevent the passage of government Bills and cannot even insist on revisions to them if the government is determined to keep them in their original form and its supporters do not waver.

The main function of the Opposition, it has often been said, is to oppose. These is a good deal of truth in this. The British devotion to parliamentary democracy is based partly on the belief that no one party or group ever has a monopoly of political wisdom. Every policy has some drawbacks, and it is thought to be a good thing that the Opposition should point them out. The need to defend their policies in Parliament may well lead ministers to think more carefully about the advantages and disadvantages of each policy before it is adopted. Apart from this, the exposure of government actions and plans to continuous criticism in Parliament is a reasonably effective way of keeping the public informed about what their government is doing. Press conferences and television interviews are often more lively and searching, but ministers are under no obligation to take part if they do not wish to do so. And it should perhaps be stressed that public information about government is valuable not only in the very general sense of contributing to an education in citizenship but also in two very specific senses. First, it alerts groups within the community to the prospect of government actions that may affect their interests. Secondly, it helps electors to form some kind of judgement on the efficiency and equity of government policies.

This activity of criticism and verbal opposition is carried on within limits that are fairly well defined and understood. The parliamentary game has rules that everyone normally observes, and these rules maintain a delicate line between what is regarded as legitimate criticism and what would be regarded as obstruction. Indeed, to some extent the Opposition co-operates with the government in arrangements that contribute to the orderly progress of parliamentary and government business. Thus, a minister going abroad for a conference may pair with an Opposition Member who is going on business in the provinces. These pairing arrangements are always strictly observed. They are often arranged by the Whips, who in both parties are responsible for the smooth running of parliamentary business and for a certain amount of 'stage management'. Other courtesies of parliamentary life ensure that snap votes are not taken at unexpected times, that all-night sittings are rarely held and that Members refrain from abusing one another in debate.

The weekly programme of parliamentary business is arranged by the government Chief Whip in consultation with his opposite number. By convention, the subjects of debate of twenty-six days of each session are chosen by the Opposition. By convention also, the government will allow the Opposition to interrupt the planned programme (provided a request is made through 'the usual channels') in order to move a vote of censure on the government in connection with a new development of government policy. By convention again, the Opposition normally refrains from harassing the government in ways that would impose a physical burden on ministers or otherwise hinder the business of governing the country.

In a more general sense, too the Opposition refrains from attempts to obstruct the government. In many democratic countries the debates on financial Bills are the occasion for a vigorous attempt by the opposition party or parties to reduce taxation or to cut the expenditures authorized for government departments. In modern Britain this does not happen. Technical revisions of Bills levying taxation are often urged, but there is no general attempt by the Opposition to reduce taxes and no attempt at all to cut government expenditure. The principle adopted is that it is better to give the government enough rope to hang itself with, and Oppositions hope that an extravagant administration will be punished by loss of popularity with the electors.

This brings us to the other main function and aim of the Opposition. Not only must it criticize the government of the day, it must also present the image of a credible alternative government. If it is to win the next general election, it must look like a united body of people who would be competent to govern the country, and if possible it must develop a theme with which to capture the attention of electors and the support of a majority of them. The government of the day is in such a strong position in Britain, and has such a near-monopoly of information and initiative, that no Opposition can hope to win power by its own efforts alone. What it can do is to look like an alternative government, to exploit every weakness of the administration and to put itself in a position to win support when the government loses momentum or popularity.

Further Reading

The standard historical and institutional account of the Cabinet system is that given in Mackintosh (1977a), *The British Cabinet*; a lively discussion of the Cabinet in practice is given in Hennessy (1986), *Cabinet*; a useful collection of articles will be found in King (1985), *The British Prime Minister*.

◇ 10 ◇

Civil Servants

Over 6 million people are now employed by public authorities in Britain. They are engaged in all kinds of activities that range from coal-mining to diplomacy and include teaching, scientific research and printing. They are employed by government departments, by local authorities, by the boards of nationalized industries, and by a variety of other agencies. In view of this, it may seem a little arbitrary to concentrate all our attention in this chapter on the 500,000 or so people who staff the central departments of Whitehall.

There are two justifications for doing so. One is that the Whitehall departments control finance and therefore, in the last resort, determine what all the other public authorities can do. The other is that the civil servants in Whitehall provide the link with the minister and with parliament; if this vast system of public administration and public enterprise is democratically controlled, it is done through Whitehall. In this chapter, therefore, we are concerned not with all those who are engaged in public administration, but simply with those who staff the central departments of state.

The Role of Civil Servants

There are four aspects of the role of British civil servants that deserve brief comment: the tradition that they should be anonymous; the principle that they should be impartial; the principle that the task of the civil servant is to carry out the policies decided upon by ministers; and the traditional assumption that it is not the task of the Civil Service to initiate change or to take responsibility for planning future lines of social or economic development.

The tradition of anonymity follows from the convention that the minister and the minister alone is responsible for the work of his department. He gets the credit for all that goes well and the censure for all that is criticized. He answers to Parliament for the activities of the department and is not expected to evade this responsibility by naming or blaming his permanent officials. The principle is that they are his servants carrying out his instructions.

There is of course an element of unreality about this principle. Ministers cannot have direct knowledge of all the multifarious activities of their departments and often find themselves defending actions taken by civil servants in terms drafted by civil servants, the minister's role being that of spokesman. A new minister in a department may have to accept responsibility for decisions taken before he assumed the appointment, and is expected to defend them even if they do not have his entire approval. Nevertheless, the principle is operative. The tradition of Civil Service anonymity is deeply rooted and is generally respected by ministers, by back-benchers and by others concerned with government. Many journalists, for instance, know the names of leading officials, but they rarely publish them. Group spokesmen are in a similar position; when they are disappointed with the outcome of negotiations, they can easily identify the responsible officials, but they do not criticize them in public; instead they criticize the minister. If things go conspicuously wrong, civil servants may be criticized publicly by a special inquiry or by the minister concerned, but this is by no means a common occurrence.

The principle of Civil Service impartiality is bound up with the tradition of anonymity. The idea is that civil servants are servants of the Crown, serving with complete impartiality whichever ministers happen to be in office. This principle was questioned between the wars by a number of left-wing writers, who argued that the middle-class backgrounds of senior officials would make it difficult for them to sympathize with Labour aims and to co-operate fully with Labour ministers. But the Labour government of 1945–51 carried through a series of reforms with complete co-operation from the Civil Service, and after that no more was heard of these criticisms; as Lord Attlee said, 'all doubts disappeared with experience' (quoted in Robson, 1956, p. 16). In point of fact, there is no evidence that civil servants are right of centre in their sympathies, let alone in their actions; a study made of the higher Civil Service reached the conclusion that higher civil servants as a group are somewhat to the left of centre in their political sympathies (see R. Chapman, 1970, pp. 115–17).

The principle of impartiality carries with it certain restrictions on the political activities of civil servants. The present position is that staff in the higher grades of the service may not take any part in national politics apart from voting and may take part in local politics only if prior personal permission to do so is given by their department. Staff in the various clerical grades may not stand for Parliament but may engage in other political activities in so far as the regulations of their department permit this. Departments were advised by the Treasury to 'grant permission or refuse it mainly according to the degree and nature of the contact with the public involved by the duties of the officer concerned, and the extent to which his political activities are likely to be known . . . as those of a civil servant whose official duties involve his taking decisions . . . affecting the personal well-being of the department's clients' (see Mackenzie and Grove, 1956, pp. 157–8). This means, for example, that clerks in local employment offices may be excluded from participation in national politics, and clerks in departments dealing with local authorities may not be able to take part in local politics.

The third principle, that ministers make policy and officials carry it out, is a very simple statement about a very complex situation. Most questions of policy emerge from the normal process of administration and are brought up from within the department for the attention of the leading officials and, if they are important enough, for the decision of the minister. When the file is given to the minister it does not end with a question mark, it ends with a recommendation, supported by reasons. The minister may accept this recommendation or he may query it. In the latter case he will normally discuss the matter with the permanent secretary and may suggest that an alternative policy would be preferable. If he does this, it would be the duty of the permanent secretary to draw the minister's attention to difficulties that might be created, and other officials might be asked to join in a frank discussion of the merits and problems of the alternative courses of action. In the end it is the minister's responsibility to reach a decision, knowing that if things go wrong he will have to justify it to his colleagues in the government and to defend it in Parliament.

Civil servants are not supposed to obstruct their ministers, and it is often said that the duty of the most senior officials is to 'know the minister's mind', so that they give him the kind of information he needs and make recommendations that accord with the general line of policy he wishes to pursue. As Ridley has said, top officials are expected to have 'a chameleon-like ability to identify with successive governments of quite different political complexion' (Ridley, 1983, p. 29). However, ministers vary greatly in their personalities, their experience and the extent of their knowledge about the work of the department. Some ministers move quickly from one department to another and in a short stay they may find it difficult not to accept the recommendations that are made to them, particularly when the problems are technical or involved. In these circumstances there may develop a 'departmental policy' that is made by civil servants and accepted by successive ministers. Readers who have seen the television programme 'Yes, Minister' will have a good idea of the relationships between top civil servants and ministers, though it should be added that a really determined minister, if backed by the Cabinet, can insist on reforms whether his officials approve of them or not.

A fourth aspect of the role of the Civil Service can be seen most clearly if a comparison is drawn with the situation in France. In that country it is taken for granted that the state, which in practice means the permanent departments of state, has a general responsibility for watching developments in the country and for providing such public services as are necessary. In recent years French ministries and commissions have compiled and published a number of reports on matters such as the expected size and location of the future population of the country, the transport needs of the country, the demand for technical and university education and – best known of all – the five-yearly national plans for economic development. The recommendations are not always translated into practice, for they are subject to scrutiny and often to substantial revision by the National Assembly. But the ministries accept a responsibility for making recommendations and their reports provide factual information on which politicians can draw.

In Britain the departments do not normally accept this kind of responsibility. They see their role as that of dealing with routine administration, of arbitrating between conflicting interests and of advising their ministers about matters of policy. They do not conceive it to be their duty to make predictions about the future, except in so far as these are necessary for particular decisions that have to be taken at the present time; and even when predictions are made it is not usually thought appropriate to publish them, lest they provide ammunition for critics. The 'national plan' published by the Department of Economic Affairs in 1965 was a break with tradition, and its total failure must have provided an additional argument for those who uphold the traditional approach.

In 1963 the limited nature of the role of the Civil Service was vigorously criticized by Brian Chapman, who argued that things were done better in France and that widespread reforms were needed if the British administrative system was to cope effectively with the increased responsibilities of government in the second half of the twentieth century (B. Chapman, 1963). The merits of the French system are not our concern. The relevance of this criticism is that it draws attention to one of the most important features of British administration. In Britain, as in most advanced countries, the first half of the twentieth century was marked by a transformation in the extent of governmental activities. But while in France and many other European countries this was paralleled by developments in the role of the Civil Service, in Britain this did not occur. Here the structure and the role of the Civil Service in the 1960s were in most respects the same as they were at the end of the nineteenth century, and it is only since then that small reforms have been made.

This relative lack of change has been possible partly because of the habit of consultation with affected interests, partly because of the habit of appointing committees of eminent outsiders to advise on delicate problems and partly because of the creation of a rich variety of autonomous and semi-autonomous institutions to deal with many of the responsibilities of the state. No attempt will be made in this book to delineate the powers and duties of the BBC, the Monopolies Commission, the Racecourse Betting Control Board, the National Insurance Advisory Committee, the Local Government Commission for England, the Bank of England, the Regional Hospital Boards, or the numerous other bodies that are engaged in public administration but cannot be regarded as government departments. But the student should realize that it is partly because of this tendency to proliferate administrative institutions that the Civil Service as such, sitting at the centre of the web, has been able to retain for so long the main features that characterized it at the end of the last century: an impartial and anonymous service, composed largely of non-specialists, enjoying remarkable freedom from public scrutiny.

Staffing Policies

The modern British Civil Service is essentially a career service of professional bureaucrats and there have been two marked turning-points in its development. The first of these was the publication in 1854 of the Northcote-Trevelyan Report, which outlined a set of principles about the organization of the Civil Service that were adopted by the government of the day and were not seriously challenged until very recently. The second turning-point is the publication in 1968 of the Fulton Report, which consciously questioned or rejected several of these principles and recommended a number of reforms. The changes in the size and composition of the service between these dates were very extensive and there were a number of intermediate inquiries and reports. Nevertheless the basic principles enunciated in 1854 remained virtually intact until 1968, and this gives the period a certain unity.

The first of these principles is that civil servants should be recruited immediately or very shortly after the end of their full-time education, by open competitive examinations directly related to the candidates' studies at school or university. The argument for this procedure was put in the following terms by Lord Macaulay (Trevelyan's brother-in-law) in a parliamentary speech on 23 June 1853: 'It seems to me that there never was a fact proved by a larger mass of evidence, or a more unvaried experience, than this; that men who distinguish themselves in their youth above their contemporaries almost always keep to the end of their lives the start which they have gained.'

The long-standing belief in the merits of competitive examination reflects the desire to select civil servants from among the most gifted members of each age-group. The dominant official view for over a hundred years has been that intelligent recruits could be trained (by apprenticeship rather than formal instruction) to do whatever is required, leaving no need, save in exceptional circumstances, to recruit people of more mature years who had experience in other occupations. Exceptional circumstances obtained during the Second World War, when the Civil Service almost doubled in size, and many of the temporary recruits were given permanent appointments after 1945. But the general principle of recruitment immediately after the completion of full-time education was made operative again after the war.

A second principle is that recruits should be given jobs for life, with complete security of tenure unless the official behaves in a scandalous way. The great majority of civil servants at the present time – meaning about four-fifths of them – have held no other job.

The third principle is that staff should be recruited for general classes of work rather than for specific posts or even specific departments. There are numerous classes, each with its own career structure, and with somewhat rigid divisions between them. Some of the divisions are horizontal, such as those between what used to be called the clerical class, the executive class and the administrative class. Others are vertical, dividing these general classes from the specialized classes of lawyers, accountants, statisticians, engineers, scientists, medical officers and so forth. Once appointed to a class, it is difficult to move to another class, though relatively easy to move from one government department to another or one location to another.

The officials who enjoy most power in all departments, and have sole responsibility for determining policy and advising ministers, are those filling the ranks of permanent secretary, deputy secretary, assistant secretary and principal. These are the grades that were collectively known as the administrative class until the reforms of 1969. They comprise less than 4 per cent of the total staff, with about 18,000 officials out of the current total of around 500,000. Most of the staff in these positions were recruited to the administrative stream directly after graduating from university. Staff in the specialized classes have virtually no opportunity to get into these policy-making ranks.

Applicants for the administrative stream have to have a degree with first- or second-class honours and must take a written qualifying examination. The subject of the degree is not thought important. Those who pass the qualifying examination then go through a selection process involving two days of verbal presentations, group discussions and interviews. The successful few join the élite and are involved with policy questions from their first years of service onwards.

The principle underlying this recruitment policy is that the top people in the Civil Service should be 'generalists' rather than specialists. It is in sharp contrast to the principles adopted in most other advanced societies. In the United States, for instance, top officials are in most cases picked for their special skills, with agricultural economists taking jobs in the Department of Agriculture and specialists in strategic studies being appointed to the Department of Defense. In France, all recruits for the equivalent of the administrative class first study the social sciences and then spend two and a half years in the Ecole Nationale d'Administration, which provides them with the specialized training that the French consider necessary for high administrative office. The British tradition has been one of suspicion towards the specialist and a preference for giving individuals of broad general education the responsibility for assessing specialized advice in terms of the public interest.

Criticisms and Attempted Reforms

These principles of Civil Service recruitment, accepted without serious question for over a hundred years, were the object of mounting criticism during the 1960s. It was in this decade that the British realized that most of the other industrial states of Western Europe had grappled with their economic problems more successfully than Britain, and to some extent the blame for this was laid at the door of the Civil Service. A series of writers alleged that higher civil servants were 'amateurs', lacking the training in the social or natural sciences that they were thought to need. It was suggested that an education in the humanities may have been appropriate when the domestic role of government was simply to hold the ring, but was inadequate in an age when the government had direct responsibility for a public sector employing 20 per cent of the country's workers, and indirect responsibility for the level of economic activity in the private sector employing the other 80 per cent.

This criticism of the education of senior civil servants was supplemented by other criticisms, also directed mainly at the administrative class. It was said that the fact that four-fifths of the entrants to this class were graduates of Oxford or Cambridge indicated class bias in the recruitment system, which was not only unfair to applicants from other universities but also deprived the administrative class of a broader range of experience that would probably have been beneficial. Critics also regretted that in peacetime the great majority of senior civil servants spend their entire careers in the Civil Service, without acquiring any direct knowledge of the world outside Whitehall. Whereas senior civil servants in France have all spent part of their training period in a government office outside Paris and part in an industrial enterprise, most senior civil servants in Britain spend their whole working lives, from the age of 21 to the age of 60, in the closed world of government head offices in central London. It was asserted that senior administrators lacked managerial skills and displayed no wish to acquire them.

In 1966, in response to these criticisms, the government appointed a Committee on the Civil Service, commonly known as the Fulton Committee, with very wide terms of reference and the clear expectation that radical changes would be proposed. This committee set out deliberately, and perhaps a little self-consciously, to remodel the Civil Service. The opening paragraph of its report stated bluntly: 'The Home Civil Service today is still fundamentally the product of the nineteenth-century philosophy of the Northcote-Trevelyan Report. The tasks it faces are those of the second half of the twentieth century. This is what we have found; it is what we seek to remedy' (Fulton Committee, 1968, p. 69).

The main concern of the committee was with the non-specialized character of the members of the administrative class. The committee regretted that most members of this class had degrees in classics or history, that they had no post-entry training in management or the social sciences and that they rarely stayed long enough in any one job to become an expert in that job. To preserve the principle that policy-makers should not be specialists, they were moved with great rapidity from one task to another, lasting on average only 2.8 years in any one position. The committee called this 'the cult of the generalist' and referred to members of the administrative class as amateurs. This last term infuriated top civil servants, who were proud of the fact that they were generalists but regarded themselves as professionals – not, to be sure, in any particular subject, but professional governors of Britain.

The most significant recommendations of the Fulton Committee were as follows:

(1) All classes should be abolished and replaced by a single unified grading structure. The correct grading of each post should be determined by job evaluation.

(2) The service should encourage greater professionalism among its staff, with post-entry training in management and encouragement for administrators to become specialists in particular areas.

(3) When recruiting university graduates, preference should be given to graduates in relevant disciplines, such as the social sciences and the natural sciences.

(4) A Civil Service College should be established to provide post-entry training for recruits, giving courses in administration, management, economics and allied subjects.

(5) Each government department should establish a planning unit, whose director would have direct access to the minister.

(6) There should be expanded opportunities for late entry, for short-term appointments and for exchange between the service, the universities and the private sector.

(7) A new department, to be called the Civil Service Department, should be created to manage the service.

(8) The rules regarding secrecy should be relaxed and the administrative process made more open to public knowledge and consultation.

Not surprisingly, these recommendations were received with hostility by top civil servants, who regarded the proposals (quite correctly) as an attempt to change the whole character of the senior Civil Service. Officials persuaded ministers that the proposal to give preference to graduates in relevant disciplines would deprive the service of some of their best recruits, and this recommendation was rejected by the government. The other recommendations were accepted by the Cabinet, given strong personal backing by the Prime Minister (Harold Wilson) and supported by the Leader of the Opposition (Edward Heath). However, the proposals had to be implemented by the Civil Service, and there followed a protracted defensive action by top civil servants to minimize the changes.

In November 1968 the Civil Service Department was established, and its first head was appointed with a mandate to see that the Fulton recommendations were translated into practice. Eight years later, when asked by a House of Commons committee to explain why the recommendation that classes should be abolished had not been implemented, he replied that he had been 'quite prepared to examine this, though I was not particularly impressed' (quoted in Garrett, 1980, p. 44). In fact, the record suggests that he was determined not to implement any more of this proposal than was absolutely unavoidable. The distinction between the administrative and executive classes has been blurred and the nomenclature changed, which adds a little flexibility to the recruitment process. However, the vertical divisions have not been abolished, specialists still have their own career

structures within the specialized classes, and policy-making is still the prerogative of non-specialists in the general administrative grades.

The second and fourth of the proposals listed above have been implemented
only in a half-hearted way. The Civil Service College was established by the
government in 1969, but it was put under the control of the Civil Service
Department. The academics on its staff were frustrated by bureaucratic control
and its first director, a social scientist, took early retirement after a few years –
to be replaced by a civil servant. The courses do not compare with those given
by the Ecole Nationale d'Administration, lasting for only twenty-two weeks
instead of for two and a half years. The course on economics lasts for only four
weeks. The college provides a useful introduction to existing Civil Service
practice, but does very little indeed to give future administrators the social
science training that the Fulton Committee had thought necessary for officials
whose task is to guide British economy policy and run the social services. The
Civil Service does practically nothing to encourage professionalism among its
staff and what Fulton called 'the cult of the generalist' still prevails in the higher
echelons.

The recommendation about the establishment of planning units within
departments has been ignored. More civil servants are recruited after a period
in other occupations, but they form only a very small proportion of all recruits.
The Official Secrets Act was not modified until 1989, and was then only slightly
liberalized. All in all, the story of the Fulton Committee and its aftermath is a
story of bureaucratic resistance to reform, with the bureaucrats winning partly
because of their tenacity and skill in administrative manoeuvres, and partly
because they have permanent posts whereas ministers (even Prime Ministers)
come and go.

A parallel story with the same conclusion is the story of the various efforts
made to reduce the dominance of Oxford and Cambridge (Oxbridge) graduates
among recruits to the administrative class. It was understandable in the days
when these two universities were clearly the biggest and best in the country,
but not when they are only two among forty-six, with roughly similar intellectual
standards throughout. The civil servants responsible for recruitment reacted to
the widespread criticisms of the situation by visiting universities throughout the
country, beginning in 1969, to encourage applications from the other forty-four.
In the 1970s they also invited senior academics to spend a day as the guests of
selected departments, with a similar objective. These tactics have been
successful. The number of applicants from the other universities has risen
greatly. The only snag is that they rarely get through the Civil Service selection
tests. In 1968 it was reported that Oxbridge candidates provided 35 per cent of
the candidates but 59 per cent of the successful ones (Kellner and Crowther-
Hunt, 1980, p. 119). In 1987 Oxbridge provided only 13 per cent of the applicants
but 54 per cent of those appointed (*Civil Service Commission Annual Report,
1987*, p. 46). An Oxbridge candidate in 1987 was nine times as likely to be
appointed as a candidate from another university. Of those appointed, 60 per

cent had degrees in the humanities compared with 23 per cent in the social sciences and 17 per cent in science and technology.

How should this bias be interpreted? Marxists would say that it reveals a determination to ensure that positions of power within the state are occupied only by defenders of the existing social order. Statistics published in the 1970s showed that most of the successful Oxbridge candidates had been educated at fee-paying schools and were therefore members of the upper and upper-middle classes. The whole selection process, it could be said, makes certain that radicals are excluded from the higher Civil Service.

This interpretation cannot be denied, but it is not the whole story. There is also a cultural bias in the selection process that favours arts graduates over others, and there is a degree of complacency in the higher ranks of the service, which is reflected in the whole system of recruitment. Broadly speaking, higher civil servants are proud of the service, believe it to govern the country well and are quietly determined to ensure that the top civil servants of the future shall be similar in character and training to the top civil servants of the present. This is entirely understandable in view of the emphasis that is placed on informal relationships and personal trust in the higher Civil Service. As a senior Treasury official told two American scholars: 'The Civil Service is run by a small group of people who grew up together' (Heclo and Wildavsky, 1974, p. 76). For better or worse, the system is self-perpetuating.

Developments since 1979

Margaret Thatcher's arrival at 10 Downing Street in 1979 brought to office a Prime Minister of radical disposition who was determined to arrest British economic decline. In her words, she wanted 'to turn Britain around'. Among her early actions was the appointment of two policy advisers with a mandate to investigate the efficiency of the Civil Service machine, and to report personally on this to the Prime Minister.

One of the advisers was Sir Derek Rayner, a chief executive with Marks & Spencer. He found the management techniques and methods of financial control in government departments to be somewhat ineffective, and made recommendations for their improvement, which were accepted by the Prime Minister. Rayner also recommended that the Civil Service Department be abolished and its functions transferred to the Treasury. The department was duly abolished, and its head given early retirement, but its functions were divided between the Treasury and the Cabinet Office. The Prime Minister put herself in charge of the section of the Cabinet Office responsible for Civil Service management.

The other adviser was Sir John Hoskyns, a former entrepreneur in the computer business and, from 1975 to 1979, a policy adviser to Thatcher and her colleagues in opposition. Hoskyns focused on the attitudes of senior civil servants to British economic affairs, which he found deplorable. In 1980 a former Head of the Civil Service stated publicly that in his view 'the task of the British Civil Service is the orderly management of decline' (quoted in Fry, 1984, p. 353). Hoskyns discovered that this view was widely shared. Senior civil servants were resigned to the relative decline of the British economy and deeply sceptical of any radical attempt to reverse it, whether the radicalism was of the left or of the right. Most top administrators had entered the service in the years immediately following 1945, and in Hoskyns's view joining the service in that period was 'like joining Napoleon's army just in time for the retreat from Moscow' (Hoskyns, 1983, p. 142). He recommended that a fairly high proportion of senior officials over the age of 50 should be removed from their posts and replaced by outsiders, brought in on contract.

This recommendation was too radical even for Thatcher. A number of top people have been pushed into early retirement, which they and many of their colleagues resent, but they have been replaced by other officials given rapid promotion rather than by outsiders. However, Thatcher has broken with precedent by controlling these promotions herself. She does not do so on a party-political basis, as civil servants do not make their partisan sympathies known, but she has strong preferences in terms of policy attitudes, style and personal qualities. As has been said, 'she is not attracted to the qualities of detachment, versatility, caution . . . traditionally prized among British senior civil servants' (Drewry and Butcher, 1988, p.164). She favours officials who are dynamic and prepared to be ruthless, at the expense of those who value consensus and continuity. There are about 40 permanent secretaries and 135 deputy secretaries in Whitehall, and by the end of her second term of office in 1987 she had made appointments to the great majority of these posts.

This is a new development that involves a complete break with the tradition that the Civil Service is autonomous in questions of staffing and promotion. It is easy to understand why Thatcher should have chosen this approach, which gives her control over the top appointments without the disruption that would have been caused if she had accepted Hoskyns's proposal that outsiders should be brought in. Nevertheless, it adds uncertainty to the career prospects of higher civil servants and is inevitably regarded as a form of politicization of a service that prides itself on its political neutrality. Officials ask what will happen if the Conservatives are defeated at the next election. Will a new Prime Minister feel unable to work with Thatcher's appointees and replace them with officials of his own choosing? It is a development with large implications and has inevitably created tension between the Prime Minister and some of her top officials. It has also caused concern and distrust on the part of the staff association of the administrative civil servants, which bears the characteristically élitist name of the First Division Association.

Another development since 1979 has been a concerted effort to reduce the size and cost of the Civil Service. Between 1979 and 1983 its size was reduced by 14 per cent, partly by privatization of some services and the discontinuance of others, but mainly by failing to replace officials as they retired or left.

Inevitably, this has meant a heavier work-load for those who remain, combined with reduced opportunities for promotion. The policy has been highly unpopular with all the staff associations. It has been accompanied by talk about reducing the privileges enjoyed by civil servants, such as indexed pensions, and by a refusal to continue established procedures for determining the size of annual salary increases. The Thatcher government does not believe in a general incomes policy, but has insisted on controlling pay awards to its own employees. Resentment about this led in 1981 to an unprecedented national rolling strike, involving senior officials as well as their junior colleagues. The strike lasted twenty-one weeks and the selective withdrawal of staff was carefully organized so as to cause the maximum possible loss to the government, by not collecting taxes and customs duties or checking social security payments. The government refused to give way on the question of pay, but it has been estimated that the overall cost was about £1,000 million whereas the cost of meeting the pay claims would have been only £50 million (F. F. Ridley, 1983, p. 46).

The consequence of these recent developments is that morale in the Civil Service has declined. Relations between ministers and officials are worse than at any previous time in the twentieth century. Civil Service unions, including the First Division Association, are now affiliated to the Trades Union Congress, in the hope of gaining support in case of further strike action. Some civil servants have suggested that they may have a duty to the Crown or to Parliament that is higher than their duty to the government of the day. A secretary in the Foreign Office gave secret information to a newspaper about the arrival of the Cruise missile in Britain, for which she was prosecuted and sent to prison in 1984. Later in the same year, a senior official in the Ministry of Defence gave secret information to a Labour MP about the Falkland Islands campaign, for which he was prosecuted but (in a sensational verdict) acquitted by the jury. In view of these cases, the Head of the Civil Service issued a note of guidance to all staff on their duties and responsibilities, which is printed in full as an appendix to this chapter.

Conclusion

The recent criticisms of the Civil Service and changes made to it are entirely understandable in the light of two inescapable facts: first, that the service must accept part of the responsibility, even if only a small part, for Britain's deteriorating economic position; and secondly, that the service has displayed the greatest reluctance to accept or to implement the proposals that have been made for its reform.

Having said this, it seems appropriate to conclude by pointing out that the Civil Service has very considerable virtues as well as certain limitations. It is, for example, entirely honest. In the entire postwar period only one civil servant has been found guilty of corruption. That is one out of half a million, over forty years.

Moreover, there are no rumours of bribes or graft. Secondly, its political neutrality is in general terms undoubtedly an advantage. Thirdly, it is singularly lacking in the addiction to red tape and formality that plagues the bureaucratic process in many countries. Civil servants write in plain English rather than in legal or bureaucratic jargon, the appendix to this chapter being characteristic in this respect. It is easy to get an interview with civil servants and they are invariably courteous in their dealings with members of the public. Tax inspectors and customs officers are rarely disagreeable. Citizens are not penalized, as they are in Canada and some other countries, if they are a few weeks (or even months) late with their tax returns. There is some tension between the long-term unemployed and the officials responsible for assessing their financial needs, but relations between civil servants and the public remain generally good. These virtues are important and should never be overlooked.

Appendix

The Duties and Responsibilities of Civil Servants in Relation to Ministers

[A note of guidance by the Head of the Civil Service].

(1)   During the last few months a number of my colleagues have suggested to me that it would be timely to restate the general duties and responsibilities of civil servants in relation to ministers. Recent events, and the public discussion to which they have given rise, have led me to conclude that the time has come when it would be right for me, as Head of the Home Civil Service, to respond to these suggestions. I am accordingly putting out the guidance in this note. It is issued after consultation with Permanent Secretaries in charge of departments, and with their agreement.

(2)   Civil servants are servants of the Crown. For all practical purposes the Crown in this context means and is represented by the government of the day. There are special cases in which certain functions are conferred by law upon particular members or groups of members of the public service; but in general the executive powers of the Crown are exercised by and on the advice of Her Majesty's ministers, who are in turn answerable to Parliament. The Civil Service as such has no constitutional personality or responsibility separate from the duly elected government of the day. It is there to provide the government of the day with advice on the formulation of the policies of the government, to assist in carrying out the decisions of the government, and to manage and deliver the services for which the government is responsible. Some civil servants are also involved, as a proper part of their duties, in the processes of presentation of government policies and decisions.

(3)   The Civil Service serves the government of the day as a whole, that is to say Her Majesty's ministers collectively, and the Prime Minister is the minister for the Civil Service. The duty of the individual civil servant is first and foremost to the minister of the Crown who is in charge of the department in which he or she is serving. It is the minister who is responsible, and answerable in Parliament, for the conduct of the department's affairs and the management of its business. It is the duty of civil servants to serve their ministers with integrity and to the best of their ability.

(4)   The British Civil Service is a non-political and disciplined career service. Civil

145

Servants are required to serve the duly elected government of the day, of whatever political complexion. It is of the first importance that civil servants should conduct themselves in such a way as to deserve and retain the confidence of ministers, and as to be able to establish the same relationship with those whom they may be required to serve in some future administration. That confidence is the indispensable foundation of a good relationship between ministers and civil servants. The conduct of civil servants should at all times be such that ministers and potential future ministers can be sure that confidence can be freely given, and that the Civil Service will at all times conscientiously fulfil its duties and obligations to, and impartially assist, advise and carry out the policies of, the duly elected government of the day.

(5)   The determination of policy is the responsibility of the minister (within the convention of collective responsibility of the whole government for the decisions and actions of every member of it). In the determination of policy the civil servant has no constitutional responsibility or role, distinct from that of the minister. Subject to the conventions limiting the access of ministers to papers of previous administrations, it is the duty of the civil servant to make available to the minister all the information and experience at his or her disposal which may have a bearing on the policy decisions to which the minister is committed or which he is preparing to make, and to give to the minister honest and impartial advice, without fear or favour, and whether the advice accords with the minister's view or not. Civil servants are in breach of their duty, and damage their integrity as servants of the Crown, if they deliberately withhold relevant information from their minister, or if they give their minister other advice than the best they believe they can give, or if they seek to obstruct or delay a decision simply because they do not agree with it. When, having been given all the relevant information and advice, the minister has taken a decision, it is the duty of civil servants loyally to carry out that decision with precisely the same energy and good will, whether they agree with it or not.

(6)   Civil servants are under an obligation to keep the confidences to which they become privy in the course of their official duties; not only the maintenance of trust between ministers and civil servants but also the efficiency of government depend on their doing so. There is and must be a general duty upon every civil servant, serving or retired, not to disclose, in breach of that obligation, any document or information or detail about the course of business, which has come his or her way in the course of duty as a civil servant. Whether such disclosure is done from political or personal motives, or for pecuniary gain, and quite apart from liability to prosecution under the Official Secrets Acts, the civil servant concerned forfeits the trust that is put in him or her as a servant of the Crown, and may well forfeit the right to continue in the Service. He or she also undermines the confidence that ought to subsist between ministers and civil servants and thus damages colleagues and the Service as well as him or herself.

(7)   The previous paragraphs have set out the basic principles which govern civil servants' relations with ministers. The rest of this note deals with particular aspects of conduct which derive from them, where it may be felt that more detailed guidance would be helpful.

(8)   A civil servant should not be required to do anything unlawful. In the very unlikely event of a civil servant being asked to do something which he or she believes would put him or her in clear breach of the law, the matter should be reported to a superior officer or to the Principal Establishment Officer, who should if necessary seek the advice of the legal adviser to the department. If legal advice confirms that the action would be likely to be held to the unlawful, the matter should be reported in writing to the Permanent Head of the department.

(9)   Civil servants often find themselves in situations where they are required or expected to give information to a parliamentary select committee, to the media, or to individuals. In doing so they should be guided by the general policy of the government on

evidence to select committees and on the disclosure of information, by any specifically departmental policies in relation to departmental information, and by the requirements of security and confidentiality. In this respect, however, as in other respects, the civil servant's first duty is to his or her minister. Ultimately the responsibility lies with ministers, and not with civil servants, to decide what information should be made available, and how and when it should be released, whether it is to Parliament, to select committees, to the media or to individuals. It is not acceptable for a serving or former civil servant to seek to frustrate policies or decisions of ministers by the disclosure outside the government, in breach of confidence, of information to which he or she has had access as a civil servant.

(10) It is ministers and not civil servants who bear political responsibility. Civil servants should not decline to take, or abstain from taking, an action merely because to do so would conflict with their personal opinions on matters of political choice or judgment between alternative or competing objectives and benefits; they should consider the possibility of declining only if taking or abstaining from the action in question is felt to be directly contrary to deeply held personal conviction on a fundamental issue of conscience.

(11) A civil servant who feels that to act or to abstain from acting in a particular way, or to acquiesce in a particular decision or course of action, would raise for him or her a fundamental issue of conscience, or is so profoundly opposed to a policy as to feel unable conscientiously to administer it in accordance with the standards described in this note, should consult a superior officer, who can and should if necessary consult the Head of the Home Civil Service. If that does not enable the matter to be resolved on a basis which the civil servant concerned is able to accept, he or she must either carry out his or her instructions or resign from the public service – though even after resignation he or she will still be bound to keep the confidences to which he or she has become privy as a civil servant.

(Communicated to the House of Commons by the Prime Minister on 26 February 1985 as part of a written answer to a parliamentary question)

Further Reading

The best book on the Civil Service is Drewry and Butcher (1988), *The Civil Service Today*; some recent developments and controversies are analysed in F. F. Ridley (1983) and Fry (1984), both articles in *Parliamentary Affairs*.

Part IV

The Process of Government

◇ 11 ◇

Administration and Policy-Making

The Administrative System

The administrator lives by the pen, and the administrative process is largely a process of communication. An administrative system is essentially a network of communication channels, and it is effective if it ensures that messages are speedily transmitted, information and advice are readily available, and the activities of those on the periphery are co-ordinated and controlled by those at the centre.

In the latter part of the last century the British system of central administration, following the Northcote-Trevelyan reforms, was both unified and simple in structure. The main functions of government were the traditional ones of defence, foreign and colonial affairs, maintaining law and order, raising revenue and encouraging trade. The most important departments were accordingly the Admiralty and the War Office, the Foreign Office, the Colonial Office, the Home Office, the Treasury and the Board of Trade. These departments were all housed within a few hundred yards of each other in Whitehall; their staff were recruited centrally and were liable to be transferred from one department to another; their expenditures were closely controlled by the Treasury. Such co-ordination as was necessary between departments was facilitated by the fact that senior officials knew one another personally. If an issue could not be settled at this level, it would be referred to the ministers, who would either settle it between themselves or take it to the Cabinet.

In the present century this system has been immensely complicated by the vast extension of the activities of the government. Many of the new activities differ from the old in that they involve administrators in a much greater measure of positive action on their own initiative. Partly for this reason, only some of the newer activities have been put into the hands of departments organized on traditional lines, the others being given to a variety of other institutions and agencies. The system as a whole is now untidy and cannot be said to be based on a clear set of principles. The following outline may serve as a rough guide, though exceptions can be found to every generalization and the reader who wants specific information should consult a textbook on public administration.

151

The first set of environmental and social services to be provided by statute were those concerned with public health, housing and education, all of which were initiated before 1900 and have been developed since. Although departments of the central government are concerned with these services and have some control over them, their actual administration was placed in the hands of local authorities, which in a legal sense are independent bodies rather than agents of Whitehall. The administration of these services is therefore partly determined by the relations between local authorities and Whitehall, which are complex. Thus, housing policy is a hot political issue at Westminster, and the national government controls it by detailed legislation. But the national government does not build a single house or issue a single loan on mortgage; and the local authorities, which do these things, have their own individual policies within the national policy, for which local councillors must answer to local electors.

A second set of services are those concerned with social welfare, which were introduced by the Liberals in 1908–11 and have been developed by subsequent governments. The administration of social insurance and pensions was made the responsibility of new government departments, which consequently handle large blocks of routine work that rarely raise issues of policy. On the other hand, when the National Health Service was established in 1946 administrative control of the service was divided between the Ministry of Health and twelve Regional Hospital Boards, each of which was based on a teaching hospital attached to a university.

A third kind of government activity, which is not entirely new but has been greatly extended in the past fifty years, is the provision of grants, subsidies and other forms of protection for various kinds of private activity. This invariably involves co-operation between Whitehall and representatives of the activity, though the institutional arrangements for this co-operation vary. Government aid to the cotton industry is determined after discussions with the Cotton Board, which is a statutory body established by the government to represent the industry. In the 1930s the policy of industrial protection led to the creation of a number of officially sponsored organizations like the Milk Marketing Board and the Iron and Steel Federation to act as channels of communication between Whitehall and the industries, and the direct government control of many industries during the war was carried out in part by the recruitment as temporary civil servants of members of these bodies. In the case of universities, as noted earlier, the grants are administered by a University Funding Council of which only the chairman is a government servant.

A fourth kind of government activity is the direct management of industrial undertakings. It was felt inappropriate to put the industries that were nationalized after 1945 into the hands of government departments. Instead, they are managed by public corporations, semi-autonomous bodies subject to certain kinds of government control but free from the continuous control by ministers, by Parliament and by the Treasury that characterizes government departments. Various reasons were given for this decision. It was suggested that the management of the industries would lack initiative and flexibility if it were tied to Civil Service procedures. It was thought desirable for those in charge to have more freedom in hiring and firing staff than is enjoyed by government departments. It was felt the industries should be free from the political pressures to which ministries are subject and it was thought that they should be sheltered from the political controversy that would arise if questions in Parliament could be tabled about every aspect of their work.

The logic of these arguments has never been entirely clear. Staffing arrangements could have been varied for industrial ministries. The industries have not been at all free from political pressure and have in fact been forced to take uneconomic decisions by ministerial order. The main difference is that MPs have found it more difficult to ask questions and acquire information about the industries than they would if a minister had been in charge, though the Select Committee on Nationalized Industries was established to bridge this gap and has enjoyed some modest success in doing so. However, the arguments prevailed, and the result is that most of the public sector of industry is now managed by public corporations whose activities are subject to a rather uneven form of control by the government. If they want to buy aircraft or import fuel or close branch railway lines they are subject to direct ministerial control, as they are in planning capital developments; but in much of their day-to-day work the control is more tenuous and patchy.

Fifth, and finally, since the last war the government has assumed overall responsibility for guiding the economy of the country. The main instrument of economic management has been fiscal policy, which from 1945 until the late 1970s was based upon Keynesian principles. The object of fiscal control in this period was to stimulate the economy in times of recession by planning for a budgetary deficit, or conversely to check inflation by increasing taxes and reducing public expenditure so as to take money out of circulation. Since 1976, and more markedly since 1979, the objectives of controlling inflation and limiting public expenditure have been given priority over the economic objectives, with the monetarist theories of Chicago economist Milton Friedman being preferred to the theories of J. M. Keynes. However, the machinery of fiscal control has not been substantially changed. The Treasury has responsibility for economic management of this kind, and the detailed control it exercises over all other government departments and the Bank of England enables fiscal adjustments to be made at very short notice.

During the early 1960s various critics alleged that the concern of the Treasury to protect the balance of payments and the value of sterling had led it to make frequent interventions in the economy with insufficient regard for the need to develop long-term plans for economic growth. This line of criticism led to the establishment in 1964 of the Department of Economic Affairs, the new department being made responsible for long-term economic planning while the Treasury retained control of fiscal policy. This was like a division of functions between husband and wife in which the wife did the shopping, paid the bills and managed the family bank account, while the husband compiled an elaborate dossier on the kind of mansion into which they might move if their financial situation ever permitted it. The Department of Economic Affairs was a failure, the 'national plan' it produced was outdated before it was published, and the department was abolished in 1969. Other aspects of economic management are dealt with by the Department of Trade and Industry, the Department of Energy and a variety of semi-autonomous agencies.

Co-ordination and Control

The foregoing paragraphs give an impression of the shape of the somewhat untidy system of central administration that now exists. Co-ordination and control within this system are the responsibilities of the Civil Service, the Treasury and the Cabinet.

Although the Civil Service (excluding the semi-industrial divisions of the Ministry of Defence) employs less than a tenth of the people engaged in the public sector, it maintains effective control over activities within the sector. Local authorities, public corporations and other public bodies enjoy legal and formal independence of government departments but they do not enjoy a great deal of administrative independence. Thus, education is the responsibility of local authorities, and the government does not employ a single teacher or own a single school. But the administration of education is shaped by ministry circulars, and teaching methods are kept in line by government inspectors, who visit schools and watch teachers at work in their classrooms. Again, public corporations enjoy a good deal of independence in their day-to-day activities but they are not allowed to do anything that conflicts with government policy and are sometimes made to do things that are directly contrary to their own interests. Thus, the railways have been told to keep open a number of uneconomic branch lines; the aircraft corporations were at one stage forced to buy British planes to help the aircraft industry, instead of American planes that would have made the airlines more competitive; a nationalized steel firm has been refused permission to import American coal, which was cheaper than any it could buy in Britain; the Central Electricity Generating Board has been told by the Department of Energy whether its power stations will be fuelled by coal, oil or nuclear power.

There is no question about the power of Whitehall in its relationships with all these other administrative authorities. A local authority that refuses to obey a ministry directive can be brought to heel by the immediate suspension of its grant, without which it cannot finance its activities. A public corporation that declines to co-operate finds that its capital projects are not approved and its chairman is subject to abrupt dismissal, a fate that has befallen two of the chairmen of British Airways in recent years.

The Whitehall departments, staffed and organized in the way described in the previous chapter, thus sit at the centre of the administrative system. Considered in historical terms, one of the most remarkable features of this system is how little the process of central decision-making has changed in the past century. The size of the Civil Service has grown by a multiple of about twenty and it is supplemented by a vast and complex array of semi-autonomous agencies, but the crucial decisions are still made by two or three hundred top officials in Whitehall who know each other personally and are in constant communication with one another. Heclo and Wildavsky have described the world of these top administrators as a village, whose inhabitants are linked by networks of gossip as well as business relationships, and where everyone has a good idea of what everyone else is doing (Heclo and Wildavsky, 1974, chs. 1, 3). It is quite different from the divided world of federal administration in the United States. There is no danger in Britain of departments working at cross-purposes, either through ignorance or because of rivalry. Differences of opinion and interest naturally occur, but they are resolved at the top rather than reflected in the pursuit of inconsistent policies.

A vitally important role in the process of central co-ordination is played by the Treasury. The power of the Treasury depends on its control of expenditure. Government departments cannot do much without spending money, and all expenditures are subject to the prior approval of the Treasury. Each year each department prepares detailed estimates of proposed expenditure for the following year, and these are discussed in detail with Treasury officials and are rarely approved without reductions being made. Moreover, no provision for a new service or new development may even be included in the estimates unless the department has secured the prior approval of the Treasury for it in writing.

Once the estimates are accepted the department is tied to them, and cannot transfer money saved under one subhead for use elsewhere unless the Treasury agrees. If there is a prospect of overspending on any subhead, the department must immediately inform the Treasury, when a decision will be taken as to whether the department should cut expenditure, should transfer money from some other subhead, or should apply for a supplementary estimate. To emphasize its control of the purse-strings, the Treasury doles out money to each department in a monthly allowance that is carefully calculated to ensure that the departments never have very much in hand.

The departments do not always accept Treasury rulings without argument, and if officials feel that Treasury decisions are not in the interest of good government they will put the matter to their minister. He may then raise it with the Chancellor of the Exchequer, and if agreement cannot be reached between them they may take the whole problem to the Cabinet. Cabinet discussions of this kind are not uncommon, and the outcome may depend on the relative political strengths of the ministers involved as well as on the merits of the issue. But Cabinet decisions are binding and are invariably accepted by all parties. A minister has no choice but to accept or resign; civil servants have no further discretion in the matter, and stoically accept what has been decided.

The Cabinet settles differences between ministers not only over finance but also over the application of government policy and the situations that arise when the policies of one department affect the interests of another. The Cabinet is the highest agency of co-ordination and must be prepared to discuss conflict until agreement is reached – not always unanimous agreement, but agreement that can be accepted by the minority as 'the sense of the meeting'.

Consultation and Advice

As explained in Chapter 7, it is the normal practice of government departments to consult representatives of affected interests before taking decisions. One reason for this is that civil servants need specialized information about the practices and problems of the group involved. A representative association is the most convenient source of such information, and even if a government department decides to collect its own data, for instance by requiring firms to make regular returns of production, the officials will need to consult the appropriate trade association about how to draw up the questionnaire. Another reason is that consultation often helps to ensure that the decisions of the department will be accepted by members of the trade or profession concerned, and that their co-operation will be forthcoming. A third point is that organized groups often act as a buffer or filter between Whitehall and the various interests, firms and individuals represented by the group, who might otherwise inundate the department concerned with letters of protest and contradictory expressions of view about what should be done. For all those reasons regular consultation with group spokesmen is now regarded as a principle of good government.

The advantages of this practice to the group spokesmen are obvious. It enables them to press the claims of their groups before decisions are taken, which is much more useful than the ability to protest after the event. It also establishes their status in the eyes of members of the group, so that their position as an organization is made secure. Of course, the privileges such spokesmen enjoy in Whitehall imply certain unwritten obligations. They are expected to maintain the confidential nature of some discussions and to respect the anonymity of civil servants; they may feel that if they fail to gain their point they ought to accept failure gracefully rather than launch a public attack on the ministry; they often slide into the role of an intermediary between the ministry and the more demanding members of the group they represent. It is natural for an organization that becomes an established channel of communication to transmit messages in both directions, and occasionally this leads the more impatient or radical members of a group to feel that their spokesmen have become excessively responsible and moderate. Some motorists feel that the AA and the RAC have moved in this direction; some animal-lovers feel the same about the RSPCA.

One of the features of this system of consultation is that each department has its own set of client organizations, mainly representing groups with common interests but sometimes representing groups with shared attitudes. Thus, the Department of Trade and Industry deals mainly with trade associations; the Ministry of Transport deals with the Road Haulage Association, the AA and the RAC, the Traders' Road Transport Association, the Transport Workers' Union and the three unions of railway workers; the Ministry of Agriculture and Fisheries deals with the National Farmers' Union, the British Trawlers' Federation, and the Country Landowners' Association; the Home Office deals with the Howard League for Penal Reform, the National Council for Civil Liberties and organizations representing immigrants; the Department of Education and Science deals with the National Union of Teachers, the Association of Municipal Corporations and the Association of Education Committees. If no organization exists to represent an interest, the government department concerned may sponsor one. Thus in 1956 the Forestry Commission stated that it was prepared to give a substantial sum to assist the establishment of a Woodland Owners' Association to represent the interests of private owners; in 1959 a grant of £30,000 was included in the commission's estimates for this purpose (with the approval of the Treasury); and a few months later the new association was reported to be urging the government not to accept any large increase in timber imports from the Soviet Union (Potter, 1961, p. 32). Equally, the government may take action to reduce the number of organizations representing an interest if they are inconveniently numerous; in 1945 'the Ministry of Works took the initiative in setting up a National Council of Building Producers, bringing together forty-one separate trade associations for common action in dealing with the Department' (Grove, 1962, p. 146).

This feature of British government is of constitutional as well as administrative importance. There is no theory or model of the constitution that takes account of the practice of consultation between government departments and the spokesmen for organized groups. Traditional theories of the constitution suggest that the influence of the citizen on the process of government is secured solely through the House of Commons, either by the general impact of elections or by the specific means of an approach to an MP, who then approaches or questions the relevant minister. In practice the citizen who wants action from the government does not normally go to his MP. He may do this, but he is more likely to raise the matter through an organized group whose spokesmen will deal directly with Whitehall. Such groups cover all activities and all categories of the population. Newly born babies cannot organize themselves, but their mothers or prospective mothers can join the Association for the Improvement of Maternity Services; parents who are dissatisfied with the provision of playing-fields for children can approach the Central Council of Physical Recreation; students discontented with their grants can ask the National Union of Students to make further representations; workers unhappy about safety precautions at the factory can approach their trade union; shopkeepers' interests are defended by the Association of British Chambers of Commerce; consumers' interests are protected by the British Standards Association and the Consumer's Association;

old people, disabled people, ex-servicemen and other groups all have spokes-men who enjoy access to government departments. This is clearly one of the central features of the modern British constitution.

Having said this, it should be added that the constitutional status of officials (i.e. their position as servants of the Crown and the minister) affects the form taken by the discussions, which are usually described as a process of consul-tation even when they are in reality a process of bargaining. One former civil servant has written about them in the following terms:

> The conversation will preserve all proper forms. The unofficials will inquire of the official, not 'Will you agree to this?' but 'Do you think the minister will agree?' The official replies: 'No, I feel sure he won't go as far as that; but I think he will probably consent to do so much, on the understanding that the rest is left over until next year.' The unofficials answer: 'Well, we think we can persuade our people to be content with that for the present.' And they part with mutual expressions of affection and esteem, each side understanding perfectly that pledges have been given and received to the effect that the department will go some way to meet its unofficial critics, and that the critics will make no trouble in the House of Commons or elsewhere because it does not at once go the whole way.
>
> (Dale, 1941, pp. 182–3)

Apart from consultation with group spokesmen, government departments also rely heavily on advisory committees. At the last count there were almost a thousand permanent (but unpaid) committees advising the departments in London, together with an almost uncountable number of local committees. Many of the members of these committees are drawn from the ranks of group spokesmen, who thus get a further opportunity to advance their views. Other members are technical experts, civil servants and independent laymen. Thus, when the Cinematograph Films Council was set up to advise the President of the Board of Trade its twenty-two members comprised four representatives of film producers, two of film renters, five of exhibitors, four of employees in the industry and seven independent members (including the chairman) of whom some were experts and some were laymen (Wheare, 1955, p. 57). In this case only the secretary was a civil servant, though often one or two officials are included in the committee. The reports of these advisory committees are not normally published; their function is simply to make specialized information and informed recommendations available to the departments.

In addition, special committees to inquire and to advise are frequently appointed, sometimes being known simply as committees and sometimes being given the status of Royal Commissions. These committees differ from the permanent advisory committees in that they are much more likely to contain a preponderance of independent members, who may have experience in the field of activity under consideration but are not appointed as representatives of groups. Committees of this kind hear evidence from interested parties and sometimes commission specialists to conduct studies on their behalf. Thus, the Royal Commission on Population commissioned economists and demographers to make predictions about population trends, and the Robbins Committee on Higher Education had studies made of several problems. The reports of committees of inquiry are normally published.

Committees of this kind are appointed for a variety of reasons. Sometimes a department realizes that something has to be done and appoints a committee as the best way of getting informed advice about what is needed. Sometimes a department has a delicate problem on its hands and wants a committee, for whose work the government takes no responsibility, to examine the alternatives and make recommendations. An example is the Committee on Homosexual Offences and Prostitution, which interviewed homosexuals and whose report caused a great deal of controversy. Sometimes a department wants to prepare Parliament and public opinion for a reform that officials and the minister consider desirable and appoints a committee partly so that the evidence in favour of the reform can be mustered and the need for the reform can be endorsed by an independent body. As Enoch Powell said, a minister may feel: 'There is a big change to be made here, quite clearly, or a big advance. It will be much easier to commend it to Parliament and the country if I have set up a group of reasonable beings, well experienced and so on, and they have come to that conclusion' (Hunt, 1964, p. 48). An example is the Royal Commission on Betting, Lotteries and Gaming, whose recommendations led to the legalization of off-the-course betting in cash and the establishment of betting shops all over the country.

Sometimes committees of inquiry are appointed without any serious expectation that their reports will be acted upon. They are appointed to pacify critics, examples being the Royal Commission on the Press of 1947 and the Royal Commission on Equal Pay for Men and Women in 1948. They are appointed to buy time, a possible example being the Royal Commission on Marriage and Divorce of 1951. Finally, they may be appointed to kill a proposal by demonstrating its disadvantages or by taking it out of the public eye: a possible example of this being the Palestine Partition Committee of 1938, whose report helped to kill the plan of partition that a former committee had proposed. But it is probably fair to say that most committees of inquiry lead to some kind of action sooner or later, even though it is unusual for a committee's recommendations to be adopted *in toto*.

It should be clear by now that, although leading civil servants are rarely specialists, neither they nor their ministers need lack specialized advice. It is pressed on them from all sides, and the custom is for government departments to welcome this. Quite apart from their need for information, it is in accordance with the traditional role of the British Civil Service that other people should come forward with controversial proposals, leaving officials with the task of giving their ministers discreet and anonymous advice on the merits of the alternative courses of action that are open.

Decision-Making and Policy

It is part of the familiar theory of British government that ministers take decisions and officials simply give advice. While this was never entirely true, it was much nearer the truth in the latter part of the nineteenth century than it is today. When departments were small, ministers could be personally acquainted with all issues of any importance. But this is no longer the case; the Civil Service is about twenty times as big as it was a hundred years ago and there are only about three times as many ministers. Now about forty ministers, helped by about fifty junior ministers, control the work of about 500,000 officials. The great majority of decisions are clearly taken without reference to a minister.

Within the Civil Service there is a well-established hierarchy of decision-making, so that a principal knows what he can decide on his own account and what he must refer up to an assistant secretary. In Whitehall one of the basic techniques of administration is the rotating file, which is carried from out-tray to in-tray by a small army of uniformed messengers. When a file reaches the official who is impowered to decide on the case he does so unless it poses a special problem of one kind or another, which is quite rare in some departments (e. g. the Department of Social Security) but quite common in others (e. g. the Foreign Office). The special problems that arise out of day-to-day administration are the seeds from which many changes of policy develop.

One kind of problem is the possibility of conflict with another department. Questions about the school dental service raise the possibility of conflict, or at any rate differences of opinion, between the Department of Health and the Department of Education and Science. Questions about regional unemployment involve both the Department of Trade and Industry and the Department of Employment. In these and similar cases the civil servant must consult his opposite number in the other department before taking action. They may be able to settle the matter between them. But, if it is not as easy as that, each must refer the matter to his departmental superior. Sometimes issues between departments can then be settled by an informal conference or a committee; in other cases this is not possible and the files go right up the hierarchy to the permanent secretaries and perhaps the ministers, with each official on the way adding his comments in the form of a minute.

Another kind of problem arises where the implementation of policy gives rise to ambiguities or to developments that had not been expected. To take a rather trivial example, local authorities were for years empowered to pay vacation grants to undergraduates following a course of vacation study. Some authorities interpreted this to mean a course that was physically supervised by tutors, while others paid grants for a course of home reading that was prescribed in advance. The result was that students in similar circumstances were sometimes treated differently, and in 1971 the Department of Education and Science transferred the administration of these grants from local authorities to universities.

Yet another kind of problem arises when the implementation of a routine decision seems likely to create political controversy. Thus, the decision to construct concrete lamp standards in front of a row of country houses took on a special significance when it was realized that one of the houses was owned by the President of the Royal Academy, an outspoken opponent of modern street furniture. In cases like this the department is likely to be mentioned in the press and questions may be asked in Parliament. The wise official will draw the attention of his superiors to such cases (an activity known in Whitehall as 'putting up an umbrella') so that they can be sure of their ground and be prepared to defend themselves against a possible storm of criticism.

Important questions arising from the administrative process reach the permanent secretary, who must decide whether or not to put them before the minister. This decision again depends on how far it impinges on other questions of policy with which the minister is grappling. A permanent secretary will not want to worry his minister unnecessarily, but he will try to keep him in touch with the questions that may lead to criticism. The minister, unlike the officials, has to deal with questions in Parliament, in press conferences and in public meetings, and he will not want to be caught off guard because he is ignorant of one of the problems of his department.

The minister, in his turn, has to decide whether to take matters to the Cabinet. Clearly he will have to do so if he cannot reach agreement with another minister, for the Cabinet is the only place in which differences of this kind can be solved. Apart from this, he will take matters to the Cabinet if they are intrinsically important or if they are likely to cause a major political row. All proposals for legislation are normally referred to the Cabinet, for even if they are not controversial in themselves they will take up parliamentary time and a case must be made for their priority. Developments that will affect the reputation of the government should be brought to the attention of the Cabinet, which is a meeting of party leaders as well as a meeting of departmental heads. Thus, when a new government takes office a minister may find that for administrative reasons it is impossible to achieve something to which his party had committed itself in the election, and this must be reported to his colleagues. Topics that arouse great public interest will tend to appear on the Cabinet agenda for a similar reason, though they may be disposed of quickly. Finally, ministers will take to the Cabinet all those knotty problems that are virtually insoluble but are likely to be used as a stick with which to belabour the government. One former Cabinet minister has said that 'most of the Cabinet's time is spent in dealing with matters which are insoluble, in the sense that there are serious disadvantages attaching to any possible course of action' (Hunt, 1964, p. 56). Notable examples in recent years include the position of Rhodesia between 1964 and 1979 and the crisis in Northern Ireland from 1969 onwards.

The agenda of cabinet meetings is controlled by the Prime Minister. The Cabinet secretariat is responsible for circulating papers, and when an item is reached the minister concerned speaks to it. The other members then speak and the Prime Minister eventually declares the sense of the meeting, no vote being taken. The style and character of Cabinet meetings depend partly on the personality of the Prime Minister. We learn from memoirs that Churchill was loquacious and sometimes rather arbitrary, allowing lengthy discussions on some items but dismissing others very briefly. We learn that Attlee, in contrast, was quiet, concise, methodical and sometimes extremely curt. We know that Thatcher is rather domineering. But these are variations within limits that are set by the pressure of business, by the influence of the secretary of the Cabinet (who is a senior civil servant) and by the traditions that all Prime Ministers respect.

So far policy-making has been discussed as if all policy questions arose out of the ordinary business of administration. In fact the majority of policy questions arise in this way. Even when a team of new ministers take office after defeating the previous government what they normally do is deal with existing departmental problems with a rather different emphasis, not come into their departments with a sheaf of new policies under their arms. Harold Laski once said that the task of a minister is to 'inject a stream of tendency' into the decisions of his department, and although the phrase is inelegant it is quite appropriate.

Other policy decisions have their origins in the ideas of ministers or the Cabinet. Some examples are the decisions to nationalize certain industries after 1945, to create a completely free National Health Service in 1946, to develop commercial television in 1954, to abolish resale price maintenance in 1963, to impose a capital gains tax in 1965, to regulate industrial relations by law in 1971 and to compel local authorities to offer council housing for sale to tenants in 1979. In cases like these the minister will get the authority of the Cabinet to draw up detailed proposals; he will discuss the idea with his senior officials, who may already have thought about alternative methods of achieving the object; and a specific set of plans will be worked out in the department. The minister will then ask the Cabinet for approval of these plans, which he must be prepared to defend against probing questions from his colleagues, who may seek to anticipate the criticisms that will be made in Parliament and in the country. If approval is given, it is then a matter for more detailed work in the department and for the preparation of legislation if that is required. If the Cabinet does not approve, the minister will have to think again, or may have to abandon the proposals for the time being. Occasionally a minister resigns when his proposals are rejected, but politicians acquire thick skins in the course of their careers, and resignations on this ground are infrequent.

Problems and Controversies

The British central administration is well organized and thoroughly co-ordinated. It operates with impressive smoothness. However, this does not mean that it is free from problems or that its policy outputs are necessarily successful. To take the most conspicuous example of failure, Britain has experienced relative economic decline in the postwar years and has moved from being one of the richest of the advanced industrial countries to being one of the poorest. In 1950 Britain was the third most prosperous country in Europe, surpassed only by neutral Sweden and Switzerland, but by 1980 its ranking had fallen to twelfth. Since the government has so much influence over the economy, successive governments have had to accept a share of the responsibility for this sad story. And within governmental circles, there has been a tendency for politicians to lay part of the blame on the administrative machine.

It is important to realize that these expressions of concern have come from politicians of varying ideological commitments. The most vociferous critics have been on the extreme left, with Tony Benn (of the 'hard left' within the Labour Party) saying repeatedly that civil servants obstruct radical initiatives and prevent Labour governments from achieving the policies set out in their election manifesto. However, from the centre-left Shirley Williams (one of the founders of the Social Democratic Party) has said something rather similar: 'The trouble with the civil service is that it's essentially a negative machine, that it exists to try to stop things happening' (quoted in Fry, 1984, p. 359). From the centre-right, Lord Boyle, a former Conservative Minister of Education, told this author in 1974 that: 'Being political head of a department is like making a journey in a Rolls-Royce; it's a remarkable machine, but you are not allowed to drive it yourself.' From the fairly far right Sir John Hoskyns has written of a 'leadership vacuum' at the heart of government, where 'a deeply pessimistic civil service looks for political leadership ... to a tiny handful of exhausted ministers. Those same ministers look in vain to their officials to provide policy options which, to be any use, would have to be too "politically controversial" for the officials to think of' (quoted ibid., pp. 356–7).

The defence of the system would take the form that it ensures stable and consistent government. Civil servants have the duty of warning their ministers that some policy proposals would be impracticable or excessively expensive. The general secretary of the First Division Association has put this very bluntly: 'The civil service provides an important and unique stabilizing role ... It is absolute nonsense to pretend, as some politicians do, that electorates vote for governments to implement their policies in full' (quoted in F. Ridley, 1983, p. 44). It follows that, although the values of commentators vary, there is not much doubt about the way the system operates.

Stability and consistency are virtues in themselves; the vital question is whether their pursuit has prevented the implementation of policies that would have benefited the British economy. This is a very hard question to answer, both because it is difficult to disentangle the precise responsibility for policies that have been adopted or abandoned and because economists are not agreed about what ought to have been done. The postwar British economy has not been a planned economy; it has been a system of (largely) free enterprise subject to four types of governmental control or intervention. First, the government has used monetary and fiscal powers to control the overall level of demand;

secondly, some basic industries have been nationalized; thirdly, regional policies have been pursued in order to help the areas of industrial decline; and fourthly, a great deal of public money has been put into subsidies of various kinds. If economic policies of these four types are considered one by one, it is possible to set out the framework for an analysis of government policies, though difficult to provide more than a very tentative assessment of them.

Policies of Monetary Management

Discussions of monetary policy have been sharpened since the Conservative victory of 1979 by conflicts between those who favour the theories of J. M. Keynes (the Labour, Liberal and Social Democratic parties, plus many Conservatives) and those who prefer the theories of Milton Friedman (Margaret Thatcher and her supporters). In fact, this theoretical disagreement may be less important than it has recently appeared to be. Friedman's main contribution has been to re-emphasize traditional theories rather than to formulate new ones. These traditional theories, emphasizing the virtues of a balanced budget, returned to fashion because changing economic circumstances made them appropriate, not because of intellectual arguments. Fiscal policies based loosely on Keynesian ideas worked tolerably well from 1945 to 1973, when the British economy was thrown off balance by the coincidence of several developments that were unrelated and largely unpredictable.

The essence of Keynesian policy, it will be recalled, is that aggregate demand should be expanded during periods of recession, by fiscal and credit policies that will result in a budgetary deficit but will also boost the economy and reduce unemployment. In times of boom, on the other hand, more restrictive monetary policies should be adopted, which will prevent the economy overheating (with consequent problems for the international balance of payments) and will provide a budgetary surplus to control inflationary tendencies. Pursuing these policies was known as 'fine-tuning the economy', and the Treasury did this in a very competent way. The 'stop–go' impact of the policies made the investment climate somewhat unstable, so that a price was paid for the benefits of fine-tuning, but the leaders of all political parties and most economists thought at the time that this was a price worth paying.

In January 1973 Britain entered the European Economic Community, and in anticipation of economic gains from this move the Heath government led the country in what was called a 'dash for growth'. Changes in the law regarding financial transactions led to a large expansion of credit facilities, which had inflationary implications. The government hoped that inflation would be contained partly by a growth in industrial output and partly by a national incomes policy that limited pay rises. Unfortunately, the dash for growth lasted only until October 1973, when the Arab–Israeli war led first to an interruption of oil supplies and then to their resumption at four times the previous price. These developments disrupted the economies of the entire Western world, and the British economy (always vulnerable because of its dependence on trade) suffered more than most. Unfortunately also, Heath's incomes policy was sabotaged by a miners' strike in the winter of 1973–4. Heath felt it desirable to fight an election on this issue and lost it, so that the incoming Labour government felt committed to abandoning the incomes policy and permitting a general scramble for wage and salary increases. The result was an inflation rate of over 24 per cent in 1975, and a subsequent need for policies of severe financial restraint.

These policies – which would undoubtedly have been recommended by Keynes had he still been alive – were first imposed by the Labour government under Callaghan, and were then sharpened by the Conservatives under Thatcher. The ideological difference between Thatcher's supporters and all the other political groups is that the former regard financial restraint as a desirable long-term policy, to avoid inflation, reduce the burden of public expenditure and sharpen the competitive edge of British industry, whereas the latter regard it as (at best) a temporary expedient that had outlived its usefulness by 1981 or 1982. There is no doubt that financial restraint has helped to control inflation, while also leading to an increase in unemployment. Productivity has improved in the sense that a smaller industrial workforce is producing more goods, but in the older industrial sectors there have been many bankruptcies.

These monetary policies may or may not have been entirely desirable. In the context of this chapter, what is perfectly clear is that they have been planned by a handful of senior ministers, influenced by broad economic developments and executed faithfully by the Treasury and other government departments.

Public Ownership

The second type of economic policy of which we should take note is the nationalization of certain industries and the subsequent control of their activities. The motives for taking industrial concerns into public ownership have been mixed: to provide an efficient supply of fuel and power to the whole country; because private enterprise could not provide the capital needed for the industry, as in the case of railways; for ideological reasons, as with steel; to save private firms from the normal consequences of bankruptcy, as with Rolls-Royce and British Leyland. Whatever the motives, the operation of these industries has been similar to that of a private monopoly (or private competitive firm in the case of Rolls-Royce, British Leyland and several smaller outfits, like Cook's Tours or the railway hotels). The Labour Party has never developed a distinctively socialist policy for running nationalized industries. (For a fuller discussion of these questions see Thompson, 1984.) There has been an increasing amount of ministerial intervention in the activities of the industries but the motives for this have also been mixed, and it would be misleading to describe them as socialist motives.

In these circumstances, the criteria for assessing the performance of the main nationalized industries must be similar to those that might be used for the assessment of private industry, namely efficiency and profitability. In these terms, it can be said that in three of the main industries – electricity supply, gas supply and air transport – the story is one of unqualified success. The Thatcher government has privatized these industries, but this is because of a general commitment to private enterprise rather than because of any perceived failings in them. The steel industry, nationalized in the 1960s, suffered a cruel blow in the 1979–83 period, when excess capacity throughout the world made it necessary for production to be concentrated in five large plants and for a number of smaller plants to be shut down. Slightly more than 60 per cent of the workers lost their jobs in this process of rationalization. The plans of the European Community point to a further reduction from five plants to four, but the government has resisted this proposal so far on the ground that the threatened plant is in a high unemployment region of Scotland.

The two nationalized industries that have led to political controversy are the railways and coal-mining. Both were under-capitalized when taken over by the state, both have received massive injections of public money for investment and both need annual subsidies on current account. The position of the railways is similar to their position in all other European countries; they are generally thought to be essential but they cannot possibly cover their costs. The controversies in Britain have arisen because of the refusal of railway unions to accept certain proposals to increase productivity, and because of other proposals designed to reduce losses by closing down branch lines in rural areas. The ministry responsible for railways has twice commissioned a consultant to prepare plans for rationalization, but on each occasion most of the recommended closures have been abandoned in face of opposition from unions and rural residents. The unions have had support from the Labour Party and the rural residents from the Conservative Party, so that a rough kind of equilibrium obtains. This issue has probably produced more heat than it is really worth, in view of the relatively small potential savings projected.

The question of the coal-mines involves larger issues. They suffer from falling demand that has fallen at a greater rate than was predicted. In round figures, the mines produced about 250 million tons of coal per year in the 1950s; were expected to level off in the 1960s with an annual production of 200 million tons; and by 1984 were down to 100 million tons, which was slightly more than could be sold. The other problem is that many of the mines suffer from decreasing productivity because their once-rich seams are now narrow and almost worked out.

The obvious answer to these problems is to close the less economic pits, but this policy is so resisted by the National Union of Mineworkers that the National Coal Board has had to proceed with great caution. In 1984 the proposal to close twenty uneconomic pits, out of a total of two hundred, led to a national strike lasting twelve months before the union capitulated. The strike was called in spite of the fact that redundant workers under the age of 50 were promised jobs in other pits and those over that age were offered redundancy payments on a scale more generous than that available in any other sector of British industry. The strike was carried on despite bitter divisions within the workforce, with 35,000 men working throughout and far more than that joining them in the last three months of the strike. The working miners were attacked by pickets and protected by police; three men were killed and hundreds injured; and over 6,000 pickets were arrested for obstruction or violence. The whole affair displayed British industrial relations at their worst.

The politics and sociology of coal-mining are fascinating to the observer who can remain detached. The miners remain emotionally attached to their dirty and dangerous work, living in closed communities, forming almost a class of their own and deeply reluctant to change jobs, to move to a newer pit, or even to commute as far as tens of thousands of London office workers commute each day as a matter of course. They are a living symbol of industrial obsolescence and resistance to change. Governments up till 1984 have been afraid of the miners because of their ability to cut off supplies to electricity power stations, but also reluctant to place the country at the mercy of the Arab states by switching to oil-fired generating plants and unwilling to face the environmental and political costs of going over to nuclear plants. The issue has been perceived not only in terms of cost but also as a choice between different types of anxiety.

It is one of the achievements of the Thatcher government to have grasped this nettle. Power stations were prepared for the anticipated strike not only by building up coal stocks but also by the installation of extra equipment to enable some of them to be switched from coal to oil. Underwater cables are being laid to connect the British and French electricity grids, which will enable French electricity (produced mainly by nuclear power) to be bought in a future emergency. New nuclear power stations are being planned. Paradoxically, it is a Conservative government showing ideological hostility to economic planning that has made more effective use than its recent predecessors of the power to make plans for the fuel and power industries.

Regional Policies and Industrial Subsidies

What are known in Britain as regional policies are a group of measures designed to attract new or expanding industrial concerns to areas suffering from the decline of their basic industries. It was decided to proceed in this way immediately after the Second World War. During the 1930s unemployed workers in areas of this kind, known as 'depressed areas', were offered removal grants to take themselves to more prosperous parts of the country in search of work. In 1945, however, it was stated by the government that henceforth every effort would be made to 'take work to the people' instead.

The policy rested upon both negative controls and positive incentives. Every employer planning to build industrial premises of more than so many square feet in area had to secure a certificate from the Board of Trade (subsequently the Department of Trade and Industry), and this certificate was not readily granted for expansion in the prosperous areas of southern England and the Midlands. Firms were put under strong pressure to move to Scotland, Wales, or northern England as an alternative. The incentives varied from time to time, consisting variously of tax allowances if investment was made in a 'development area', actual grants for investment in such areas and the provision of empty buildings for rental at a low rent to industrialists.

These policies were successful in the sense that more employment was created in the development areas than would otherwise have been the case. Whether this benefit was worth the overall cost to the country is very doubtful indeed. In the postwar years, Britain has been the only one of the Western industrial states to have deliberately restricted the growth of what would naturally have been its most progressive and prosperous industrial areas. In the case of London, an engineering centre where productivity per worker is higher than anywhere else, government policies have driven industry away and have resulted in an overall reduction of the population by about 12 per cent. The West Midlands, as the main centre of the British car industry, has suffered because several applications to expand the industry there were rejected, in support of a policy to scatter car production around the peripheral areas of the country. The economic cost of these policies has been very high.

One of the problems of pursuing a sensible regional policy in Britain is that there are no regional institutions with authority to draw up plans and press for their implementation. Consider the case of the industrial North-west, where the Industrial Revolution started in the late eighteenth century with the manufacture of cotton cloth and where clothing and fabric industries have grown up on the basis of cotton. It was clear from the 1920s onwards that the competitive position of the British cotton industry would eventually be destroyed by the use of cheap labour in Asian countries to produce similar goods. At no time has there been an effective agency to plan for the redevelopment of the North-west. The Cotton Board has served as a spokesman for the existing cotton firms, and has been concerned to prolong their life as long as possible and to secure government grants to make redundancy payments to workers when production had to end. Local MPs have been concerned to look after their individual constituencies, rather than the region as a whole. The various municipalities have also had parochial interests, and in any case are unable either to spend much money on economic development or to exert much pressure on the government.

As it happens, Terylene was invented by scientists in the North-west in 1942. This opened up the possibility of establishing an artificial fibre industry in the region, which could supply a modified clothing industry. However, this being wartime, the patent was sold to Dupont of America, who subsequently established a large world market (including Britain) for the product, under the trade name of Dacron. When nylon factories were established in Britain they were sited not in the North-west but in other parts of the country, such as South Wales, which did not have clothing or fabric industries. Possibly this contributed to the fact that the collapse of the cotton industry was accompanied by the decline of the associated textile industries. In thirty years Britain has moved from being a net exporter of clothing to being a net importer, getting clothes from Italy and France as well as from low-cost countries like Hong Kong. The collapse of cotton has also been accompanied by the collapse of the region's major port, Liverpool – which now has the highest unemployment rate of any city in England.

British governments are not directly responsible for this unfortunate chain of events, but they should certainly bear part of the blame. If they accepted responsibility for helping areas of economic decline, which they did, why did they not prepare a plan to help the North-west? The answer is partly that the Civil Service, as presently constituted, does not have the personnel or the capacity for this kind of planning; partly that governments have not set up alternative structures that might have this capacity. The result is that regional policies have hindered the operation of free enterprise without gaining the advantages that might have flowed from economic planning.

Industrial subsidies have been given under various programmes ever since 1945. It is an unfortunate fact that more money has gone to firms in trouble than to prime the pump for expanding firms, but political pressures from both sides of industry have combined with the wish to avoid unemployment to produce this effect. In the absence of any long-lived agency for economic planning, insulated to some degree from day-to-day political pressures, this result was difficult to avoid.

Some of these grants have done little more than prolong the agony of failure, an example being the money given to obsolete shipyards on the Clyde. Other grants have helped industrial concerns to tide over a period of difficulty, from which they have recovered. An interesting example is that of British Leyland, which has received enormous sums of money since it was taken into public ownership in 1975, but which eventually started to show a profit in 1984. To some extent, the Thatcher government has used British Leyland to demonstrate two propositions that are dear to its heart: that dynamic management can tame the trade unions and that modern technology (in this case the use of robots) can transform industrial productivity.

Other grants again have been proposed or given to help new firms or new projects to get under way. The record here is somewhat mixed, as the judgement of politicians and civil servants has sometimes proved good and sometimes proved poor. An interesting example of poor judgement occurred in the immediate aftermath of the war. An Army intelligence unit surveying German industry proposed that Britain should get the Volkswagen plans and plant as part of its war reparations. British car firms looked this gift horse in the mouth and turned it down on the ground that the car would not sell, and the

Labour government declined to set up the plant under public ownership for similar reasons.

Another peculiar decision was made in the car industry in 1975, when the government agreed to pay Chrysler a sizeable sum to continue to operate its uneconomic plants in Britain, apparently because one of the plants was in an area of high unemployment near Glasgow. As there was excess capacity in the car industry this was done at the expense of other British car manufacturers as well as at some cost to taxpayers. When the Peugeot concern took over Chrysler's European operations two or three years later, Peugeot's first action was to close down the Glasgow plant and auction off its machinery.

Yet another costly decision was made when the government agreed to finance the design and manufacture of Concorde, which was a certain loss-maker from the beginning. Every plane that is sold involves a loss to British Aerospace, while every normal scheduled flight of Concorde involves a loss to British Airways.

However, there have also been numerous success stories. Action under the Labour government of 1964–70 resulted in saving a British computer industry that is independent of American control. The National Enterprise Board, established in 1975, has helped a number of firms by providing loans to tide them over difficult periods or giving them injections of capital in return for blocks of shares. This board was also responsible for taking Britain into the enterprise of manufacturing microchips, establishing for this purpose a firm called Imnos.

One example of regional policy is that when Imnos proposed to establish its first manufacturing plant in Bristol, the home of Concorde and a city noted for advanced technology, this proposal was rejected by the government in favour of a site in South Wales, where unemployment was higher. This discrimination against the Bristol area is reminiscent of the refusal of the 1964 Labour government to provide money for the modernization of the port of Bristol, on the explicit ground that this might damage the interests of the nearby industrial areas of South Wales. It is clear that Bristol, along with Birmingham, Coventry and London itself, has suffered seriously from the centralization of economic policy-making in Whitehall. There is repeated evidence of a bias against centres of potential growth that was common to both Conservative and Labour administrations up to the 1980s.

In the 1980s regional policy has been wound down and industry has been permitted to expand in the areas of its choice. The result has been a remarkable boom in high technology industries located in southern England combined with a partial recovery of the West Midlands, but a growth of long-term unemployment in the older industrial areas of northern England and Scotland. The national economy as a whole has benefited, but at the expense of decay and poverty in the areas of industrial decline.

Conclusion

These comments on government economic policies have had to be kept brief because this is a book about British government rather than one about the British economy. It is hoped that the comments nevertheless give an impression of some of the policies that have been pursued and of the strengths and weaknesses of the British administrative system in formulating and implementing them.

Further Reading

For a general account of the administrative system see Brown and Steel (1979), *The Administrative Process in Britain*; for a penetrating analysis of the role of the Treasury see Heclo and Wildavsky (1974), *The Private Government of Public Money*; for a valuable account of the policy-making process see Richardson and Jordan (1979), *Governing under Pressure*; for useful case studies of policy-making see Grant (1981), *The Political Economy of Industrial Policy*, R. Williams (1980), *The Nuclear Power Decisions: British Policies 1953–78*, and Richardson and Moon (1985), *Unemployment in the UK: Politics and Policies*.

◇ 12 ◇

Parliament and the Administration

Constitutional Theory

It is a basic principle of the British constitution that the function of Parliament is not to govern the country, but to control the government. As noted in Chapter 2, the responsibility for government and administration rests with the Queen's ministers, but developments in the past three centuries have rendered them accountable to Parliament (and in particular to the House of Cornmons) for most, though not all, of their actions. Parliament is, in fact, the only institution that has power to control the actions of government departments, provided their officials do not break the law. There is no equivalent in Britain of the United States Supreme Court or the German Constitutional Court, both of which have power to declare executive actions contrary to constitutional principles. Nor does Britain have a system of administrative courts, like the French Conseil d'Etat or the Italian Consiglio di Stato, which can review administrative decisions and decide whether or not they were justified. In Britain government departments can do largely as they like, provided they have parliamentary approval and keep within the letter of the law. In constitutional theory there is a division, not of powers, but of functions, ministers being responsible for governing the country and Parliament being responsible for calling ministers to account as well as for legislation (which will be dealt with separately in the following chapter). The accountability of the government is said to be ensured by two constitutional conventions: the convention that ministers are collectively responsible to Parliament for the policy of the government as a whole and the convention that each minister is individually responsible to Parliament for the work of his department.

There is a degree of unreality about this constitutional theory, which assumes a dichotomy between the government on one hand and Parliament on the other. In fact nearly one hundred Members of Parliament at the present time are members of the government and more than two hundred other MPs are loyal supporters of the government. The real dichotomy in British politics is between the government and the Opposition, not between the government and Parliament. But this is not yet reflected in constitutional theory and it will be convenient in this chapter to begin by examining the established principles and conventions.

Collective Responsibility

The essence of this convention is (1) that members of the government should present a united front to Parliament in defence of their policies; and (2) that if the House of Commons defeats the government on a vote of confidence the Prime Minister should either ask the monarch for an immediate dissolution of Parliament or should resign, together with all his ministers. The convention was developed in the years between 1780 and 1832, and in the middle decades of the nineteenth century it led to the resignation of a series of governments. Between the first Reform Act of 1832 and the second Reform Act of 1867 no government survived for what is now regarded as a government's normal life, from a general election until the Prime Minister askes for a dissolution, at a time of his own choice, towards the end of that Parliament's allotted span. In this period the convention of collective responsibility was an effective weapon that ensured parliamentary control of the executive, and ten governments in thirty-five years were brought to an end by adverse votes in the House of Commons. It was largely on the evidence of this period that commentators and politicians based their claims, in the latter part of the century, that the British system of government was one in which the actions of the government were effectively controlled by Parliament.

In fact, even as these claims were gaining general acceptance, the development of party discipline was changing the situation. Between 1900 and 1979 only three governments were forced out of office as the result of parliamentary defeats. In January 1924 Liberal and Labour MPs joined forces to defeat the Conservative government (which had lost seats in a general election a few weeks earlier). The Conservative Prime Minister resigned and a minority Labour government was formed with Liberal support. In December 1924 the Liberals combined with the Conservatives to defeat the Labour government. The Prime Minister dissolved Parliament and the Conservatives won the ensuing election. In March 1979 the Labour government was defeated by the combined votes of Conservatives, Liberals, Scottish Nationalists and Ulster Unionists. This was followed by a dissolution and a Conservative victory in the election.

On these three occasions no single party commanded a majority in the House of Commons, so that the government of the day was at the mercy of the smaller parties, which held the balance of power. However, throughout the greater part of the present century the leading party has had an overall majority in the House of Commons, and party discipline has been so effective that no ruling party in that situation has been brought down by a vote of no confidence. This has held good even when the governing party has commanded only a tiny majority. The

Labour government of 1950–1 survived with a majority of only six, and the Labour government of 1964–6 got by with a majority that varied between four and one. The maintenance of a majority in the division lobbies in this kind of situation puts a severe strain on government supporters, who have to be prepared to attend no matter how inconvenient it is to them, even to the extreme of being brought into the precincts of Parliament by ambulance and being counted by the tellers while lying on a stretcher. But so far they have always measured up to these demands.

This does not mean that the convention of collective responsibility is obsolete, for clearly it still exists; a government that is defeated on a vote of confidence has no choice but to resign or to dissolve Parliament. But, as a general rule, governments in the twentieth century are defeated not by Parliament but by the electorate, and this affects the significance of the convention of collective responsibility. A government that faced the constant possibility of defeat in Parliament would be more likely to have to resign or ask for a dissolution when things were going badly for it than when things were going well; in this sense responsibility to Parliament would provide an immediate sanction for a failure of government policy. In the modern British political system this sanction is absent. As a general rule a government is not more likely to resign or dissolve Parliament when its policies meet with a major reversal than when it is prospering, but less likely to do so. The public has a short memory, and a government's best strategy in times of crisis is to ride the storm and hope that it will be able to recapture public support before the next general election is held. The Labour government of 1945–50 survived through the fuel crisis of 1947, the devaluation of the pound in 1948, the collapse of its Palestine policy in the same year and the fiasco of the groundnuts scheme in 1949. In 1950 it was returned to power, though with a reduced majority. The Conservative government of 1955–9 succeeded not only in surviving after the débâcle of Suez, but in winning an increased majority at the next general election. James Callaghan's government of 1976–9 tried desperately to stay in office until the parliamentary term came to an end in October 1979, in the hope that a good summer would induce the electorate to forget the hardships caused by industrial disruption during the previous winter.

The role of the convention of collective responsibility in British government may perhaps be summarized in the following terms. It does not provide a continuous sanction for the blunders and failures of government, as it did in the middle decades of the last century. On the other hand, it continues to play a vital role in the British political system, ensuring that governments resign immediately they lose their parliamentary majority in an election. On these admittedly rare occasions when the governing party leads the others by only a hair's breadth the convention may prompt the government to modify its plans, as in 1965 when the Labour government decided not to go ahead at that time with its declared policy of renationalizing the steel industry. At all times the convention gives some procedural advantage to the Opposition; if it puts down a motion of censure on the government, this has precedence over other parliamentary business, and the government will be obliged to rearrange the timetable to find time for it.

Finally, the convention compels ministers to maintain the appearance of unity; they are expected to resign from the government if they are not prepared to defend its policies in public. Instances are fairly rare, but the principle is undoubedly effective; in 1985 Michael Heseltine resigned from his post as Minster of Defence because he could not accept the Cabinet view that a British firm making military helicopters should be taken over by an American firm, and did not believe that his contrary view had been given a fair hearing. There have been one or two recent instances of ministers disagreeing in public, as in 1975 when Cabinet ministers opposed to British membership of the European Community were permitted to campaign for a negative vote in the referendum on that issue. But there is no general tendency for Prime Ministers to relax their insistence on unity.

Individual Responsibility

This convention has two strands, one of which is in full operation, the other of which is something of a myth. The first strand is that the minister in charge of a department is answerable to Parliament for all the actions of that department. As Gladstone said: 'In every free state, for every public act, some one must be responsible, and the question is, who shall it be? The British constitution answers: "the minister, and the minister exclusively"' (Gladstone, 1879, Vol. 1, p. 233). The positive aspect of this is that Members of Parliament wishing to query the actions of a department, either privately or publicly, know that there is one person who cannot evade the duty of answering their questions. The negative aspect of it is that it protects the anonymity of civil servants and shields them from political controversy. This strand of the convention can be seen on four days a week when Parliament is in session, for the first hour of each sitting is devoted to Question Time, at which ministers answer questions put to them in advance by MPs and have also to deal with supplementary questions that arise out of their answers.

According to the second strand of the convention, ministers must accept responsibility for the actions of their department not only in the sense that they must be ready to explain and defend them but also in the sense that they must resign their appointments if serious blunders or failures are exposed. This, at any rate, is what is implied by many commentators and what is widely thought to be part of the practice of British government.

In fact, resignations of this kind are extremely rare. Mistakes are constantly being made, and from time to time they are exposed or admitted, but it is exceptional for a minister to resign on this account. The most conspicuous failures of postwar British governments have led to stormy debates in

Parliament and to scathing comments in the press, but they have not led to the resignation of the ministers concerned. The total failure of British policy in Palestine between 1945 and 1948 did not lead the Foreign Secretary to think of resigning, even though he had said in a rash moment that he would stake his political future on his ability to deal with the problem. The fiasco of the groundnuts scheme in 1949 did not lead the Minister of Food to resign, though he was urged to do so by the opposition and the majority of newspapers. The humiliating collapse of British policy towards Egypt at the time of the Suez expedition was not followed by the resignation on political grounds of any of the ministers concerned, though ill-health forced the Prime Minister to resign a few weeks later. The waste of vast sums of public money on the design of missiles and aircraft that have never been produced has not led to the resignation of any of the Ministers of Aviation and Defence who were responsible for it. The list could be extended to include the various failures of economic policy in the past thirty years, the slaughter of eleven prisoners in a Mau-Mau detention camp in Kenya, the gross errors made in estimating the development costs of Concorde and many other examples.

Looking at the matter another way, S. E. Finer traced only sixteen cases of a minister resigning as the result of parliamentary criticism of his department between 1855 (when the first case occurred) and 1955 (Finer, 1956). Since there were no cases between 1955 and 1980, this makes sixteen cases in 125 years. The smallness of the number indicates that it is only in exceptional circumstances that failure leads to loss of office, and Finer suggested that what made these cases exceptional was not the gravity of the failures but, in general, the fact that the ministers had lost popularity or respect within their own party. However, in 1982 the Foreign Secretary, Lord Carrington, resigned because he and his advisers had failed to predict that Argentine forces would invade the Falkland Islands. Carrington's action was emphatically not an example of Finer's rule, as he was held in very high regard by his colleagues and he resigned in spite of personal requests from the Prime Minister that he should stay in office. Two more junior ministers at the Foreign Office resigned with him.

Of course, the exposure of departmental failings may affect a minister's career even though it does not lead to his resignation. In the next ministerial reshuffle he may find that he is transferred to a less attractive ministry or even relegated to the back benches. The point is that most failures do not have any such consequence, and whether they do or not is apt to depend more on the general standing of the minister with his party and Prime Minister than on the extent of parliamentary criticism. In view of this, it cannot be said that the convention of individual ministerial responsibility to Parliament renders the minister liable to loss of office if the work of his department comes under fire.

The first part of the convention, however, is of considerable importance. The fact that ministers have to answer for their departments gives MPs the right to demand information about administrative decisions, whether these be related to large issues of policy or to dealings with individual citizens. MPs frequently exercise this right, sometimes by questions in Parliament, more often by private correspondence. It enables MPs to investigate the grievances and press the claims of their constituents at the highest level, and knowledge that this has been done is a comfort to constituents even if the decision cannot be changed.

In the second place, the ability to hold ministers to account for their actions in Parliament facilitates the work of opposition MPs. They can use parliamentary questions to expose weaknesses in the government's policies and lack of efficiency in the administration. If the matter that is brought to light is both serious and urgent, the Opposition may be able to secure the adjournment of the House and hold a full debate on the same day. Failing this, the Opposition can move a vote of censure or debate the issue on one of the twenty-six days on which Opposition motions have priority. If the matter is potentially damaging to the government's reputation, members of the Opposition can return to it time and time again by asking questions on its different aspects. In this way the Opposition can bring the government's weaknesses to the attention of press and public and so hope to win votes in the next election.

If these three points about individual responsibility are considered in conjunction with the earlier points made about collective responsibility, it is clear that ministerial responsibility to Parliament is one of the central features of the British political system. It does not normally lead to the resignation or dismissal of ministers, but it does mean that they have constantly to explain and justify the work and plans of the administration to a critical assembly, and it provides an important channel of communication between those who govern and those who are governed.

The MP and the Administration

The ordinary Member of Parliament, whether he be a government back-bencher or a member of one of the opposition parties, has various methods open to him by which he can check or criticize the work of the government. The most straightforward method is to put down a parliamentary question. The questions have to be submitted in advance, in writing, but Members are given the opportunity to follow them up by supplementary questions.

This procedure is significant in two different ways, beyond its utility in providing MPs with an opportunity to extract information about the implementation of government policies. It has an impact on the Civil Service and it gives MPs an additional channel through which they can hope to embarrass and criticize ministers. There is no doubt that the behaviour of civil servants is affected by the knowledge that, if they make a mistake or offend a member of the public, the matter may subsequently be raised in Parliament. The name of the civil servant will not be publicly disclosed, but no official likes the prospect of having to justify his actions to his superiors in response to an urgent demand by the minister, knowing that the reputation of the department rests, for the moment, on his shoulders. It is not without significance that every draft answer to a parliamentary question is normally scrutinized and checked by the permanent secretary of the department. It is true that, since the size of the Civil Service has increased far more rapidly in the past fifty years than the number of questions asked, the chances of any individual decision leading to a parliamentary question must have diminished. But there is no evidence that this has led civil servants to stop worrying about the possibility of a question, and no serious reason to doubt the truth of the following comment by a senior official of the Department of Employment:

> One may say of the British official that, if he is engaged on a job with no immediate outlet to minister and Parliament, he will still be working tacitly with the sort of notions of relevance that would mean something to them; he must try to so order things that, of all that can happen, only those things happen which are susceptible of explanation in the parliamentary context. (Sisson, 1959, p. 123)

The opportunity to embarrass ministers is afforded more by the supplementary questions than by the original written questions. Civil servants are experts in drafting answers to written questions that protect the department and the minister, but they cannot always predict the supplementaries, which the minister will have to answer off the cuff. In recent decades, as parliamentary conflicts have tended to become sharper, supplementary questions have become more numerous. In the early years of the twentieth century there was one supplementary for every two or three main questions, but by the 1970s there were on average two supplementaries for every question – a fivefold increase in the proportion of supplementaries (Borthwick, 1979, p. 488). The supplementary questions have become a means of harassing ministers and scoring partisan points. While they have to take the form of questions to be within the rules of order, there has been a tendency for them to become longer so as to contain assertions and implicit accusations as well as questions. In the 1930s and the years immediately following the war the average supplementary occupied only five lines in the official reports of debates, but in 1974 the average supplementary occupied ten lines (ibid., p. 488).

The increasing tendency to use Question Time in an adversarial way is most conspicuous on Tuesday and Thursday afternoons, when the Prime Minister answers questions. These questions range over a wide selection of topics and are sometimes used as an attempt to ambush the Prime Minister, following seemingly innocuous questions with unpredictable supplementaries on delicate issues. For instance, on one occasion a question about whether the Prime Minister had any plans to visit Derbyshire was followed by a supplementary asking whether she realized that job opportunities for Derbyshire workers employed by Rolls-Royce were being jeopardized by her government's refusal to sell certain types of arms to Chile. Prime Minister's Question Time is in consequence a test of wits that may become an ordeal. It does little or nothing to improve the quality of policy-making but it is a remarkable aspect of British democracy that Prime Ministers should be willing (or feel compelled, as the case may be) to expose themselves twice weekly in this way.

In addition to asking questions MPs have various opportunities to debate the wisdom of governmental policies. They do so at the beginning of each session, when there is a debate lasting five or six days on the government's legislative programme for the year. They do so during debates initiated by the Opposition on twenty-six days each year, these days formerly being called Supply Days and now known simply as Opposition Days. They do so when the government finds time to discuss an important and urgent current issue, sometimes on its own initiative and sometimes on the request of opposition parties. All these debates are normally adversarial in character, though debates on urgent current issues sometimes find the main parties in substantial agreement. This is particularly likely to be the case when the issue is one of foreign affairs.

In addition, there is an adjournment debate of thirty minutes at the close of each day's business, with MPs balloting for the right to choose issues and open the debate, except that on one day a week the Speaker of the House chooses the opening speaker. The matters raised in these short debates tend to be local issues, or specific questions about the implementation of national policies. Attendance tends to be small, as most Members leave at the conclusion of the main business of the day around 10 p.m. The discussions are not usually adversarial in character.

Finally, there is a procedure by which Members can secure the adjournment of normal business in order to obtain an immediate debate on an urgent issue of national importance. Under Standing Order 9, the Speaker will allow a motion for the adjournment of the House if he is persuaded that the issue is of public importance, is within the competence of a minister, could not reasonably have been debated earlier and could not reasonably be left until time could be found for it in the normal timetable of the House. These are stringent conditions, which are met only once or twice a year. But occasionally there is a sudden development that arouses the concern of Parliament – a crisis in foreign affairs, a breakdown of public order, a decision to deport an alien at short notice – and in these circumstances the motion may be put. If forty Members support the motion, no matter how many Members oppose it (they are not counted), the motion succeeds and is the subject of a three-hour debate the same evening or the following afternoon.

Specialized Committees of Investigation

The main factor that limits the influence MPs can exert through the channels so far mentioned is the average member's lack of specialized knowledge of governmental affairs. Ministers have all the resources of their departments behind them and can often fend off attacks by being armed with more detailed facts and figures than their opponents can possibly muster.

To remedy this weakness, reformers in the postwar period have repeatedly urged that the House of Commons should develop a set of specialized committees, aided by professional staff, with the power to call for papers and cross-examine civil servants. There can be no doubt that committees of this kind, which have flourished over many decades in the United States, are the only channel through which a large representative assembly can exercise effective and continuous control over the work of government departments. Without this opportunity to find out for themselves what is being done in departments, members of the assembly are in a poor position to offer detailed and constructive criticism.

The British reformers who have argued for this development have included the more intellectual of the Labour back-benchers, the more liberal of the Conservative back-benchers, leaders of the smaller parties and academic students of politics. They have argued in terms of what was described in Chapter 2 as the liberal theory of the constitution, saying that as Parliament is the sovereign representative of the electorate, it ought to have effective control over the administration. Opponents of reform, who have until very recently included the leading members of both main parties, have argued in terms of what was described in Chapter 2 as the Whitehall view of the constitution. They have maintained that ministers have the responsibility of governing the country, leaving Parliament with the important but nevertheless more limited duty of criticism. This attitude was expressed very clearly in the Report of the Select Committee on Procedure of 1958–9, which made the following comment about a proposal to establish a committee on colonial affairs:

> There is little doubt that the activities of such a committee would ultimately be aimed at controlling rather than criticizing the policy and actions of the department concerned. In so doing, it would be usurping a function which the House itself has never attempted to exercise. Although the House has always maintained the right to criticize the executive and in the last resort to withdraw its confidence, it has always been careful not to arrogate to itself any of the executive power.

Until the late 1960s, the House of Commons had only three specialized committees of investigation, none of which corresponded in scope to the activities of a department. These were the committees on Public Accounts, Estimates and Nationalized Industries. Of these, the Public Accounts Committee has the most precise function. Its task is to consider the annual report of the Comptroller and Auditor-General on departmental expenditures. If this report criticizes particular departments for transgressing the very detailed rules that govern administrative expenditures, the Public Accounts Committee is likely to issue a kind of public reprimand to the senior civil servants responsible. This procedure serves as a way of confirming the principle that Parliament has ultimate control over the budget, even though this control is exercised retrospectively.

The function of what used to be called the Estimates Committee, but now has the much more logical title of the Committee on Expenditure, is to scrutinize government expenditures with a view to assessing whether or not the taxpayer has got good value for money. Until 1965 the committee had only a small staff of clerks and could do no more each year than to pick out a few examples of government expenditure for examination. In 1965 the committee's membership and staff were increased, and five specialized subcommittees were established. This move was in line with Whitehall's new emphasis on managerial efficiency in the public services, and in recent years the committee has produced a stream of useful reports.

The Select Committee on Nationalized Industries was set up in 1956 to examine the reports and accounts of public corporations in charge of the nationalized industries, and it has interpreted its terms of reference in a broad way. Taking one industry at a time, it has conducted fairly thorough inquiries into matters of administration and policy, and has felt free to examine officials of the relevant government departments as well as officials of the public corporations. The committee has rarely divided on party lines or approached issues in a partisan way, and this has helped it both to secure the co-operation of civil servants and to command respect in Parliament for its reports.

The undoubted success of this committee lent support to those reformers who wished to see the establishment of specialized committees of Parliament covering a wide range of government activities. It was argued that this reform would make Parliament's influence over administration more effective as well as increasing the knowledge and extending the experience of back-bench MPs. However, the extension of the committee system had to wait for the support of a sympathetic administration.

This support was forthcoming in 1966, when it was announced that several new committees were to be established on an experimental basis, the experiment to be reviewed after a few years. The first two committees dealt respectively with agriculture and with science and technology. These were followed in 1968 and 1969 by new committees on education, on race relations and immigration, on Scottish affairs and on overseas development.

Of these committees, three were devoted to the affairs of particular government departments, while the other three dealt with a broader range of topics. Committees in the first category – those dealing with agriculture, education and overseas developments – made less impact than the others. Having terms of reference that coincided with the responsibilities of departments, they were viewed with suspicion by senior civil servants in those departments. The latter were simply not happy to see a group of MPs acquire specialized knowledge about departmental affairs, which might serve as a basis for penetrating criticisms of departmental policies. Relations between the Committee on Agriculture and the Department of Agriculture, Fisheries and Food were particularly strained, and this committee was abolished after just over two years, early in 1969. The Committee on Education was also limited to two years, from 1968 to 1970. The Committee on Overseas Development had a smoother passage and continued until 1979.

The other committees were more successful. The Committee on Science and Technology dealt with matters that are not normally subject to partisan controversy, and some of its members had scientific expertise that could be used more effectively in committee than on the floor of the House. The committee's investigations of alternative designs for nuclear power stations were widely welcomed as a useful contribution. The Committee on Race Relations and Immigration was successful for a rather different reason, namely that the topics with which it dealt were politically sensitive issues for which the ministers and civil servants concerned were happy to share responsibility. This committee made a number of valuable studies.

The result of this experiment with specialized committees of inquiry was therefore mixed. The committees themselves functioned well, with members taking a constructive interest in the issues involved and with hardly any divisions on party lines. However, one would be hard pressed to identify their impact on policy-making and administration. The committees on agriculture and on education were somewhat resented by the departments, and their recommendations were ignored. The reports of the other committees contributed to the general pool of ideas about their respective subjects, but it is almost impossible to trace a causal relationship between recommendations and action. The reports contributed to the education of Members of Parliament, but there was rarely time for them to be debated on the floor of the House. Those who wanted further reforms of Parliament could point to useful work done, whereas sceptics could and did say that the results were hardly worth the effort.

The next stage in the story opened in 1978, when a report of the Select Committee on Procedure recommended a completely new committee structure in the House of Commons, giving committees a comprehensive coverage of government departments and also enlarging their powers. The then Leader of the House, Michael Foot, was opposed to these recommendations, but they were supported by back-benchers of all parties and also by Conservative front-benchers. In the 1979 general election the Conservative Party committed itself to the proposed new structure and one of the first decisions taken by the new Parliament was to endorse the majority of the recommendations.

Under the new system, there are fourteen new specialized committees, covering the subjects listed in Table 12.1. The long-standing Public Accounts Committee continues unchanged, but the other committees mentioned above have their work taken over by one or other of the new committees. These committees are small in size, having either nine or eleven members each (apart from the Committee on Scottish Affairs, which has thirteen members). They appoint their own chairmen, and in the first session seven appointed Conservative Members to that position while the other seven appointed Labour Members. They each have several professional advisers, who are paid on a daily basis. These is also a Liaison Committee, consisting of the fourteen chairmen. Their terms of reference enable the committees to discuss the activities of

Table 12.1 *Specialized Committees of Parliament Established in 1979*

Topic	Numbers of members	Number of professional advisers
Agriculture	9	4
Defence	11	4
Education, Science and Arts	9	4
Employment	9	4
Energy	11	9
Environment	11	7
Foreign Affairs	11	4
Home Affairs	11	2
Industry and Trade	11	2
Social Services	9	5
Transport	11	2
Treasury and Civil Service	11	7
Scottish Affairs	13	1
Welsh Affairs	11	3

nationalized industries and of the whole range of semi-autonomous public authorities that come under the ultimate control of government departments.

With the establishment of these committees, the House of Commons has gone a considerable way towards accepting responsibility for the continuous scrutiny of the work of government departments. It is a step away from the Whitehall view of the constitution and towards the liberal view. Several positive things can be said about the work of the new committees. They have proceeded in a business-like way, getting advice from professional staff and consultants, taking evidence from spokesmen for pressure groups and cross-examining civil servants. They have rarely divided on party lines, so that they have escaped from the adversarial conflict that marks most debates on the floor of the House. They have worked hard, meeting frequently and each producing several reports a year.

The limitation of the new committees is that they have no powers of action except to submit reports to the House. They have no powers over legislation, which are the prerogative of a quite different set of committees, to be discussed in the following chapter. Parliament may or may not find time to hold debates on committee reports, and in the majority of cases is not able to do so. It is clear that the committees add considerably to the amount and (more important) the quality of specialized information about policy-making and policy implementation that is available to Parliament, but it is too early to say how much practical difference this will make to the conduct of British government.

Further Reading

Norton (1981), *The Commons in Perspective*, is the most accessible account of Parliament at work; Marshall (1989) *Ministerial Responsibility*, is an excellent guide to conventions and practice; for some essays on parliamentary reform see Judge (1983), *The Politics of Parliamentary Reform*; for detailed accounts of the new specialized committees see Drewry (1985), *The New Select Committees*.

◇ 13 ◇

Changing the Law

Legislative Procedure

The law of Britain consists of Common Law, as interpreted by judges over the centuries, and Statute Law, as enacted by Parliament. In this context the word 'Parliament' signifies the two Houses together with the monarch, for all three must agree to a new law before it can be placed on the Statute Book. The procedure is for a Bill to be introduced in one of the Houses, where it must pass three readings and a Committee Stage, for it to be sent to the other House for the same treatment, and for it then to be presented to the monarch for assent. In constitutional law the monarch retains the right to refuse assent but in practice she has no choice in the matter. After the Royal Assent the Act is entered in the Statute Book and immediately becomes part of the law of the land.

Parliamentary Bills are of two kinds. The great majority, in the present century are 'public Bills', which affect the community generally. The others are 'private Bills', which relate to a matter of purely private or local interest; for instance, an individual may promote a private Bill to free his property from some legal restriction as to its disposal, or a local authority may do so to acquire the powers necessary for the damming of a river or the conversion of a burial ground into a park. There is no special procedure for private Bills that is quasi-judicial in nature. First, the promoters of the Bill must notify all persons and organizations whose interests may be affected by the Bill. After a formal first reading there is a second reading that is also formal unless someone objects to the Bill in principle, as might happen, for example, in the case of a bill that would extend the power of a municipal authority to engage in trade. If the Bill passes the second reading, it is then referred to a special committee of four or five Members, before which the proponents and opponents of the measure argue their case with the assistance of counsel. This is the important stage, and if the Bill gets through this committee it is usually passed without further amendment.

In the case of public Bills the second reading in the House of Commons is the most important stage. The first reading is a pure formality. On the second reading there is a debate on the principles and purpose of the Bill, which may last for several days. The Bill is then referred to a committee, which considers it clause by clause. Finance Bills and some other Bills of exceptional importance are heard in committee of the whole House. Bills relating only to Scotland are referred to the Scottish Committee and other public Bills are normally referred to one of the six standing committees of the House, which are not specialized in function or title and are know simply as Standing Committees A, B and so on through to F.

Each standing committee deals with Bills on a wide variety of topics, and for this reason it is commonly thought that there is only a random relationship between the subject of a Bill and the interests and expertise of the members of the committee that considers the Bill. The truth is very different. Each committee is composed of a nucleus of twenty members, chosen by the Committee of Selection in proportion to the strength of the parties in the House, together with up to thirty members who are appointed for the consideration of one Bill only and are chosen for their interests and qualifications. Given the nature of party management in Parliament, these additional members are also chosen in rough proportion to party strengths, but they are people who have an active interest in the Bill to be discussed. Furthermore, the Committee of Selection does not appoint the twenty nuclear members of a standing committee until after it is known what Bill will first be discussed by that committee, and the choice is usually influenced by that knowledge. If the subject of the second Bill is markedly different, several of the nuclear members may resign from the committee and be replaced by others who are better qualified to discuss the second Bill, and so on through the session. It follows that the standing committees of the House of Commons are much more specialized in composition than appears at first sight. The minister responsible for the Bill in the House always sits on the committee, advised by his officials, while the Attorney-General and Solicitor-General are entitled to take part in the proceedings of all standing committees so as to advise on legal points. The standing committees are therefore well-informed bodies. They consider each Bill clause by clause, though they are sometimes limited by shortage of time. In order to keep up the pace of legislation that is required in modern Britain, the government has occasionally to use the closure in committee, together with other procedural devices known as the guillotine (which stops debate on a clause after a predetermined time) and the kangaroo (which takes the committee in jumps from one important clause to another).

When a Bill comes out of committee it is reported to the House, at which stage the House discusses and occasionally reverses the amendments made in committee, as well as having the chance to add detailed changes of its own. There quickly follows the third reading, at which only changes in wording are permitted, and the Bill is then sent to the House of Lords for similar (though briefer) treatment, unless it is one of those non-controversial Bills that go through the Lords before they are presented to the Commons.

The Origins of Legislation

A century ago most Bills were initiated by Private Members. However, since 1867 governments have progressively increased their control over the legislative process so that Private Members are now given only the most limited opportunities to introduce Bills. Every alternate Friday in the first twenty weeks of each session is reserved for Private Members' Bills, and as the House rises early on Fridays this means that in practice Private Members have no more than 10 per cent of parliamentary time at their disposal for legislation. This is often regarded as an inevitable consequence of the great extension of government activities that the past century has seen, but in fact the British Parliament is dominated much more completely by the government than are the legislatures of most other liberal democracies. In the United States Congress all Bills are technically introduced by Private Members and most Bills are actually initiated by them; in Sweden Private Members' Bills usually outnumber government Bills (though they do not deal with such important subjects); in the Fourth French Republic the ordinary deputy had a good deal of room for initiative; and even in the Fifth Republic the members of the National Assembly enjoy somewhat more scope for legislative enterprise than do their British counterparts.

The present practice in Britain is for back-benchers to ballot for the opportunity to introduce Bills. Only twenty of the 650 MPs win a place in the ballot each session, and a member does not have much chance of getting his Bill a decent hearing unless he is in the top half of this twenty. Some MPs have draft Bills in their pockets to introduce if they win, while others use the opportunity to sponsor a Bill drafted by a pressure group or by one of their colleagues. Success in the ballot entitles a Member to introduce a Bill for its first and second readings, but progress beyond this stage depends upon the goodwill of the government. In an average session only about eight or nine Private Members' Bills pass into law. To get a Bill enacted requires skill, patience, determination, a measure of support from more than one party and the sympathy of the ministers most directly affected. An interesting example is the Obscene Publications Bill, which was originally drafted by Roy Jenkins in the autumn of 1954. In the spring of 1955 this got a brief first hearing in the House but lapsed at the end of the session. In the following winter it was reintroduced by a friendly MP who had won a place in ballot, but was 'talked out' by the Under Secretary for Home Affairs, who spoke for so long that the House passed to other business without there being time for a vote. A year later a third Member sponsored it and it was passed on second reading, after which it would normally have been referred to a standing committee that was so choked with other Bills that it would never have got round to discussing this one. The Bill was saved from this fate by R. A. Butler, the new Home Secretary, who arranged for a select committee to be established to discuss the Bill in detail. This took time, and the committee did not produce its report until the spring of 1958, by when the Bill had once again lapsed, as all uncompleted legislation does at the end of each session. In the ballot the following autumn none of the twenty successful Members proved willing to sponsor the Bill and the whole operation was back to square one, from which it was rescued a few months later by the Home Secretary, who offered government time for a new second reading, on the understanding that the principles as well as the details of the Bill would be open to debate. What emerged from this was a compromise Bill that was not unacceptable to the government and eventually passed into law, after a good deal of hard bargaining in the committee and report stages, in July 1959. The whole process has been likened to a game of snakes and ladders lasting five years (Jenkins, 1959).

Although Private Members' Bills are not numerous, some of them are very important. Recent examples include the 1967 Sexual Offences Act, which legalized homosexual practices between consenting adults, the Act that authorized abortion more or less on demand and the Act that abolished censorship in the theatre.

Government Bills are much more numerous, and their passage through Parliament is more certain. In an average session about seventy are introduced and nearly as many are enacted. Their origins are various, and may be discussed under the headings of: (1) party policy; (2) Cabinet decisions; (3) committee reports; (4) outside pressures; and (5) administrative needs.

(1)   Legislation based directly on policy statements put out by the parties tends to be at the head of the programme after a general election has led to a change of government. The 1945 election brought a government into office that was committed to a set of reforms that had been under discussion for many years. In the following five sessions Parliament passed more major Acts than it has ever passed in a period of comparable length. The coal, gas, electricity and transport industries were nationalized, the civil airlines were established, the National Health Service was set up, national insurance was reorganized, and an elaborate Act regarding town and country planning was passed. But this was altogether exceptional. When the Conservatives regained power in 1951 the only major Acts that followed from their party programme were those to denationalize road transport and the iron and steel industry. Some other important changes were made, such as the abolition of petrol rationing, but these did not require legislation apart from the making of orders under powers already granted to ministers.

The Labour victory of 1964 produced a Bill to extend rent control and a number of financial measures to deal with the balance-of-payments crisis, but Labour's electoral programme was reflected more in administrative changes and the appointment of committees than in the passage of legislation. The Conservative victory of 1970 led to the Industrial Relations Act, the Housing Finance Act and the enabling legislation consequent upon Britain's entry to the European community. When Labour returned to power in 1974 the main immediate legislative consequences of its election manifesto were the repeal of Conservative laws regarding industrial relations and housing, but in the following two years several new measures were introduced that had their origins in party promises. These included measures to increase security of employment and to extend the compensation payable to workers who were made redundant. The Thatcher victories of 1979, 1983 and 1987 were followed by a stream of legislative changes introduced to give effect to party policy, notably measures to restore nationalized undertakings to private ownership, to compel local authorities to offer municipal housing for sale to tenants, to place ceilings on the expenditure of local authorities, to abolish the authorities governing the seven largest cities and to reform the education system. Statistically, only a small proportion of government Bills have their immediate origins in party policy statements. An analysis of legislation between 1970 and 1979 has shown that only 8 per cent of Bills in 1970–4 followed directly from the Conservative election manifesto, while only 13 per cent of Bills in 1974–9 followed from the Labour election manifesto (Rose, 1980b, p. 72). However, some of the most important Bills begin life in this way.

(2)   Many other Bills are party-political in origin in the sense that they are sponsored by ministers or by Cabinet committees who become convinced that changes are needed. For instance, Conservative Cabinets between 1951 and 1964 decided to grand independence to a large number of British colonies, to disband the Central African Federation, to abolish resale price maintenance, to establish machinery for economic planning and to extend the control of restrictive practices in trade. The annual Finance Act is also a highly political measure, as are the various legislative attempts to control prices and incomes.

(3)   Other Bills are based on the reports of committees of inquiry. Examples are the Clean Air Act, which followed the Beaver Committee on Air Pollution, the Act to reorganize the government of Greater London, which followed the report of the Herbert Commission, the Act to liberalize the laws regarding gambling, which followed the report of the Royal Commission on Betting, Lotteries and Gaming, the Act designed to drive prostitutes off the streets, which followed the report of the Wolfenden Committee, and the Local Government Act of 1972, which drew on the analysis (though not the conclusions) of the Redcliffe-Maud Commission. None of these Bills was partisan in character, and in each case the government would have welcomed the support of the Opposition for a measure that an impartial committee had recommended. In most cases, though not in the case of London government, Opposition support was secured for the principle of the Bill even if not for its details.

(4)   Some Bills result from outside pressures, usually overt but occasionally covert. The Act that led to the establishment of commercial television is an outstanding example of a piece of legislation promoted largely as the result of the activities of a well-organized pressure group who acquired influence through friends and contacts in the governing party and the Cabinet. The parliamentary debates on this Bill were frank, lively and well publicized, but the previous negotiations had been devious and fairly secret. However, this example is

exceptional. Most legislation that has its origin in outside pressures results either from open campaigns by promotional groups, such as the RSPCA or the Abortion Law Reform Society, or from frank discussions between government departments and spokesmen for economic interests.

The RSPCA is without the most successful promotional group in Britain. It has keen supporters in both main parties and enjoys the great advantage that animal welfare is not a cause to which anyone objects, so long as it is not taken to the length of interfering with a traditional sport like hunting. Other promotional (as opposed to interest) groups that have attempted, successfully or not, to promote legislation since 1949 are the National Campaign for the Abolition of Capital Punishment, the Marriage Law Reform Society, the League Against Cruel Sports, the Abortion Law Reform Association and the National Temperance Federation.

Interest groups also propose legislation from time to time on behalf of their members, sometimes by drafting a Bill for introduction as a Private Member's Bill, sometimes by approaching the government department most directly concerned. In 1951 the British Veterinary Association drafted a Bill to make the use of anaesthetics compulsory for operations on domestic animals, which was eventually passed as a Private Member's Bill in 1953. In 1954 the Society of Authors was partly responsible for the first draft of the Obscene Publications Bill, discussed above. An initiative taken by the Joint Committee of Ophthalmic Opticians resulted in the passage of a Bill requiring opticians to be registered. A similar initiative taken by a society representing estate agents has led to a good deal of debate but has not so far resulted in legislation, because there are differences of view within the profession, and the government, while willing to find time for a Bill that meets the wishes of the profession, has not been willing to impose its own view on the profession. A good deal of legislation, over the years, has resulted directly or indirectly from proposals made by trade unions. The Catering Wages Act of 1948 was introduced by the government to meet long-standing complaints by unions about the treatment of workers in the catering trades. The Offices Act of 1960 was designed to meet some of the complaints by white-collar unions about the conditions of work in offices. The Trade Disputes Act of 1965 was passed at the request of the unions to remove the possibility that a union might be sued for damages if it broke a contractual agreement for the purpose of injuring a third party.

(5) A good deal of legislation has its origins within the administration. Government departments find that problems arise that cannot be solved without a change in the law, and the officials persuade their minister that a Bill must be drafted. Each year there is a substantial body of legislation about fairly technical matters that is essentially 'administrative legislation', drafted by government departments after consultation with the affected interests, and controversial only in so far as spokesmen for groups that are not entirely happy with it try to get it amended in Parliament. Examples are Bills dealing with wage negotiations, with weights and measures, with national insurance and with public health.

From a Proposal to the Law

After a government department has decided to sponsor a piece of legislation, there is much work to be done. The minister and the senior officials concerned with the Bill will have agreed upon its general principles and the latter should 'know the minister's mind' sufficiently well to be able to negotiate with affected groups without having constantly to refer back to their chief. Consultation with all the groups likely to be affected by the Bill is essential, and is recognized as an integral part of the British system of government. A minister whose department omitted to consult a significant group would undoubtedly be criticized in Parliament for this omission, for the group would not fail to find a back-bencher willing to express its objections.

Of course, consultation with groups does not imply acceptance of all their suggestions and criticisms. The government's task is to balance group claims against one another and to assess them in terms of the national interest. But a wise minister will give group spokesmen every chance to press their claims, for three reasons. First, he needs to know all the practical difficulties involved in the proposal so as to get the details right, to avoid ambiguity and to reduce the opportunities for evasion of the law. Secondly, he will want to get as much support as he possibly can for the Bill from those directly affected by it and to assess the arguments and strength of any probable opposition. Even when groups dislike the proposal in principle, it will pay the minister to put his case to them, if they are influential, and perhaps to moderate their opposition by offering them concessions on points of detail. If he does not do so, his Bill will have a more difficult passage through Parliament and his party may lose a certain amount of public support. Thirdly, the minister will be concerned about future relations between his department and the groups. For better or worse, government departments and interest-group spokesmen have to live with one another, and both sides normally do everything they can to keep the relationship harmonious.

It is an established convention that a Bill is not published in advance of its presentation to Parliament. These consultations and negotiations therefore normally take place on the basis of either a report of an official committee or a White Paper explaining the government's intentions. In the case of Bills that are unlikely to arouse party controversy the whole process may be based on discussions and departmental papers, without anything being published in advance of the Bill. The following quotation from the 1948 *Year Book* of the National Farmers' Union illustrates the kind of detailed discussion that often takes place before a Bill sees the light of day, though (as noted earlier) the NFU is more fortunate than most interest groups in that it does not have to contend with rival or hostile groups of any significance. The degree of influence claimed may therefore by untypical, but the extent of discussion is not unusual.

The Agriculture Bill was introduced . . . in December 1946. For as long as two years before this date discussions had been going on between the Union and the

Minister of Agriculture as to the form which this Bill was to take . . . When the Bill was introduced it represented, in substance, the result of discussion and a large measure of agreement . . . There were, however, still many points upon which the Union wished to see the Bill amended, and during the first six months of the year an intensive campaign was conducted inside and outside Parliament to persuade the government to adopt these amendments. On three points only were we unsuccessful.   (Potter, 1961, p. 207)

When the draft Bill is in shape the minister must get Cabinet approval for it, together with a firm place in the parliamentary timetable. He will previously have secured provisional support for the Bill and some promise of parliamentary time, but the timetable is crowded and draft Bills are sometimes delayed from one session to the next for this reason. The political climate also changes, and Bills may be deferred if the government is going through an anxious period or if the Bills seem likely to provoke more controversy than had previously been anticipated. Occasionally a measure that has been given provisional approval by the Cabinet alarms government back-benchers, who communicate their feelings through the Whips and at meetings of the specialized party committees. Many Conservative back-benchers disliked a 1957 proposal to liberalize the law regarding shop closing hours and substantially the same group were opposed to a later proposal to abolish resale price maintenance. In the former case the government dropped the Bill; in the latter case the minister concerned defended his policies before the party committee and then before the whole 1922 Commitee, gaining enough support to let him continue with the Bill, which was subsequently passed.

Bills that are deferred by a government or left stranded by a change of government are consigned to the pigeon-holes of Whitehall. But the majority avoid this fate and, after Cabinet approval, are put into legal shape by the parliamentary draftsmen and duly presented to Parliament.

Party Discipline and Legislation

Ever since the development of effective party discipline in the 1860s, the great majority of government Bills have been enacted without substantial change. As early as 1908, the American scholar A. L. Lowell commented that 'to say that at present the Cabinet legislates with the advice and consent of Parliament would hardly be an exaggeration' (quoted in Walkland, 1979, p. 251). Richards reports that in the first twelve years after the Second World War governments introduced 732 Bills in Parliament and secured the passage of 703 of them (Richards, 1959, p. 110). This is a success rate of 96 per cent. Statistics of this kind have led some commentators to conclude that the House of Commons acts as little more than a rubber stamp in the legislative process, using the debates as yet another opportunity to appeal to the electorate rather than as an occasion for legislative revision.

Table 13.1 *Government Bills Checked or Wrecked by the House of Commons Since 1970*

Year	Bill	Result
1972	Industry Bill	Significant amendment
1975	Housing Finance (Special Provisions) Bill	Emasculation
1976	Dock Work Regulation Bill	Emasculation
1977	Scotland and Wales Bill	Forced withdrawal
1977/8	Scotland Bill	Three vital amendments
1978	Wales Bill	Vital amendment
1978	Budget	Two important amendments
1981	Local Government Finance Bill	Forced withdrawal
1982	Local Government Finance (No. 2) Bill	Significant amendment
1984	Rates Bill	Significant amendment
1986	Shops Bill	Defeat of Bill

This kind of conclusion is understandable but is less than the whole truth. If Richards's figures are viewed from another perspective, they show that in those twelve years of maximum party discipline governments had to abandon twenty-nine legislative measures in the face of parliamentary opposition. Other Bills were amended in significant ways. Since the late 1960s party discipline has become somewhat less effective, and governments have had repeatedly to accept unwelcome amendments, to introduce ministerial amendments to ward off criticism, or even to withdraw a Bill altogether. Between 1970 and 1979 the government of the day suffered forty-eight defeats on legislative issues on the floor of the House of Commons, together with more defeats in committee.

Table 13.1 lists some of the more important defeats on legislative issues that governments have experienced since 1970. Some of these defeats were remarkable. Thus, in 1977 the House of Commons forced the government to abandon its first attempt to establish national assemblies in Scotland and Wales. When a second attempt was made, this time with provision for referendums on the issue, the insertion by back-benchers of the requirement that a majority in the referendum must include 40 per cent of all electors to count as a positive endorsement effectively wrecked the chances of establishing these assemblies. In 1978 a Commons revolt on the budget lowered the standard rate of income tax. In 1986 a government with a majority of over a hundred was defeated in its attempt to liberalize the shop closing laws so as to permit Sunday trading.

The House of Commons therefore plays a crucial role in the legislative process, even though, as a consequence of party loyalty and governmental control of parliamentary time, it exercises less power than the Cabinet. Since

1974 the House of Lords has also played a significant role, making itself awkward to Labour governments between 1974 and 1979 and to the Conservative government since 1979. The government still dominates the scene, but Parliament cannot be written off as a rubber stamp.

Delegated Legislation and European Legislation

For various reasons there has been a considerable increase in postwar years in the volume of legislative orders and regulations that are drafted by government departments and pass into law unless Parliament disagrees within a certain stipulated period. The main reasons are the increased complexity of the regulations needed, the need to change them from time to time and the shortage of parliamentary time. The House of Commons now passes between sixty and seventy-five public Acts each session, for which it has about eighty days of debate available. It would clearly be counter-productive to overwhelm Parliament with all the details that are necessary for modern legislation in the economic and social fields, and it is much more sensible to have the details added by the departments concerned after Parliament has agreed on the principles. Equally, it would be a waste of time for the full legislative procedure to be employed whenever national insurance contributions or benefits are increased, to take only the simplest example.

In consequence increasing use has been made of the device of authorizing the minister concerned to add (and when necessary change) the details after the main Act has been placed on the Statute Book. To give an idea of the volume of legislation involved, in 1900 there were 202 pages of new statute law and only a little delegated legislation, whereas in 1965 there were 1,817 pages of new statute law and 6,435 pages of delegated legislation.

The rules and orders thus made are known collectively by the rather odd title of 'statutory instruments', and the general procedure is for them to be laid on the table of the two Houses of Parliament and to become law after so many days unless either of the Houses passes a motion to reject them. Amendment is not a possible option. From 1944 to 1973 the responsibility for scrutinizing all these orders rested with a committee known as the Select Committee on Statutory Instruments, which would draw the attention of the House (at certain specified times) to any orders that it considered inappropriate or improper. In 1973 this committee was replaced by a Joint Committee on Statutory Instruments, composed of seven members from each House. In 1973 also a Standing Committee on Statutory Instruments was established, with the main function of considering the merits of orders referred to it by the Joint Committee. It is clear, however, that the scrutiny provided by these committees falls short of what would be desirable in terms of liberal principles of representative government. The volume of delegated legislation is just too great for Parliament to be able to give it thorough attention, and there is no prospect of any change in this situation. It can only be said that the members of the committees do their best.

The question of European legislation is more complex. Within the European Community, the European Commission has power to draft legislation that is binding on member-states, though it is subject to ratification by the European Council of Ministers. The various national parliaments have no legal powers or functions at all in this process. What has been done in Britain is to establish a Select Committee on European Legislation, which has the function of considering draft legislation proposed by the European Commission and reporting to the House of Commons. The House of Lords has a similar committee, together with several subcommittees, and as the Lords' committees have more time and more manpower available than the Commons committee the scrutiny of proposed European legislation has generally been more effective in the Lords. The Houses of Parliament can then, separately or jointly, ask the minister concerned to oppose measures that they consider harmful to British interests when these measures come up for ratification in the European Council of Ministers. The minister is not obliged to act on such requests and might find it difficult to do so if he were involved in a bargaining procedure within the Council. However, the minister will in most cases abide by the wishes of Parliament and, in so far as he has a veto in the Council of Ministers, can then be expected to block the proposed measure.

Up to now, European legislation has been modest in quantity and limited to somewhat unimportant matters. However, it may be expected to increase in both scope and importance in the years to come. Moreover, it is planned that after 1992 the Council of Ministers will take all decisions by majority vote in a weighted system of voting that takes account of the population of each member state, so that British ministers will lose their veto power. In due course, therefore, the British Parliament's ability to influence European legislation will be diminished. This is one of the costs of the move towards European unity.

Further Reading

The best introductions to this topic are Walkland (1968), *The Legislative Process in Great Britain*, and Norton (1981), *The Commons in Perspective*, Ch. 5; Private Members' Bills are discussed in Richards (1970), *Parliament and Conscience*; some valuable essays on the topic will be found in Walkland (1979), *The House of Commons in the Twentieth Century*.

◇ 14 ◇

Government at the Local Level

Although the British system of government is highly centralized, it is not feasible for environmental and social services to be provided in a country of 55 million people except through the medium of local agencies. In Britain these agencies have varied and still vary considerably in their character. When water, sanitation and educational services were developed in the nineteenth century, this was at first done through specially constituted authorities with overlapping areas. The system was then rationalized and democratized in 1888 and 1894. The whole country was divided into counties and county boroughs, each of which was a multi-purpose authority controlled by an elected council. Within the counties there was established a second tier of district authorities providing local services like street lighting, and these were also controlled by elected councils.

This system was not without problems, but it was tidy in the sense that there were no overlapping areas and it was democratic in the sense that the authorities were under the immediate control of elected representatives. However, from the 1930s onwards national governments have followed a pattern of removing services from the control of the counties and county boroughs and placing them under new specially constituted agencies, directed by people who are appointed rather than elected. The relief of poverty was placed into the hands of the National Assistance Board, replaced later by the Supplementary Benefits Commission. Hospitals were transferred from elected authorities to the National Health Service, administered through twelve Regional Hospital Boards based on a unique set of regions. The distribution of electricity was made the responsibility of regional electricity boards and the distribution of gas made that of regional gas boards, the areas of those regions being coterminous neither with each other nor with the areas of the hospital boards. Some years later, regional water boards were established, with different areas again.

It follows that the British system of government at the local level has a marked lack of uniformity. First, there are branch offices of national government departments, such as the Inland Revenue and the Department of Social Security. The ministerial head of each department is ultimately responsible to

Parliament for the work of these branch offices, and the Parliamentary Commissioner for Administration can investigate their actions if accusations of maladministration are levelled against them.

Secondly, there are the regional organizations of the public utilities mentioned above. They are directed by boards whose members are nominated rather than elected. Ministers are not responsible to Parliament for the work of the boards and there are no other democratic checks on their activities except for some rather ineffectual local advisory committees. Complaints about maladministration within these organizations cannot be investigated by a government official or parliamentary committee. They operate like private monopolies, whose discontented customers can sometimes take them to court but do not have any public machinery for the redress of their grievances.

Thirdly, there are county councils and district councils, each controlled by elected councillors who play a much more direct role in local administration than MPs play in national administration. The councillors are part-time politicians, unpaid except for a very small allowance, who have important administrative functions in regard to education, housing, town planning and a range of other services.

Fourthly, there are the local and regional organizations of the National Health Service, which have to be put into a category of their own. The service is an enormous undertaking, being the largest employer in Western Europe, and its organizational structure is elaborate. The Secretary of State for Health is ultimately responsible for its work, though he is not accountable to Parliament for its day-to-day activities. It has a Health Service Commissioner with the power to investigate accusations of maladministration, and it is possible (though not at all common) for patients to sue doctors or hospitals in cases of inappropriate treatment that caused harm.

It has become fashionable to give all these local and regional agencies the collective title of 'the local state', while maintaining the traditional terms 'local authorities' and 'local government' for the elected councils, their staff and their activities. In this book there is space to deal only with the local authorities, and to deal with these only in a general way, emphasizing their distinctive characteristics and their relations with the national government. The generality and relative brevity of this treatment should not be thought to imply that local government is unimportant. British local authorities employ over 2.5 million staff, compared with only about 500,000 civil servants, and they provide many services that are essential to the citizen. The nature of the treatment is determined by the fact that local government is a complex topic in its own right, which cannot be dealt with fully here without unbalancing the book. Readers who want fuller information about it, or about the other agencies of the local state, are referred to texts on public administration and local government.

The Character of the Local Government System

The British system of local government cannot be characterized as easily as can either the centralized system that exists in France or the decentralized system of the United States. France has a system of local administration. The country is divided into ninety *départements* and in each of these administration is controlled by a prefect, who is an official of the Ministry of the Interior and is moved from one area to another in the course of his career. The prefect and his staff are responsible not only for the administration of local services, which vary only a little from one *département* to another, but also for the enforcement of the law, the collection of taxes and the administration of a number of national services in the area. They are influenced by local politics and local pressures, but they are part of the government of France.

The United States, on the other hand, has a system of genuine local self-government. The government of an American city is not a part of either the state government or the federal government. In most states a city government has a considerable measure of independence, with power to levy taxes, to raise loans, to decide on the level of services it will provide and to change its own form of organization, provided the electors agree (and within limits set by the state constitution). The result is that American local authorities vary a great deal in their mode of organization and their policies in regard to housing, town planning and other matters.

British local government does not fit neatly into either of these categories. It has the appearance and trappings of a system of local self-government but not much of the reality. The Corporation of the City of Hull, for instance, cannot be said to be part of the British government; it is an independent corporation that was established in the fifteenth century, which owns a great deal of property and appoints its own Sheriff and Lord Mayor; it does not administer national services and it has, indeed, very little contact with the various branch offices of government departments that are established in the city. On the other hand, the Hull Corporation cannot change its own constitution, which is regulated by Act of Parliament; it cannot exercise any powers other than those delegated to it by Parliament; and it is subject to constant regulation and inspection by government departments.

The system is idiosyncratic and has not been based on any clear principles. The reader seeking a guide to the theory of British local government will search the libraries in vain, for no such book exists. What can be found instead is a plethora of volumes on the history and structure of local government. These are replete with analyses of recent reforms and discussions of the case for further reforms, for one of the characteristics of the system is that it is constantly thought to be in need of change. Between 1945 and 1980 the debates about local government revolved upon three distinct issues: the conflict between the case for financial independence and the case for financial equality; the conflict of interests between the cities and the surrounding rural and outer suburban areas; and the conflict between the case for greater efficiency (which is believed to require large units of administration) and the case for local democracy (which is believed to require small units). Since 1980 the debates have centred on a new and more politicized kind of conflict between a national government determined to impose financial restraint on local authorities and a number of urban authorities determined to resist this policy.

The arguments about financial independence have been firmly resolved in favour of dependence on grants from the national government. The main problem about giving local authorities control over taxes that would yield enough income to finance their activities, such as taxes on income or retail sales, is that this would result in large inequalities of income between poorer and richer areas. There are other problems too, notably the deep reluctance of the Treasury to surrender its monopoly of such taxes, but the problem of inequality is the crux of the issue. The position in recent years has been that local authorities derive between half and two-thirds of their net income from a block grant paid by the national government. This grant is determined by a complex formula that has been changed from time to time, but which has as its constant feature a large equalizing element. The result is that the money available for local government services enables authorities all over the country to provide services of roughly equal standard. Citizens living in poorer areas may have to accept a poorer environment, but they do not suffer appreciably in the quality of their schools, housing, road maintenance and other basic services. Most people in Britain regard the sacrifice of financial independence by local authorities as a small price to pay for this kind of equality.

The conflict of interests between the cities and the rural areas is inevitable in a crowded country like Britain. If cities have no room for new housing estates within their boundaries, they can only rehouse people from overcrowded slums by building in the surrounding county – which will usually be resented by residents of the county area affected. The conflict between groups exists no matter where the boundary is, but the location of the boundary is apt to determine the outcome. There are other issues too, and they have dogged the debates about structure and boundaries for many decades. In 1972–3 the Heath government cut through these debates by imposing a new structure, in which enlarged county councils acquired power over numerous urban areas that had previously been independent of them. From the political point of view this reform can be viewed as offering a compromise, whereby county residents could no longer wash their hands of urban problems but might (depending on the balance of populations) be able to dominate the newly enlarged county council.

The new structure also dealt with the problem of governing conurbations by creating six entirely new counties, known as metropolitan counties, to cover the contiguous urban areas surrounding Birmingham, Liverpool, Manchester, Sheffield, Leeds and Newcastle-upon-Tyne. The changes were promoted by the government not only as a way of solving boundary problems but also as a way of creating larger units of local government that could develop planning departments and make use of modern technology to raise the level of administrative efficiency.

Whether these structural changes were worthwhile is a question on which most specialists have returned an unfavourable verdict (see, for example, Alexander, 1982, ch. 3). The larger counties may be in some technical respects more efficient as administrative units, but relations between the upper and lower tiers of local government have produced conflict and the system as a whole is more cumbersome and more expensive to operate than the system it replaced. Moreover, popular participation in local government was reduced by the reform, partly because one of the overall consequences of the change was greatly to reduce the number of elected councillors, partly because there is less public interest in larger units of local government than in smaller units. Controversies about structure were therefore not ended by the 1972–3 changes, and they came to the fore again in 1985 when the Thatcher government introduced legislation to abolish the six metropolitan counties along with the Greater London Council. The powers enjoyed by these seven authorities were mostly transferred to the smaller district councils covering the same area.

The Character of Central-Local Relations

National control of local government determines how local authorities are organized, what services they must provide, what other services they may provide if they choose to do so and how most of their services must be administered. The services they must provide include education, police, sanitation and public health. If an authority fails to provide one of these services at a level that meets the minimum standards set by the relevant ministry, the ministry may take powers to act in default, at the expense of the local authority. In 1954, for instance, the Coventry City Council refused to organize a civil defence service on the ground that civil defence, as understood in Britain, would be irrelevant to the problems of nuclear warfare. The Home Office thereupon took powers to organize a civil defence force in Coventry and send the bill to the City Council, a move that eventually persuaded the council to fall into line. In 1957 the St Pancras Borough Council decided to abandon its civil defence department for the same reason that had motivated Coventry, and with exactly the same result.

Some other services are optional, but the limits of a council's activities are set by the doctrine of *ultra vires*, according to which no authority is entitled to engage in any activity unless it has been specifically empowered to do so by Parliament. An authority that tries to exceed its legal powers may be stopped from doing so by a court order, as happened in 1921 when the Fulham Borough Council proposed to establish a municipal laundry under its power to provide public washhouses. Local laundry firms objected and the council had to abandon the project. If an authority proceeds unheeded in an activity that is *ultra vires*, the sanction is applied at the end of the financial year when the authority's accounts are audited by an official of the central government known as a District Auditor. If he finds that certain expenditures were unjustified, his duty is to disallow their payment from public funds, in which case those members of the authority who voted for the expenditures have to pay for them out of their own pockets. To avoid this fate, local authorities that are in doubt about the legality of a proposed measure often ask the relevant government department for a ruling before a final decision is taken.

The best-known example of disallowance occurred in 1921–2 when the Poplar Borough Council paid some of its workmen a wage considerably higher than the standard wage, on the ground that the council wished to be a 'model employer'. The District Auditor's view was that councillors had no right to be generous at the ratepayers' expense and the councillors had to pay the difference between the standard wage and the actual wage paid. Another interesting example occurred in the 1950s in Manchester. It was the custom for one of the local theatres to present a performance of the Shakespearian play that was included in the school examination syllabus each year and for the Manchester City Council to send schoolchildren of the appropriate age-group to see this. One year no performance was offered. The council thereupon decided to commission a performance for the special benefit of their pupils, thinking that this expenditure would be covered by their two powers: (1) to commission and subsidize theatrical performances; and (2) to pay for schoolchildren to see educational plays. When they asked for a ruling, however, they were told that this plan would be *ultra vires*, as the first power could be invoked only if the performances were open to all members of the public, and the second power covered only the purchase of tickets for a play that was in any case being given. A more trivial example occurred in 1963, when the District Auditor forced members of the Castle Donnington District Council to pay the cost of two telegrams they sent during the Cuban crisis, one to Kennedy and one to Khrushchev, appealing for peace. A much more serious and controversial example occurred in 1972, when the majority of councillors in the Derbyshire town of Clay Cross refused to raise the rents of council-house tenants in accordance with the requirements of the Housing Finance Act. They were subsequently ordered to pay the difference between the two levels of rent themselves; refused to do so; were disqualified by a court from holding political office; refused to take notice of the court's decision; and remained in *de facto* control of the town until the Clay Cross Council was abolished completely a few months later.

Control over the way in which services are administered is backed by the readiness of the national government to reduce or cut its grant to an authority that ignores orders. As an example, one of the rules about local police forces is that appointments to the post of Chief Constable should be approved by the Home Office. In 1947 this post fell vacant in Salford and the City Council decided to promote its Deputy Chief Constable to the vacancy. The Home Office refused to approve the appointment because it was a matter of Home Office policy that Chief Constables should always be appointed from some other police force. When Salford confirmed the appointment in spite of this its grant was immediately cut off and after a few weeks financial pressure forced it to give in.

Needless to say, things rarely come to this pass. Local authorities accept control by Whitehall as a condition of life and their conduct of local affairs is shaped by ministry regulations, by a constant stream of ministry circulars and by the reports of ministry inspectors. Their schools are inspected by the Department of Education and Science; their housing plans are subject to the approval of the Department of the Environment; their police forces are inspected by the Home Office. In so far as there is variety and experiment in local government, it can be said to be by permission of Whitehall. Nevertheless, there is in practice a fair amount of variety. Government departments vary considerably in the extent to which they use their powers to foster national uniformity. The Department of Health, for instance, is said to have a *laissez-faire* attitude to local authorities, believing that, provided they meet the requirements of the law, they should be allowed to enjoy a good deal of freedom in the way they develop local health services (Griffith, 1966, pp. 515–18). An example is the department's attitude to the fluoridation of water supplies; the department has long believed this to be a desirable development and has sent a number of circulars to local authorities advising them to undertake it; but though some councils have not accepted this advice the department has taken no steps to make them do so. On the other hand, the Department of the Environment exercises a great deal of control over local authorities, and the Department of Education and Science uses its powers to minimize differences in the standards of educational provision. To this end, the department controls the output of teachers from colleges of education, the number of teachers each authority may employ, teachers' salaries, investment in school buildings and the provision of ancillary services. It also has a large staff of inspectors who visit schools and advise local authorities on teaching methods.

Local authorities naturally differ in the use they make of their discretionary powers. Authorities vary in the services they provide for old people, for mentally defective people and for the deaf and the blind. Authorities also differ in their policies for the provision of council houses or flats to be let at subsidized rents. A great deal of argument takes place about the rate and method of building, the location and the rents of council housing. In many areas housing is the most controversial service provided by local government.

Another area in which there is scope for local initiative is in the provision of recreational and cultural facilities. Some authorities spend a lot on parks and recreation grounds; some run repertory theatres and subsidize symphony concerts; some have splendid art collections; some have libraries of gramophone records as well as books and a few have loan collections of lithographs and artists' prints. There is ample opportunity here for councillors who want to improve the amenities of their town. The short answer to questions about the character of central–local relations, therefore, is that local authorities have the appearance and to some extent the legal status of independent authorities; despite this the degree of practical independence they enjoy at any time depends almost entirely on the policies of central government departments; and at the time of writing, although their activities are much more tightly restricted than they were fifty years ago, they nevertheless retain a substantial degree of initiative in fields that can make a real difference to the lives of their citizens.

The Control of Local Expenditure

Since 1979 the relations between central and local government have been given a new twist by the commitment of the Thatcher government to controlling and if possible reducing the overall level of public expenditure. From the beginning, this government imposed tight restraint on capital expenditure by local authorities, and in particular imposed a sharp reduction on the number of new dwellings constructed for municipal tenants. As capital projects by local authorities have been subject to governmental permission throughout the postwar period, this policy of restraint did not require any new legislation.

By 1980, however, the government had become concerned about the level of local authority spending on current account, and the Local Government Act of that year authorized the Department of the Environment to penalize authorities by cutting their grant (which then comprised approximately 60 per cent of their revenue) if they exceeded spending limits set by the department. The sanction was severe, in that the reduction in the central grant was larger than the amount by which expenditure exceeded the target, compelling the local authority concerned to raise property taxes (commonly known as rates) disproportionately. This provision had the desired effect of checking local government expenditures in areas controlled by Conservative councils, but was less successful in areas controlled by Labour councils. Many of the latter, particularly in the larger cities and the metropolitan counties, followed a deliberate policy of exceeding the government's expenditure limits and raising taxes to cover the ensuing deficit. It was reported in the autumn of 1981 that over half the local authorities in England had exceeded the specified limits.

From the point of view of countering inflation, this did not matter, as the extra sums involved were both raised and spent locally. However, the government's macro-economic policies were designed not only to counter inflation but also to stimulate business enterprise by reducing the overall burden of taxation. In terms of this objective, sharp increases in local property taxes mattered a good deal. The proportion of property taxes paid by business firms has increased in the postwar period, rising from 43 per cent in 1938 to 61 per cent in 1975 (Dearlove, 1979, pp. 240–1). In 1980–1 the Confederation of British Industry responded to widespread rate increases in urban areas by launching a nation-wide campaign to reduce the burden on business, applying pressure to both local authorities and the national government (for details see May, 1984). In November 1981 the Secretary of State for the Environment delivered himself of the following comment in Parliament: 'The fact is that a £1 billion overspend is not the marginal excess of legitimate freedom. It is the extravagant consequence of political licence. It is too large, too persistent and too flagrant' (quoted in Bulpitt, 1983, p. 213).

The government then introduced new measures in the Local Government Finance Bill, one section of which contained the following provisions: (1) that the government would set a limit for the level of property taxes in each area; (2) that any authority wishing to raise taxes beyond this limit would have to hold a referendum on the question; and (3) that the extra taxes above the limit would fall mainly on householders rather than on business.

This attempt to activate the ordinary citizen in the struggle against institutional power was entirely in line with the liberal and populist attitudes of the Thatcher government, reflected later in its attempt to limit the power of trade union leaders by requiring them to be subject to regular election by members. However, the Local Government Finance Bill ran into trouble. It met with fierce opposition from the Association of County Councils and the Association of Metropolitan Authorities, two powerful interest groups that had been fully consulted on local government matters by previous national governments but largely ignored since 1979. They were supported by many Conservative back-benchers, who disliked the provision for referendums. Within a month it became clear that the Bill was unlikely to get through the House of Commons and the government withdrew it. A modified version of the legislation, omitting the provision for referendums, was then introduced, but this also ran into opposition from Conservative back-benchers and was reduced in scope before it was enacted.

By this time the whole issue of central-local relationships had become thoroughly politicized. In London, for instance, the Labour Chairman of the Greater London Council (a young left-winger called Ken Livingstone) made it clear that he regarded it as the task of the GLC to act as a centre of opposition to Conservative rule. One issue was the subsidy for public transport services paid by the GLC, which was raised to a level that the government thought unreasonable. The GLC was taken to court on this issue by one of the district councils in London, representing a part of the city that was served by British Rail rather than the London Underground, so that its residents gained relatively little from the reduced fares made possible by the subsidy. In a highly controversial judgement, it was ruled that the GLC's subsidies were extravagant to the point of being illegal. Amid a storm of argument, the GLC then found a legal loophole that allowed it to continue sizeable subsidies, albeit on a somewhat smaller scale than those that had been disallowed. Other urban authorities, including the six metropolitan counties, also gave large subsidies to public transport services out of the receipts of property taxes.

In 1983 the Conservative Party included a provision in its election manifesto declaring that, if returned to power, it would abolish the Greater London Council and the six metropolitan county councils, a move seen by most commentators as overtly partisan. In 1984 the government extended the battle by taking powers to set legal limits to the budgets of local authorities with a record of overspending, it being provided that any councils refusing to comply with the limits would be in violation of the law.

This produced agonized debates in several of the councils affected, including the GLC. It so happened that several Labour members of the GLC were attempting to secure selection as parliamentary candidates at the time the deadline for the budget was reached in April 1985. These councillors faced the predicament of wanting to vote against a legal budget for ideological reasons (a step which could be expected to find favour in the eyes of constituency selection committees), while also knowing that if a legal budget were not passed they would be liable to disqualification from holding any political office. After an all-night debate, a legal budget was finally agreed with minutes to spare.

In Liverpool, an even more militant council refused to endorse a legal budget at the required time, which posed a dilemma of political authority in a particularly sharp way. A government can give orders and pass laws, but it needs the co-operation of other authorities and the compliance of citizens if these orders and laws are to be translated into effective administration. The Liverpool City Council, providing public services for over half a million people, is too important a body to be ignored or abolished. The government had the option of dismissing the councillors and appointing commissioners to run the city, but this would involve several disadvantages; it would alienate people attached to the principle of local democracy, would burden the government with the responsibility for direct administration of the city with the highest unemployment rate in the country, and would raise the difficult future question of when it would be safe (from the government's point of view) to hold fresh elections for the council. After much controversy, the Liverpool City Council overspent its legal budget and covered the gap by securing a loan from a consortium of Swiss banks.

In consequence of these developments, relations between the national government and many local authorities have acquired an adversarial and ideological character that is completely new to Britain. This raises questions about the whole future of local government, which require some discussion of the merits and value of local democracy and self-government, as hitherto practised in Britain.

The Merits of Local Self-Government

If the issue is considered in terms of democratic principles, it can be said that the idea of local democracy implies three things. First, it implies that elected representatives should have effective control of decision-making in local government. Secondly, it implies that these representatives should be fully accountable to the electorate and responsive to public opinion, through competitive elections and a fairly high level of communication between councillors on one hand and electors and pressure groups on the other. Thirdly, it implies what J. S. Mill called civic education, meaning widespread knowledge of local government activities and a reasonably high degree of popular participation in community affairs.

The first of these conditions has clearly been achieved in Britain. Control of policy rests with the council, in which the members are elected for three-year terms of office. Councils operate through a set of specialized committees such as the Education Committee, the Housing Committee and the Parks Committee, each of which keeps a continuing watch on its branch of local administration and reports to council each month. The chief officers of the authority act as secretaries of the respective committees and can expect to have a good deal of influence on what is decided, but they are not entitled to vote. The council as a whole is limited in its freedom of choice by the requirements of the central government, but within these limits the power to make decisions rests clearly in the hands of the elected representatives.

There is much more doubt about the second condition. In rural areas there is little competition to serve on local councils and most elections are uncontested. A rough check indicated that in the mid-1970s about 40 per cent of all local councillors in England and Wales had been returned unopposed at their last election. When the author lived in the East Riding of Yorkshire he went for years without a chance to vote in county elections. When there was a contested election he did not actually use his vote, as minimal campaigning and the poverty of the local press left him without any useful information about the candidates, all of whom were standing as independents.

In urban areas elections are usually contested and fought on party lines. However, in most cities voting in local elections is determined on the basis of national party loyalties and the swing of votes between one election and the next is determined by the relative popularity of the national parties. There are exceptions, but as a normal rule local issues play very little part in local elections. The turn-out in local elections is much lower than in national elections, averaging about 40 per cent instead of about 75 per cent. In view of all these circumstances, it cannot be said that local accountability is very effective in Britain. Jones and Stewart make much of it in their defence of local self-government (Jones and Stewart, 1983), and it is certainly true that (when elections are contested) electors have the opportunity to return a verdict on the performance of their councillors if they wish to do so. But the argument is weakened by the fact that in practice electors rarely behave in this way.

The third argument for local democracy is that it contributes to civic education. The evidence about this is mixed. Local government provides an opportunity for people to participate in the political system, either by standing for election or by working for pressure groups that operate at the local level. Pressure groups of this kind have become increasingly influential in the last two decades, though they are not yet as active as their American equivalents. There are certainly opportunities for the civic education of the active minority.

General public knowledge about local government is limited. It has been hindered in the past by the secrecy in which many local authorities have wrapped their activities and it is still hindered by the nature of the mass media. As noted in Chapter 1, local newspapers are less important in Britain than in most other countries because almost everyone reads one of the national papers. Local papers are read partly for their advertisements and partly as evening papers, in which case they tend to give prominence to national news because what people want is a follow-up to the news items they have read in the morning. Relatively few local papers try to make a story out of the activities of their local council. Television programmes are not localized and do not report municipal news at all.

In this situation local government cannot be said to contribute much to the civic education of the masses. Most people show less knowledge of, and less interest in, local issues than national issues. Local politics simply do not have the vitality that they have in the United States, where elections are more keenly contested, electors are often given the opportunity to vote in referendums on local issues, and the press and other mass media feature local news. For all these reasons, only limited importance can be attached to arguments about local democracy in Britain.

It does not follow, however, that the country would be equally well governed if the functions of local authorities were henceforth taken over by civil servants. 'Democracy' and 'self-government' are not synonymous terms, as the recent history of Africa makes clear. Several other arguments can be put forward in support of the rather muddled British system of local self-government.

First, it would seem to be undesirable if political power throughout Britain were completely monopolized by the party that enjoys a temporary majority in the House of Commons. In a period of Conservative rule at Westminster, it must be a good thing that there are some positions of authority controlled by the Labour Party and some opportunity for Labour politicians to translate their ideas into practice. From the point of view of the citizen, it must be desirable that Labour supporters in industrial cities should be able to feel that the city council is on their side, even though the national government is controlled by their political opponents. The same argument would apply to Conservative supporters in the southern counties during periods of Labour government at the national level.

Secondly, local self-government provides opportunity for diversity and experimentation. There are significant differences between school systems in different counties, even though these are limited by the activities of government inspectors and the fact that all children have to be prepared for national examinations. There are differences in the administration of libraries, the collection of rubbish, the planning of housing estates and many other matters. Local authorities learn from one another, and this is a real benefit even though it is impossible to quantify.

Thirdly, there is a considerable advantage in what, for want of a better name, can just be called 'localism'. Communities vary in their needs and their atmosphere, and it must be desirable for personal services at the local level to be controlled by people who are familiar with the area and can tailor the delivery of services to fit local circumstances.

For these reasons, a strong case can be made for the continuance of local self-government. If it is to continue, it seems evident that local authorities should have enough autonomy to make the work of local councillors sufficiently satisfying for talented people to be attracted to this kind of unpaid public service. Moreover, local authorities need more stability of expectations than they have been granted in recent years. If they prepare a budget that conforms to governmental guidelines, they have a right to expect that the rules of the game will not be changed during the course of the financial year, which has happened on several occasions since 1979.

As this book goes to press, it seems that the local government system may indeed be moving towards greater stability, but under a new set of rules framed by the central government. On the one hand, the Local Government and Housing Act of 1989 imposes new rules about the internal workings of local authorities. There are rules about the partisan make-up of local government committees, designed to ensure a fair balance between the parties represented on the whole council. There is a ban on the practice that some local authorities have adopted of giving voting rights to co-opted members of committees. There is a ban on people employed in a range of executive or professional positions in local government seeking election as local councillors, to terminate what the government regards as an abuse that has become more common in recent years.

On the other hand, the government is insisting that local authorities become more open and competitive in the provision of services. Council tenants have not only been given the option of buying council houses but, if they live in blocks of flats, of deciding by majority vote to switch from the municipal landlord to a private landlord if one approved by the central government comes forward with a suitable offer. Council schools have been given the chance to opt out of local government control if a majority of parents wish their school to become independent, with direct grants from the central government. Local authorities are being required to engage in competitive tendering for the provision of certain local services, including school meals, street cleaning and refuse collection. In these ways local authorities are being transformed, whether they like it or not, from being monopolistic providers of public services in their area to being 'enabling authorities' (N. Ridley, 1988), with an overall responsibility for ensuring that the services are provided, by themselves or by others, in ways that are cost-efficient and popular with the consumers.

Critics of the government allege that all these new rules constitute an interference with local government and a reduction in local autonomy. Supporters of the government maintain that the purpose of the changes is to liberalize and open up the local government system. Both arguments are largely valid. It remains to be seen whether the system will settle down, under these new rules, to a period of greater stability than it has had in the past two decades.

Further Reading

An account of the structure of local government is given in Alexander (1982), *Local Government in Britain since Reorganization*; a discussion of local government at work will be found in Elcock (1982), *Local Government*; the case for local democracy is argued in Jones and Stewart (1983), *The Case for Local Government*; the case for the Thatcher government's approach is argued in N. Ridley (1988), *The Local Right: Enabling not Providing*; there are numerous studies of politics in particular communities, ranging in size from Glossop (population 20,000), analysed in Birch (1959), *Small-Town Politics*, to Birmingham (population over a million), analysed in Newton (1976), *Second City Politics*; a valuable historical analysis of central–local relations will be found in Bulpitt (1983), *Territory and Power in the United Kingdom*.

◇ 15 ◇

Conducting Foreign Policy

The discussion so far in this book has focused entirely on the internal government of Great Britain. It is now appropriate to turn our attention to the management of Britain's relationships with other states and to the associated problem of providing for national defence.

Executive Control of Foreign Policy

The conduct of foreign policy is in the hands of the Foreign and Commonwealth Office, which has has that title since the previously separate Department of Commonwealth Relations was merged with the Foreign Office in 1968, but will henceforth, for simplicity, be referred to by its traditional and familiar title of the Foreign Office. The Foreign Office is second in importance only to the Treasury in the British administrative hierarchy, and the views of the Foreign Secretary carry great weight in Cabinet discussions. These two departments are concerned with 'high politics', as distinct from the 'low politics' of the departments dealing with such issues as health, agriculture, transport and municipal government.

The Foreign Secretary, like the Chancellor of the Exchequer, keeps in close touch with the Prime Minister, who may be called upon to answer parliamentary questions dealing with foreign affairs in the twice-weekly sessions of Prime Minister's Question Time and who often deals directly with other heads of government on critical issues of policy. In the middle of the nineteenth century Foreign Secretaries such as Palmerston and Lord John Russell could conduct foreign relations in considerable independence of their Prime Minister (see Vital, 1968, p. 54), but this has not been possible in the twentieth century and is unthinkable today. In critical periods postwar Prime Ministers have even taken foreign policy largely into their own hands, as Eden did over the nationalization of the Suez Canal, Heath did during Britain's negotiations to join the European Community, and Thatcher did when Argentina invaded the Falkland Islands. Six of the nine postwar Prime Ministers – all except Churchill, Douglas-Home and Callaghan – have at one time or another taken charge of particular diplomatic issues.

To say this is not to suggest that the Foreign Office has been elbowed aside on these occasions. The British Prime Minister is not in the position of the US President, who has his own very sizeable staff in the White House and is able to appoint personal emissaries whose powers may overshadow those of the Secretary of State, as Henry Kissinger's powers did for several years. The Prime Minister has only a minimal staff at 10 Downing Street and until 1982 was entirely dependent on Foreign Office staff for advice and assistance in regard to diplomatic affairs. Since 1982 Margaret Thatcher has had her own diplomatic adviser in the Prime Minister's Office, a development which was intended and was seen as something of a rebuff to the Foreign Office, but her advisers have been men who have spent most of their careers in the diplomatic service and the importance of this move should not be exaggerated. Thatcher has indeed shown an increasing tendency to engage in personal diplomacy in the late 1980s, as she has become the most senior of the world's leaders and has enjoyed a close friendly relationship with President Reagan, but the effective conduct of foreign policy requires a considerable staff and that staff is provided by the Foreign Office.

The Foreign Secretary is assisted by three ministers of state and three parliamentary under-secretaries, so the ministerial team is a strong one. The Diplomatic Service is also strong. On the one hand, it is considerable larger than the diplomatic services of other states of similar size and power, such as West Germany, France and Italy. On the other hand, its members are recruited separately from the members of equivalent ranks of the home Civil Service, and as entry standards are very high the Foreign Office prides itself on hiring the *crème de la crème* for its staff. There is substance to this claim; the Foreign Office has often been criticized for its lack of long-term planning, but hardly ever been criticized for poor execution of policy. When Argentina invaded the Falklands, Britain needed a two-thirds majority vote in the UN Security Council to condemn the invasion. The odds were heavily against this, but the British mission achieved it. A senior American delegate described this feat as 'a stunning example of sheer diplomatic professionalism' (Hastings and Jenkins, 1983, p. 101).

The Influence of Parliamentary and Public Opinion

Parliament exerts unfluence over foreign policy in exactly the same way as it exerts influence over domestic policy; through parliamentary questions, debates on policy issues, and the potential sanctions of being able to force a ministerial resignation or to pass a vote of no confidence in the government's handling of foreign affairs. In practice, however, most MPs are less interested in foreign affairs than in home affairs. The average voter has little interest in foreign policy and it is rare for MPs to be subject to constituency pressures in this field. It is relatively difficult for MPs to acquire an expert knowledge of diplomatic matters and there is little incentive for them to do so. The normal timetable of the House of Commons provides for the Foreign Secretary (or his deputy, if the Foreign Secretary is in the House of Lords) to answer questions only once every three weeks.

This relative quiescence of Parliament is encouraged by the fact that the political parties have rarely disagreed over foreign policy. There are running disagreements within the Labour Party over nuclear arms, but when in power the Labour Party has followed the same policy as the Conservative Party on this issue. The only two occasions since 1945 when there has been outright disagreement between government and opposition over foreign affairs were over the Suez invasion in 1956, and in 1971–3 over Britain's application to join the European Community. The conflict over Suez was short-lived, as the invasion was called off within two weeks. The front-bench conflict over the European community was moderated by the fact that both main parties were divided on the issue. In the crucial vote the number of Labour MPs who defied their Whips to support British entry, namely sixty-nine, exceeded the number of Conservative and Ulster Unionist MPs who defied their Whips to oppose entry, namely thirty-nine, to such an extent that the government's narrow margin of support was actually given to it by Labour dissidents.

A different kind of example of parliamentary influence was provided by the emergency debate that took place immediately following the Argentinian invasion of the Falkland Islands. In this debate the vehement demands for a strong British response, coming from all parts of the House and from the Leader of the Opposition, virtually compelled the government to make immediate plans for a British task force to re-take the islands. These demands were not unwelcome to the government, but the political situation in the following weeks would have been very different if the main political parties had taken conflicting views on the issue.

The fact that the government can normally expect to get parliamentary support for its foreign policies does not mean that Parliament can be taken for granted. In times of crisis, parliamentary questions and debates can be very penetrating. This has been true of all of the critical issues that have arisen in the post war period, including British policy in Palestine, the emergency in Malaya, the Berlin blockade, the Mau Mau campaign in Kenya, the Korean war, the conflict with Egypt over the Suez Canal, relations with Israel and the Arab states, the violent confrontation with Indonesia, the civil war in Nigeria, Rhodesia's unilateral declaration of independence, relations with the European Community, the dispute with Iceland over fishing limits, and the crisis over the Falkland Islands. The Foreign Secretary and the Minister of Defence have to be prepared to answer parliamentary questions day after day when crises are in progress. Their situation stands in sharp contrast to the easy time that the US Secretary of State and Secretary of Defence had in regard to Congress during the Vietnam war, for neither of them had to submit to congressional questioning between October 1964, when Congress authorized the dispatch of American forces to Vietnam, and February 1968, when it became apparent that the Americans were unable to defeat the Viet Cong.

If parliamentary criticism of the government reveals weaknesses in governmental policy or behaviour that cannot be disguised, the Foreign Secretary may feel obliged to resign. This was illustrated dramatically in 1982, when the Foreign Secretary, though himself in the House of Lords, felt he had to resign in response to forthright criticism from back-bench Conservative MPs in the 1922 Committee of the failure of the Foreign Office to predict that Argentina would invade the Falklands. The failure was not Lord Carrington's fault, but Foreign Office policy had ended in disaster and Carrington felt honour bound to accept responsibility for this. Two other Foreign Office ministers, themselves in the Commons, resigned with him.

Since 1979 the House of Commons has had select committees on both foreign affairs and defence, as noted in Chapter 12. These are small specialized committees with wide powers to investigate and report on aspects of policy and administration within their fields. They have not yet had any marked influence on policy, but the Foreign Affairs Committee played an important role in 1980–2. At that time the Canadian government asked Parliament to approve a set of amendments to the British North America Act of 1867 which included a proposal to transfer all subsequent powers of amendment to Canada. These amendments were opposed by the majority of the Canadian provinces and this rather delicate issue was immediately referred by the House of Commons to its committee, which heard evidence from experts on constitutional law. After considerable study and debate, the committee unanimously recommended that the Canadian proposals be rejected because they did not have support from sufficient provinces. After protracted controversy within Canada, the proposals were amended in ways that satisfied all but one of the provinces. The amended proposals then went through Parliament without difficulty. The Foreign Affairs Committee was invaluable in this affair, not only because it was able to call expert witnesses and prepare an incisive report but also because it enabled the House of Commons to avoid having an embarrassing debate on the floor of the House that might have had a damaging effect on Anglo-Canadian relations.

Outside Parliament, there are numerous pressure groups that seek influence over foreign policy. At one level, there are élite institutions like the Royal Institute of International Affairs, the International Institute of Strategic Studies, the Royal United Services Institution and the Foreign Affairs Club. They help to shape informed opinion about diplomatic issues, which is also shaped by (and reflected in) *The Times*, the *Economist* and the several other intellectual journals and newspapers.

Alongside these groups with a general concern for the national interest in foreign relations, there are several organizations with a more particular focus, often supported by business firms that have an interest in particular parts of the world. Among these are the China Association, the Sino-British Trade Council, the South Africa Club, the West Africa Committee, the British Atlantic Committee, the Anglo-German Association and Britain in Europe. Such groups sponsor meetings with an educative effect and also press information and views on senior Foreign Office officials and interested back-bench MPs.

In addition to these groups with a geographical focus, there are also groups with a particular slant on foreign affairs. There are, for instance, several groups concerned with British aid to the Third World, whose activities in Britain are co-ordinated by the Voluntary Committee on Aid and Development. There is the British Council of Churches, which promotes various Christian causes in relation to foreign policy. There is the United Nations Association, whose activities are mainly educational; Amnesty International, whose varied activities are designed to help political prisoners abroad; and the Corporation of Foreign Bondholders, whose members have special interests to be defended. All such groups communicate their views to the Foreign Office and to sympathetic MPs.

At the level of mass opinion, pressure groups tend to be radical in outlook and to be more interested in defence issues than in foreign policy as such. The largest of them is the Campaign for Nuclear Disarmament (henceforth CND), that has been in business since the late 1950s and in its more successful phases has enjoyed the support of tens of thousands of active sympathizers. The CND and various allied groups have gained a great deal of publicity for their cause over the years, though without ever persuading more than a minority of the public to accept their point of view. The polls have varied from time to time, but in the late 1980s they suggested that about 15 per cent of the electors accepted the arguments for unilateral nuclear disarmament by Britain. There is no evidence that the Ministry of Defence or the Foreign Office have ever modified their policies to take account of the pressures generated by these groups.

The most successful of the radical pressure groups would appear to be Anti-Apartheid, which has played some part (though other factors were also at work) in persuading British governments to stop all regular sporting contacts with South Africa. It has never been likely, however, that it would persuade the government to adopt economic sanctions against the Republic; too many British interests would be harmed by such a policy, which has little support among élite opinion.

Issues in Foreign Policy

For the past two centuries Britain's foreign policies have been deeply influenced by economic and geographical factors. Since the industrial revolution transformed British society and led to a rapid increase in its population, Britain has been dependent on imported foodstuffs and raw materials to feed its people and supply its industries. Needing to get these goods from remote parts of the world, it has also been dependent on trade routes and freedom to navigate the seas. At the same time, its position as a group of islands has protected it from invasion by foreign armies. So long as the Royal Navy had control of the seas, Britain was safe. Its traditional policy has therefore been to avoid fixed alliances that would restrict its freedom of action, while intervening in European affairs when this seemed necessary to prevent any one rival power becoming supreme among its neighbours.

These policies were pursued successfully from 1815 until 1914. In the period between the wars Britain was much weaker in terms of both economic power and defence capacity, but the diplomatic implications of these weaknesses were disguised by the isolation of the United States, the Soviet Union's domestic problems, and the confused state of European relationships. It was not until 1945, that, with the British economy ruined by the war and the emergence of the United States and the Soviet Union as super-powers, it became clear that the United Kingdom could no longer sustain the role of a great world power, independently responsible for its own defence.

Since 1945 British diplomacy has been dominated by three problems: the need to maintain the American commitment to the defence of western Europe; the need to dismantle the colonial empire; and the need to establish new relationships with its European friends and allies. In summary, it may be said to have been successful in dealing with the first problem; fairly successful in dealing with the second; and rather unsuccessful in dealing with the third.

A frank discussion of Anglo-American relationships is often confused by a cloud of wishful British thinking about the 'special relationship' that is said to exist between the two countries. In fact, British friendship and co-operation, though important to the United States, is no more important than the friendship and co-operation of West Germany, Italy or France. Much is often made of the friendly personal relationships that have existed between Macmillan and Kennedy or Thatcher and Reagan, but these are balanced by the poor relationships that obtained between Eden and Eisenhower and Wilson and Johnson. American foreign policy was actively hostile to British interests over the Suez crisis, was apparently neutral over the confrontation with Indonesia and was only hesitantly supportive over the Falklands crisis. There is evidence of a close relationship in the exchange of international intelligence, in numerous academic exchanges and in certain kinds of co-operation in the training of naval, military and air force personnel, but at the diplomatic level talk of a special relationship is generally unhelpful.

If this is discounted, the fact remains that Britain has been entirely successful, in conjunction with West Germany and other allies, in maintaining the American commitment to an active and immediate defence of western Europe against Soviet aggression. This is a very expensive commitment for America, with over 300,000 military personnel (roughly the strength of Britain's entire armed forces) stationed in Europe. As the Soviet Union is the only perceived threat to British security, the maintenance of this commitment is vital to Britain. It is partly for this reason that the British government has, perhaps unnecessarily, made occasional gestures that look like subservience to American policy, such as the partial boycott of the 1980 Moscow Olympic Games, verbal support for American policy towards El Salvador, or the decision to allow American planes to bomb Libya from bases on British soil. In the late 1980s American public opinion has been increasingly concerned about the cost of the commitment and there is mounting pressure to persuade the European members of NATO to shoulder a larger share of the defence burden. As Allen may well be correct in predicting that the European states will be unwilling to incur substantial extra costs 'unless such an action is forced upon them by a unilateral US decision' (Allen, 1988, p. 181), and as Congress may quite possibly take such a decision, this could be a serious point of tension within the western alliance in the near future. If such tension develops, resolving it is likely to be the top priority of British foreign policy in the 1990s.

The process of decolonization undertaken by Britain after 1945 was managed speedily and quite effectively. In 1947 India and Pakistan were created as independent states and in the same year it was decided to move the African colonies towards independence as soon as practicable, beginning with the colonies in West Africa because they had no British settlers to complicate the procedure. The East African colonies followed quickly thereafter and it was only in Central Africa that serious difficulties emerged.

There, the colony of Southern Rhodesia (subsequently called simply Rhodesia and now called Zimbabwe) had been governed for decades by representatives of the white settlers, who numbered about 210,000 in the 1960s, without any share in political power being given to representatives of the native African population, who numbered nearly four million. After it became clear that the British government proposed to extend the franchise to Africans, the settler government made a unilateral declaration of independence in 1965. The British government could not prevent this without using armed force, which no parliamentary party was willing to support. Sanctions were imposed and made international, but these proved to be as ineffectual as economic sanctions invariably are. It was not until the adjoining Portuguese colony of Mozambique became independent in the hands of a radical government, and started to give active assistance to black guerrilla bands operating in Rhodesia, that the white government agreed to a British proposal, worked out at the 1979 Commonwealth Conference, to hold free elections with the franchise extended to all adult citizens. The result was the independent state of Zimbabwe, with the settlers holding only a few guaranteed seats in its legislative assembly.

In certain other colonies there was violence before independence, but successive British governments, whether Labour or Conservative, dealt with these problems in a highly pragmatic way. When British forces in Palestine had to cope with Jewish terrorists as well as with Arab terrorists, the British abandoned the colony (strictly speaking a Mandated Territory) precipitately, leaving chaos behind them. When the British got tired of dealing with Greek Cypriot terrorists in Cyprus, they negotiated a settlement that gave Cyprus independence while leaving Turkey with the right to intervene militarily if the Turkish minority were threatened by Greeks, as subsequently occurred. When rebel forces in Aden proved particularly awkward, the British withdrew speedily.

In Kenya, with a sizeable number of British settlers to be protected, the government engaged in a three-year struggle against Mau-Mau terrorists. This campaign was waged largely by native troops and police and was entirely successful. It was only in Malaya that the British army had to be used in a prolonged fight against rebel forces, and British governments had a good reason for pursuing this struggle. Whereas most colonies were of limited economic use to Britain, the rubber industry made Malaya extremely valuable. By some estimates, the profits Britain derived from Malaya exceeded the profits from all the other forty or more colonies put together. With a good deal to fight for, British troops conducted a small-scale but prolonged campaign against a sizeable band of Chinese terrorists, aided substantially by the fact that the Malays, who comprised 50 per cent of the population (against 40 per cent Chinese) were entirely on the British side. After eleven years of struggle, the terrorists were completely defeated and the British subsequently handed over a peaceful country to an independent government composed of an alliance of Malay, Chinese and Indian leaders.

Other colonies were moved towards independence without serious trouble, the only areas retaining colonial status in 1989 being Hong Kong (to be returned to China in 1997), Gibraltar, the Falkland Islands and eleven territories with very small populations. Gibraltar and the Falkland Islands remain as colonies because their inhabitants strongly prefer British rule to rule by Spain or Argentina.

The controversial feature about the Commonwealth is not the decolonization process as such, which has been completed with relative efficiency, but the decision to retain the Commonwealth as a loose and amorphous multi-racial institution after decolonization, instead of cutting Britain's institutional links with its former colonies, as France, after a period of indecision, has cut links with its. Critics maintain that this decision has had two disadvantages for Britain.

First, it is said that the biennial Commonwealth Conference has proved to be a time-wasting affair, chiefly remarkable for the opportunity it gives to the leaders of former colonies to castigate Britain for alleged failings, such as the British refusal to invoke economic sanctions against South Africa. However, it should be noted that the Conference helped Britain to resolve the crisis over Rhodesia and that there are intangible benefits to be gained from personal contacts between heads of government that may be more important than the occasional moments of embarrassment. It is relevant that the very extensive British economic interests in southern Africa make it important to maintain friendly relationships with the governments of the area and to do what can be done to promote peaceful reform in South Africa.

Secondly, it is said that concern about Commonwealth relationships was an important factor in persuading the British government not to join the European Economic Community when it was formed in 1957. This is a much more serious criticism. It seems clearly to be true, and the decision was a fateful one from which Britain has suffered ever since. The terms of entry secured in 1971 were not very favourable to British economic interests; and for that matter were not very favourable to Commonwealth interests either. If Britain had entered at the beginning it could undoubtedly have protected its interests more efficiently, could probably have secured a less expensive agricultural policy, and might have been able to play a part in devising European institutions that were less dominated by bureaucrats than the present ones are. The decision not to enter was the most serious mistake of British foreign policy since the Second World War.

British policy towards western Europe has been consistently problematical. By standing aloof from the far-sighted attempts made after the war towards European unity, Britain squandered the immense goodwill it had throughout the continent, Germany excepted, in 1945. It has watched France and Germany forge an alliance that enables those two countries to dominate European diplomacy, leaving Britain on the sidelines. It could only get rather poor terms when it entered the Community and its has since proved an uneasy member of that Community. Awkwardness over the Common Agricultural Policy was justifiable, and indeed Mrs Thatcher deserves credit for inducing the Community to adopt a less extravagant policy in 1988. But adopting a consistently negative attitude towards the attempt to build a more united Europe is no way to make friends and influence people.

As one of the poorer members of the Community, Britain would actually gain economically from a more unified system of European government. In any common market, some regions, often in the centre of the area, tend to gain more from freedom of trade than other regions, often at the periphery. If there is a decentralized system of government within the market, the poorer regions get less in taxation than the richer regions because they have a smaller tax base, while having high expenditures on unemployment relief and other social services. If there is a centralized system, on the other hand, there will be an automatic process of fiscal redistribution from the taxes of the wealthier regions, through the public services, to the poorer regions. This is the main reason why the economic differences between the regions of centralized states like Britain and France are smaller than the differences between the regions of federal states like Canada and the United States.

Now, within the European Community, France, Germany, Holland and northern Italy have all gained more from the common market than Britain, Ireland or southern Italy. It is a matter of simple economic logic that the latter would therefore benefit more than the former from the fiscal redistribution to be secured from centralized public and social services. There are of course other issues besides economic logic that are important in the determination of policy. Cultural differences between regions are important and so are ideological differences. A fact that makes the Community seem a somewhat alien body to British politicians is that power within it is largely concentrated in the hands of the bureaucrats of the European Commission, who are not accountable to elected politicians for their decisions (see Shackleton, 1984, pp. 172–6). The

British have not found it easy to adapt to the procedures within Community institutions and this is one reason why British politicians have shown little recognition of the economic advantages that Britain might gain from a greater degree of European unity. An additional reason, no doubt, is the unpopularity of the Community among many British electors. British nationalism is too strong a force for the British to take easily to the idea of giving up more of their national independence.

Another way of viewing the impact of British membership of the European Community is to consider its impact upon the making of foreign policy within Britain. This impact has had two clear effects. One is to increase the influence of the Prime Minister, who quite frequently has to speak for Britain at Community meetings. The other is to involve government departments other than the Foreign Office and the Ministry of Defence in diplomatic negotiations. Ministers and officials of the Ministry of Agriculture and the Department of Trade and Industry, to name only the two most obvious examples, are constantly in touch with their opposite members in the Brussels bureaucracy and in other European governments. In 1977 the Central Policy Review Staff found that only 46 per cent of the personnel working in Britain's external relations were employed through the Foreign Office 'and only 14 per cent were members of the Diplomatic Service' (Clarke, 1988, pp. 80–1). The growing importance of European Community activities means that these percentages have probably declined since 1977, and will decline further. By 1922, for instance, the Community will acquire legal jurisdiction over aspects of environmental policy within Britain.

In the long run, negotiations within the European Community may cease to be regarded as aspects of foreign policy and come simply to be looked on as part of Britain's domestic government. In the course of time, the Community will almost certainly develop its own foreign policy, towards which some steps have already been taken. A common attitude has been developed, for instance, towards the Arab–Israeli dispute. The member-states applied sanctions against Argentina during the Falkland Islands crisis, even though some of them had reservations about British policy. The Community was also united in taking diplomatic action against Iran when the Ayatollah urged Muslims to murder a British author. In most negotiations over international trade and international fishing rights, the Community already speaks with a single voice. In these various ways, the Community is becoming more powerful and the Foreign Office is losing more and more of the near-monopoly it once enjoyed in respect of Britain's external relationships.

Issues in Defence Policy

Defence policy has proved to be the most controversial aspect of British foreign policy since the last war. For a long time after 1945, Britain maintained the defence posture of a world power, with commitments in the Mediterranean, the

Persian Gulf and the Far East as well as in the North Atlantic and the approaches to British coastal waters. The trouble with this policy was that Britain could not afford it, so that its limited forces were stretched much too thinly. It was not until 1968 that Britain abandoned its naval base at Singapore and announced that it was withdrawing from all defence commitments east of Suez.

Since that time, British defence policy has been based on the assumption that the only serious threat to British security is the threat of a Soviet invasion of western Europe. British forces are committed to NATO and British military training is shaped by the belief that the next war, if there is one, will be against the Soviet Union. British tanks are designed to fight Soviet tanks and the ships of the Royal Navy are specifically planned to deal with Soviet ships and submarines in the North Atlantic. From the point of view of the British armed forces, the Argentine invasion of the Falklands came just in time, as the assault ship essential to the British landing there was nearing the end of its useful life and was not due to be replaced. This policy makes excellent sense in the current state of the world, but it sharpens the question of why Britain needs an independent nuclear deterrent.

The decision to manufacture a British atomic bomb was taken by the Labour government in 1947, before the United States was fully committed to the defence of western Europe, and can be regarded as a logical step in the circumstances of the time. However, the case for the bomb in military terms ended in 1949 with the creation of NATO, and in the 1950s and 1960s the deterrent (including not only the bomb but also what became more costly, an effective means of delivering it) was justified primarily in diplomatic terms. The avowed object was to enhance British prestige and to give Britain 'a seat at the top table' in international negotiations.

In the 1970s and 1980s, it became apparent that this diplomatic argument afforded only a very weak justification for a commitment that had become extremely expensive because of the cost of nuclear submarines capable of firing long-distance rockets. The British were not, after all, included in the SALT negotiations between the United States and the Soviet Union over strategic arms limitations, nor did it seem likely that British interests were harmed by this exclusion. In recent years it has been accepted that the only plausible justification for continuing to maintain the deterrent is to provide insurance against the possibility that the United States might one day retreat into isolation, leaving western Europe to fend for itself. This is clearly a remote possibility, but defence planners do not forget that America has a poor track record, having stood on one side from 1914 to 1917 and again from 1939 to December 1941. If Britain had been invaded in 1940, the United States would have remained neutral. The fact that one does not expect one's house to be burned down, it is argued, should not prevent one from buying an insurance policy to cover this possibility.

The paradoxical aspect of the nuclear deterrent, seen in this light, is that although Britain can make its own hydrogen bombs it is dependent on the United States for missile delivery systems. It therefore has to buy the most expensive part of the deterrent from the very country whose possible defection is the only reason for having the deterrent. It is not surprising that the deterrent has become controversial within Britain.

The case against the deterrent is greatly weakened, however, by the terms in which it is usually put. The critics would have a rather strong case if they concentrated on the cost of the deterrent in a period when Britain's conventional forces have become smaller (see McGrew, 1988, pp.108–9) and there is strong American pressure for a greater contribution by the European members of NATO to the conventional forces available for the defence of western Europe. As a westwards onslaught by the Red Army is the only contingency which NATO planners fear, it could reasonably be argued that Britain would get better value for money by strengthening its conventional forces and weapons than by updating its nuclear deterrent.

However, the great majority of nuclear critics couch their argument in moral terms rather than in terms of cost-effectiveness. Nuclear weapons are evil, they maintain, and Britain should have no truck with them. The critics not only want the British deterrent to be scrapped, they also want Britain to shut down the US bases for nuclear weapons on British territory. Such action would undoubtedly infuriate the Americans and might well lead them to re-assess all their plans for western defence. The anti-nuclear lobbyists therefore put themselves into the paradoxical position of advocating a policy that might possibly lead to an American withdrawal from western Europe, even though this would immensely strengthen the case for an independent European deterrent which only Britain and France could provide.

This issue has become significant in British electoral politics because the Labour Party committed itself in 1981 to a policy of abandoning the nuclear deterrent and ordering the Americans to remove nuclear weapons from British bases. This policy is unpopular with the British electorate and contributed to the scale of Labour's defeat in 1983 and 1987. Because of this, Neil Kinnock made it clear in 1988 that he wanted Labour to modify its stance before the next general election. He was rebuffed in this aim at the 1988 party conference but he was successful in 1989. In any case, by the time of the next election the British government will have committed itself so firmly to purchasing the Trident submarine and missile system that no withdrawal would be feasible. The independent nuclear deterrent, with a modernized delivery system, is therefore certain to continue into the 1990s.

Further Reading

The best account of the policy-making process is that given in Wallace (1976), *The Foreign Policy Process in Britain*; the clearest account of the postwar history of foreign relations is still that in Northedge (1974), *Descent From Power*; the best discussion of the current situation is that in Smith, Smith, and White (eds.) (1988), *British Foreign Policy*.

Part V

The Citizen and the Government

◇ 16 ◇

The Rights of the Citizen

In Part III of this book we considered the roles played by citizens as voters, as party members and as members of pressure groups, and discussed the opportunities open to citizens to stand for election. In these chapters the citizen was viewed as an active or potentially active participant in the political process. This final part of the book will deal with the position of the citizen in his more passive role as a person who is governed. In the present chapter we shall consider his individual liberties and his rights in relation to the administration and the agencies for law-enforcement. In the following chapter we shall discuss the character and the role of the police, with particular reference to the growth of political violence. Finally, in Chapter 18 an attempt will be made to assess the problems and capacities of British government in the present period.

The rights and liberties of the citizen in Britain will be discussed in the following order: first, the basic civil rights of free speech and freedom of political action; secondly, the rights of the citizen in relation to the police and the courts; thirdly, the rights of the citizen in relation to government departments and other administrative authorities; fourthly, the right of ethnic minorities to be protected against discrimination; and finally, the significance for British citizens of the European Convention on Human Rights.

The Legal Basis of Civil Liberties

British civil liberties rest on a different basis from those in most other democracies. Elsewhere, civil rights are normally specified in writing, either in constitutional declarations of rights or in provisions of the legal code of the country. In the United States the fundamental civil liberties are set out in the constitution, the ten constitutional amendments that were added in 1791 (which are collectively known as the Bill of Rights) and the amendments that were passed after the Civil War with the intention of extending equal rights to blacks. In France civil rights were first specified in the Declaration of the Rights of Man and the Citizen of 1789, and the continuing French attachment to these rights is shown by the references to the declaration in the preambles of the constitutions of both the Fourth and the Fifth Republics. In other countries guarantees of rights are much more recent, depending on the dates on which regimes purporting to be liberal were first established.

The position in Britain is different because Britain has not gone through the common experience of overthrowing an oppressive system of government by force of arms and establishing a constitutional regime more or less *de novo*. Britain has enjoyed the rule of law for at least three centuries, since long before its political system was in any sense democratic, and the rights of citizens have been established not by the declarations of politicians but by the decisions of judges, interpreting the Common Law of the land. It follows that one could search the Statute Book in vain for acts conferring upon citizens the rights of free speech, freedom of association, or freedom of movement. These rights rest simply on the age-old assumption by British courts that a citizen is free to do as he likes provided he does not commit any specific breach of the law. A consequence of this situation is that the extent of civil rights can be assessed only by considering particular types of freedom and particular limitations that have been established over the years on the exercise of these freedoms.

Freedom of Speech

It is assumed by the courts that anyone is free to say or write what he likes provided he does not break the laws designed to protect the rights and security of his fellow-citizens. The laws of libel and slander are one check on this freedom; if a statement is made by A about B that is untrue and defames B's character, B may sue A in the civil courts and may be awarded substantial damages if he wins the case. But it is not libellous to publish a true statement unless malice can be established; nor is it libellous to hold a person up to ridicule, as is done in satirical programmes on television; nor is it libellous to say that a manufacturer's products are useless, as is done by consumers' associations.

A case lies for libel or slander only if an individual is named. What protection does the law afford to a group of citizens who are the collective victims of defamatory statements? One possibility is that the Director of Public Prosecutions may launch a prosecution for seditious libel. However, the last occasion on which this was done was in 1947, when the editor of a Lancashire local paper was prosecuted for publishing an anti-Semitic leading article. When the case was heard both judge and jury were so reluctant to restrict the freedom of the press that the result was an acquittal

Another possibility, if the statement is made in a public place, is that the speaker might be prosecuted for using insulting language. This was done in 1937, when a fascist speaker in the East End of London was successfully prosecuted for a speech at a public meeting in which he said that 'Jews are the lice of the earth and must be exterminated from our national life'. But the police generally lean over backwards to avoid prosecuting political speakers, no matter how offensive their remarks.

The legal situation has been somewhat changed by the passage of the Race Relations Act of 1965, which makes it a criminal offence to stir up racial hatred in a public place by written or spoken words. This led to a good deal of comment arising from the ingrained British dislike of anything approaching political censorship, and *The Times* observed that

> the clause can be seen to set the criminal law moving once again towards a position from which it has been retreating in Britain for about 300 years: judging the criminality of utterances by reference to their subject matter and content rather than by reference to their likely effect on public order. (*The Times*, 8 April 1965)

However, the British police share the values underlying this comment, and few cases have so far been brought under this section of the Act. Of these the most publicized case was against a speaker at a public meeting who described coloured immigrants as 'niggers and wops' and made some singularly unpleasant remarks about them. At the trial the jury failed to agree, and at the retrial the speaker was acquitted.

Other restrictions on freedom of speech are the laws against blasphemy, obscenity and incitement to violence. The law against blasphemy is a relic from earlier times that is now virtually obsolete. The law against obscenity has been liberalized by the passage of the Obscene Publications Act of 1959, under which a charge of obscenity can be successfully countered by proving (with the aid of expert witnesses) that the publication has literary merit. It was on this ground that the publishers of the unexpurgated edition of *Lady Chatterley's Lover* successfully withstood a prosecution alleging that this was an obscene publication. The law against incitement to violence will be discussed below, in connection with public meetings.

Freedom to March in Procession

It is both traditional and common in Britain for people wishing to demonstrate their views on a political issue to march in procession bearing placards. For many years members of the labour movement have done this on May Day. In the 1930s unemployed workers drew attention to their plight by marching from the north of England to London. In the 1960s tens of thousands of people marched about the country to indicate their dislike of nuclear weapons.

People are entitled to do this because the Queen's highway exists to facilitate travel from one place to another, and as each citizen enjoys the right to use the highway it necessarily follows that 10,000 citizens have the right to do so together. They have to be careful about stopping, because that may constitute obstruction, but so long as they keep on the move they are, with certain limitations, within the law.

There are three limitations on this right, one dating from the eighteenth

227

century and two fairly new. The first is that no processions or public meetings may be held within one mile of the Houses of Parliament while Parliament is in session. In practice it is common for meetings to be held with official permission in Trafalgar Square, but the one attempt made in recent years to move off from the square towards Parliament was briskly and effectively broken up by the police. The second limitation arises from the Public Order Act of 1936, which was passed because of the disorders caused by fascist meetings and processions in London. The Act gave any chief of police power to change the route of a procession if he had reason to think that it may otherwise lead to serious disorder, or to impose other conditions on the marchers to prevent disorder. Since then most organizers of marches have given the police notion of their intentions.

This arrangement protects the rights of demonstrators even though it may compel them to change their proposed route, for once the police have agreed to a march they are obliged to protect the marchers against hostile counter-demonstrations. In the 1970s the National Front, a racist organization, staged numerous marches that were attacked by radical left-wing groups. The National Front marchers were entitled to police protection because notice of their marches was given in advance, and the result was a series of violent clashes between left-wing demonstrators and the police, often leading to hundreds of injuries. In one clash a demonstrator and a police officer were killed. The cost of protecting the freedom to march was extremely high in these cases, and in 1985 an Act was passed requiring all march organizers to give a week's notice of their intentions, and empowering the police to ban such marches if they are deemed likely to constitute a threat to public order.

Freedom of Meeting

Since individuals are free to talk with one another, it follows that large numbers of them are free to gather together in a public meeting, provided they can find a place to meet. If they can hire premises, there is no problem. If they gather on the public highway, however, they will be guilty of obstruction, unless they have police permission. As motorists know to their cost, the highway is intended only for movement, and a motorist who parks in a cul-de-sac is technically guilty of obstruction although a procession of demonstrators holding up traffic on a main road are innocent of any such thing. It is commonly thought that people enjoy a legal right to hold meetings in public parks, but in fact meetings of this kind are dependent on the permission of the authorities who control the parks: the Department of the Environment in London and local authorities elsewhere. However, in practice such permission is fairly freely granted and, one way or another, groups who wish to hold a public meeting rarely find it dificult to do so.

The general principle governing public meetings is that people may say what they like provided it is not likely to lead to a breakdown of public order. If this likelihood arises, the police may ask the speaker to desist or in some circumstances they may arrest him. The offences with which he may be charged include disturbing the peace, inciting others to commit a breach of the peace, behaviour with intent to provoke a breach of the peace, behaviour whereby a breach of the peace is likely to be occasioned, insulting behaviour and (if he refuses a request to stop) obstructing a police officer in the execution of his duty. As a form of shorthand it is convenient to group these offences under the heading of incitement to violence.

The law regarding incitement to violence is generally administered in a liberal way, though the following examples show that there is a slight area of uncertainty at the margin. In 1914 George Lansbury was arrested after a meeting at which he had urged suffragettes to continue their militant tactics and was subsequently found guilty of inciting others to commit breaches of the peace. In 1961 Bertrand Russell and other leaders of the Committee of One Hundred were condemned on the same charge when they tried to hold a meeting in Trafalgar Square without official permission, though on other occasions members of this committee advocated civil disobedience without prosecution.

In 1936 a Mrs Duncan proposed to hold an open-air meeting to protest against government treatment of the unemployed in a street outside a training centre for unemployed workers. When she had held a similar meeting in the same place fourteen months earlier this had been followed by a disturbance in the centre. Believing that the same result might follow again, a police inspector told her that she must move 175 yards away if she wished to hold a meeting. When she ignored this instruction she was charged with obstructing a police officer in the execution of his duty and was subsequently fined. This case caused some public concern because it was felt that it gave the police too much discretion. In fact it was necessary for the court to be convinced that the police officer had reasonable grounds for believing that the meeting might cause a breach of the peace, for otherwise the order he gave Mrs Duncan would not have been 'in the execution of his duty'. But it is clear that persons proposing to hold a meeting on the public highway are well advised to get police permission in advance. The police are usually co-operative, but if they have no advance notice and they ask the speaker to 'move on', either because they fear a disturbance or on grounds of obstruction of the highway, the speaker has no choice but to obey the instruction or face arrest.

Another interesting example is that of the series of fascist meetings in Dalston, north London, in 1947. These were held in a cul-de-sac with police permission, but they caused violent reactions from the audience, many of whom came to the meetings with the express intention of breaking them up. The speeches were full of abusive and provocative anti-Semitic remarks, which could be regarded as an incitement to violence when uttered in an area with some Jewish residents. But all the violence was directed towards the speakers and the police took the view that, although a speaker should be prosecuted if he incites his audience to violence against a third party, he is entitled to take the risk of provoking violence against himself. It was felt that the traditional right of uttering unpopular opinions should be defended, and in the later meetings of the series the speakers were accordingly surrounded by a cordon of policemen facing outwards towards the audience. On the other hand, in 1963 a fascist speaker in another area was successfully prosecuted for provoking a breach of the peace among an audience that was almost entirely hostile to him, and it is clear that the application of the law in this field depends very much on the attitudes of the police.

Freedom of Political Association

There have been no restrictions on the organization of voluntary associations in Britain since the repeal of the Combination Acts in 1824. Trade union leaders had to engage in a long struggle to secure immunity from court actions over the organization of strikes that have an injurious effect on the interests of other people, but the right to form unions has not been curtailed and pressure groups and political parties have been completely free from legal restrictions. As noted in Chapter 6, political parties are not known to the law and their organization and activities are entirely untrammelled. The Communist Party has never been banned, as it has been in West Germany and some other democratic countries. Neither has the British Union of Fascists been declared illegal, though during the last war some of the leading members of the union were interned because the government regarded their loyalty to the nation as suspect.

What is almost equally important, individual members of parties have not suffered persecution or hardship on account of their views. Britain has never seen anything like the McCarthyite period in the United States, when men were driven from their jobs and sometimes driven to suicide by the lack of tolerance for their suspected sympathies or connections (past or present) with the Communist Party. Nor would the British accept as normal a variety of practices that are so accepted in the United States, such as the screening of applicants for a wide variety of posts that could not possibly be 'classified' for security reasons, or the occasional suspension of teachers for expressing heretical views on political or religious matters.

Of course, the British government has to exercise some control over internal security. In 1948 the development of the Cold War led the government to initiate a new policy of screening civil servants in posts involving security risk. Five years later it was reported that 17,000 officials had been screened, which was rather less than 3 per cent of the total number of civil servants at that time. Of these 111 were regarded as possible risks to security and 9 were still under consideration. Of the 111, 69 were transferred to equivalent posts elsewhere in the Civil Service, 19 resigned and 'only twenty-three were dismissed, and these because their qualifications were such that they could be employed only in secret work' (Street, 1963, p. 222). In the two years following there was only one resignation and three transfers. This is not a disturbing record, and there is no evidence or suggestion that civil servants with extreme political views suffer in their careers if they are engaged in non-secret work. Outside Whitehall, the only reported case of an individual being penalized on political grounds occurred in 1956 when a lawyer working for Imperial Chemical Industries was dismissed because the government refused to place secret contracts with the firm unless he were denied access to the secrets. The case created such a furore in Parliament and the press that it is unlikely that any similar incidents will occur.

These facts underline the general tolerance of British society, as does the unemotional way in which the British receive news that scientists or public servants have given secrets to potential enemies. The cases of Klaus Fuchs, Nunn May and Burgess and Maclean created interest, a measure of understanding and in the last case a good deal of amusement, but little or no sense of moral indignation. Maclean's family went to join him in Moscow, Fuchs was allowed to work for East Germany after he was released from prison, and Nunn May was offered a post in industrial research a few weeks before his sentence ended.

The British take their liberties and their tolerance so much for granted that they do not always realize how rare these conditions are in the world or how much they contribute to the quality of British life. They are among the most precious fruits of three centuries of political stability and security.

Freedom from Arrest and Imprisonment

This is a field in which it is difficult to be specific in short compass because of the complexity of the law and the very large number of relevant cases that could be cited. However, it is possible to establish one or two general points.

In the first place, it is a principle of British law that all persons are presumed to be innocent until they are found guilty by a court. This has various implications. For instance, it implies that persons suspected of a crime should not be physically harmed by the police before they are brought to trial. The extensive guarantees of fair treatment by American law are of no use to those who are killed while being arrested, to say nothing of the fact that innocent pedestrians may be killed or wounded because police bullets miss their mark. Very few incidents like this have happened in Britain because, at least until the late 1970s, British police have been unarmed. This makes them almost unique among the police forces of the world, and has been possible only because of the relative lack of violence in British society. Unfortunately, the situation changed during the 1970s. It became necessary to train special squads of police marksmen to protect embassies and airports against international terrorists, and the considerable growth in the propensity of armed robbers to open fire on the police forced the authorities to adopt the policy of issuing guns to the police in dangerous situations. At the time of writing about 20 per cent of the British police are trained marksmen, to whom guns may be issued in special circumstances on the authority of a senior officer. However, arms are not carried normally and when they are issued the police have to account for every bullet used.

Secondly, the principle implies that people should not be detained without trial. In fact, a person other than a suspected terrorist cannot legally be detained in Britain unless he is charged with a specific offence, and if he is then kept in custody he must be brought before a magistrate within twenty-four hours. In the great majority of cases he will then be released on bail until the time of his trial. Since November 1974 (the month when IRA bombs killed more than twenty people in a Birmingham pub) it has been possible for the police to detain suspected terrorists for questioning for up to seven days without charging them, a power that was declared excessive by the European Court of Human Rights in 1988. Notwithstanding this judgement, the British government has insisted on maintaining the power, using (for the first time) its right of 'derogation' in respect of judgements by the European Court.

Thirdly the principle implies that there should be some method whereby a person kept illegally in custody may secure his release. This method is the writ of *habeas corpus*, which can be issued by any High Court judge at any time, on his being informed that a person is being kept in custody without authorization. An application for such a writ takes precedence over all other business in court and application may also be made directly to a judge in chambers. This writ, incidentally, is of use not only against detention by the police but also against detention in, say, a mental home.

Another principle is that 'the Englishman's home is his castle'. The police are entitled to enter a house only if they have a search warrant after making a sworn statement regarding the need for it, unless they are in hot pursuit of a criminal. If the police exceed their powers they can be sued for damages. Thus, in the case of *Peters v. Shaw* (1965) a merry-go-round proprietor sued a policeman who had entered his caravan without permission while looking for persons suspected of commuting a felony on the fairground; the proprietor was awarded damages and costs against the policeman (*The Times*, 6 May 1965). In another case a policeman entered a garage to inquire about a lorry there, which had previously been obstructing the highway. The owner ordered the policeman off the premises, but instead of leaving immediately he started to produce a document to prove he was a police officer. The owner then ejected him by force, was prosecuted by the policeman for assault, but was acquitted because the policeman had no right to stay on the premises after he had been told to leave (Street, 1963, p. 24).

Another principle is the right to a fair trial before an impartial judge or jury. British judges are appointed for life from the ranks of successful barristers, so that they cannot be subjected to any kind of political pressure. The right to trial by jury has been firmly established for a very long time, and juries are independent bodies who cannot easily be bullied or persuaded into taking a decision that they do not consider right. There have been numerous cases, from the eighteenth century onwards, of juries acquitting an accused person in spite of the strongest advice given by the judge that the facts pointed towards a conviction. Further provisions designed to ensure a fair trial are the provision of legal aid to persons who cannot afford to pay for representation by counsel and the right of appeal to the Court of Appeals and, with permission, to the House of Lords (where the case is heard by a small group of Law Lords appointed for this purpose).

Of course the police have some powers not granted to ordinary citizens, but these are strictly limited. They have no right, for instance, to take a person to a police station or detain him there for questioning, against his will, unless they arrest him. The papers frequently report that a person has spent some hours at a police station 'assisting the police with their inquiries', but this happens either because the individual wishes to co-operate with the police, or because he thinks it will pay him to appear to co-operate with the police, or because he does not know his rights and was not told of them. It should not be thought that British police behaviour is always beyond criticism when dealing with suspected criminals.

The difficult period is that between the time when a suspect is taken to the police station for questioning and the time when he appears in court. In this period the behaviour of the police is supposed to conform to a pattern determined partly by the Judges' Rules and partly by police regulations. According to this ideal pattern, the police must permit the suspect to call a lawyer unless this is likely to interfere with the administration of justice; must respect his right not to answer questions unless he freely chooses to do so; must ensure that he is provided with reasonable comfort and refreshments; must not tell the suspect that the police believe him to be guilty; must not use threats or promises or any undue pressure to induce the suspect to make a statement; and must give the suspect a clear warning that any statement he makes may be taken down and used in evidence.

The police have to deal with some pretty rough characters in circumstances of considerable tension, and it would be surprising if this code of conduct were always followed exactly. In practice it is clear that the police sometimes trade on the ignorance of the people they examine and sometimes engage in verbal bullying or cajolery in order to secure information, or even a confession, on which they can base a charge. Occasionally they also resort to intimidation and the milder forms of violence. Moreover, there are grounds for believing that police behaviour is tending to deteriorate. Given the general increase in violence during the 1970s and 1980s, this is not surprising. The police now have to cope with armed robbers, with terrorists bent on murder, with violent political demonstations, with mass picketing that frequently produces violence, with mugging in the streets of London and with repeated crowd violence at football matches. Only twenty-five years ago, these phenomena hardly existed in

Britain. Now the police are increasingly obliged to use their fists and batons in the course of their duty and there is a danger that some of them may become coarsened by this experience. In any assessment of police behaviour (which will be discussed further in the following chapter) it is essential to realize that the great majority of the police are not heroes or saints, not bullies or pigs and not disembodied instruments of the law, but men and women doing a difficult job whose performance is inevitably influenced by the cumulative impact of their experiences.

The rules of police conduct should not therefore be taken as an infallible guide to practice. Their great value is that they constitute a norm to which appeals can be made. If the police deviate from them, the matter may be raised in court. If the defence can show that a statement was involuntary in the sense that it was induced by threats or promises, the jury is apt to dismiss the statement as being of no value; and if it is the basis of the prosecution's case the result is likely to be an acquittal.

Citizen's Rights in Relation to the Administration

The rights so far discussed in this chapter are essentially rights to be left alone by agents of the state. The development of social and economic legislation in the twentieth century has given citizens rights of a different kind: the right to a pension, to benefits while unemployed or sick, to housing at a controlled or subsidised rent, to tax relief in respect of some kinds of expenditure. The disputes about rights of this kind could not appropriately be settled by the ordinary courts, for a variety of reasons. First, the courts would be hopelessly clogged by the vast number of cases that arise. Secondly, the citizen needs a remedy that is quicker and cheaper than court procedure makes possible; it would be useless for an unemployed man to have to hire a lawyer to make a claim for a few pounds' benefit. Thirdly, the issues are administrative rather than judicial; it is desirable for those hearing the case to have some technical knowledge and it is often thought appropriate for them to be guided by departmental policy when reaching decisions.

For these reasons, disputes of this kind go not to the ordinary courts but to a variety of administrative tribunals. It is almost impossible to generalize about the composition and procedure of these tribunals because they are so varied. Some are chaired by lawyers, others by ordinary administrators. Some contain members appointed to represent interested groups such as trade unions or employers, while others do not. At some the appellant may be represented by a lawyer, at others he may bring a friend but not a lawyer.

This kind of variation is confusing but may be inevitable if each body is organized to deal with a particular set of problems. By and large, the tribunals are quick and cheap, and the people who have most to do with them are not dissatisfied. What sometimes causes concern, however, is that they violate the elementary principle that no person should be a judge in his own case. The members of tribunals that hear appeals against the decisions of a ministry are nearly always appointed by the minister concerned, and aggrieved citizens are apt to think that they would have got fairer treatment from a court of law.

Criticisms of this kind led to the passage of the Tribunals and Inquiries Act of 1958, which extended the rights of appeal and obliged tribunals to inform appellants both of the reasons for their decisions and of the possibilities for further appeal. The most common situation is that it is possible to appeal to a court on points of law but further appeals on questions of fact or interpretation have to go to another administrative tribunal or to the minister himself. It is therefore not surprising that, although in general the system works tolerably well, there remains a minority of cases that leave citizens with a deep feeling of grievance. British civil servants enjoy a well-deserved reputation for tolerance and fairness, but they wield such extensive powers that some people are bound to get bruised. A former Conservative minister has said in his memoirs that 'Every MP and social worker knows of men and women who are living with a sense of grievance at the hands of authority, some of whom have had their lives ruined by persecution complexes' (Bevins, 1965, p. 66). For this reason many critics have looked to foreign experience to see if any other countries have lessons for Britain in this field.

The general conclusion has been that they have. In many other democratic countries the citizen's rights against the administration are more thoroughly protected than they are in Britain, and in some countries people can appeal against acts of administrative discretion against which the British citizen has no appeal whatsoever (except to write to his MP).

Two main examples have been recommended as ones that might be followed. One is the French system of administrative justice. In France cases involving the way public servants use their powers are heard in a special administrative court (which has many branches) known as the Conseil d'Etat. This court has succeeded in doing what British courts have never tried to do, namely to apply the rule of law to the whole field of administrative discretion. For instance, there are in both countries numerous statutes that give a minister the power to make orders, issue licences, revoke licences and so forth 'if he is satisfied that' it is in the public interest to do so. British courts have always taken the view that if the minister declares himself to be satisfied he has complied with the condition, so that his decision is beyond challenge by the court. The Conseil d'Etat, on the other hand, takes the view that the minister has complied with the condition only if his satisfaction is based upon reasonable grounds that can be explained and justified. The Conseil has the power to require the minister or his officials to justify their decisions in this way, supplemented by power to declare the decisions null and void if the attempted justification is unsatisfactory and to award damages to the aggrieved citizen if this is thought appropriate.

Decisions about town planning make an interesting example. Whenever a local authority or government department in Britain plans to acquire property by compulsory purchase to make room for a new development the property-owners have the right to ask for a public inquiry into the scheme. Such an inquiry will be conducted by an inspector who is appointed by the minister and is usually an official of the department concerned. The inspector makes his recommendations in a report that the minister is bound to consider, under the terms of the Town and Country Planning Act. But, having considered the report, he may accept or reject the recommendations, as he thinks fit, and his decision is final. Under this procedure an objector may well feel that the scales are doubly weighted against him; the inquiry is conducted by a member of the department most closely involved the plan, and even if the result of the inquiry should be favourable to the objector the minister could still decide to ignore the inspector's advice and go ahead with the plan. The procedure gives ample time for lobbying and counter-lobbying, which indeed is its main purpose, but it does not bring the minister's actions under judicial or quasi-judicial control.

If Britain had a system of administrative justice like the French system, the situation would be quite different; the objector would be able to appeal against the minister's decision and the latter would be required to justify it to the satisfaction of the administrative court. Numerous other examples could be cited but it is unnecessary to do so, for there can be no doubt that French citizens have recourse to a more effective system of control of administrative actions than British citizens enjoy. However, it has never been likely that a British government would institute a system of administrative courts; the Civil Service would put up the strongest resistance to such a reform and ministers could not be expected to go out of their way to create a rod for their own backs.

A much more modest form of check on administrative behaviour operates in Denmark and Sweden. In these countries there is an officer known as an Ombudsman who has the specific task of investigating grievances against the administration. He is appointed by Parliament after each general election but he then enjoys security of office till the next election. His main function is to investigate complaints against the behaviour of the central administration. He has power to call for persons and documents and if he concludes that the complaint is justified it is his duty to inform the parties to the case and to publish his findings. He has no power to nullify the decision or to award damages to the complainant, but the press takes a keen interest in his reports and if a department were to ignore his recommendtions this would immediately create a public outcry.

In 1965 the government decided to create an office of this kind in Britain, with the title of Parliamentary Commissioner for Administration. The commissioner is appointed by the Crown but is at the service of Parliament. The main difference between his position and that of the Scandinavian Ombudsman is that the commissioner acts only on the request of an MP. Citizens wishing to complain must therefore find an MP (not necessarily their own) who is willing to pass the matter on to the commissioner. The commissioner has power to call for oral or written evidence and to examine departmental files. If he finds that the complaint is justified and the department responds to his invitation to put the matter right, that is the end of the matter; if the department does not so respond, the commissioner reports the whole matter to Parliament, which has established a select committee to consider such reports.

The jurisdiction of the Parliamentary Commissioner was at first very limited, for his original terms of reference made it impossible for him to criticize the exercise of administrative discretion provided all the forms had been correctly complied with and there had been no error in the interpretation of the facts. However, in the first year of his work the commissioner found an instance of maladministration that attracted nationwide publicity and gave both legitimacy and prestige to his office. For over twenty years the Foreign Office had refused to pay the compensation due to concentration-camp victims, a group of ex-servicemen who had been incarcerated in the notorious Sachsanhausen camp as prisoners of war, on the ground that their treatment had been less severe than that meted out to the other inmates. Though numerous previous appeals had failed, the Parliamentary Commissioner found that the Foreign Office had no good reason for the position it had taken and his report resulted in substantial compensation for the men involved. With his prestige strengthened by this case, the commissioner was able to secure a substantial extension of his terms of reference in 1968, which enabled him to criticize the exercise of administrative discretion if its consequences were clearly unfortunate and to criticize administrative rules if a complainant had sustained hardship through the correct application of a rule that the commissioner deemed to be unfair.

This constitutional innovation has proved to be a success. The work of the commissioner has led to a significant extension of the rights of the citizen in relation to the administration. As a consequence of this success it was decided in the 1970s to appoint commissioners with similar powers to deal with complaints about the National Health Service and complaints about the activities of local authorities.

The Rights of Ethnic Minorities

The British tradition in regard to civil rights is that these rights inhere in the individual citizen as a subject of the Crown. The object of judges and legal reformers over the past two centuries has been to ensure that these rights are adequately protected against encroachment by agents of the state and that the protection is afforded equally to all citizens, irrespective of class, sex, religion and political opinion. Until very recently there has never been any suggestion that particular groups of citizens needed legal protection against discriminatory treatment by other private citizens.

The situation has changed in recent years as a consequence of the arrival since the late 1950s of large numbers of Commonwealth immigrants from Asia, east Africa and the Caribbean. By 1989, these immigrants and their descendants constituted a group of ethnic minorities comprising 2.4 million people, a total that will increase to over 3 million by the end of the century. Sadly, but almost inevitably, problems of racial discrimination have developed and have created a need for special measures to protect the minorities.

The government first promoted legislation to this end in 1965, this action being undertaken (in the words of an American lawyer) 'very promptly by American standards, precipitously according to British tradition' (Claiborne, 1979, p. 11). It was an entirely new field of legislation for Britain, and the minister responsible for it made an important change in response to public pressure after the Race Relations Bill had been published. In its first draft the Bill provided for criminal sanctions against anyone found guilty of racial discrimination in public places. However, the Campaign against Racial Discrimination, an organization that spoke on behalf of the main immigrant groups, joined forces with a group of Labour lawyers and numerous MPs to urge that criminal sanctions be dropped from the Bill and replaced by a conciliation process for which a statutory board or commission would be responsible. This change led to the creation of the national Race Relations Board and a number of local committees, and it was undoubtedly an improvement on the original proposal. Criminal sanctions would have been difficult to enforce and dysfunctional because of their unpopularity with the general public, whereas the revised procedure was well received and established a body of public officials with a duty to conciliate and educate. In another section of the Act criminal sanctions were included for the new offence of incitement to racial hatred but, as noted earlier, there have been few prosecutions under this section and even fewer convictions.

The 1965 Act was limited in its scope, covering only discrimination in public places, discrimination in tenancies and incitement to racial hatred. However, in 1968 the second Race Relations Act extended the scope of the law to cover employment, housing, the sale and rental of business premises, the sales of all goods at both wholesale and retail levels, the provision of all services and membership of trade unions and professional associations. It was also decided to introduce a complete ban on racially discriminatory advertisements and to establish a new body called the Community Relations Commission, with responsibility for improving race relations by education and the co-ordination of voluntary activities in this field. In 1976 the body was replaced by the Commission for Racial Equality, with wider powers.

If these British arrangements for protecting the rights of ethnic minorities are compared with American arrangements, some interesting differences emerge. First, British law-makers moved much more quickly than their American counterparts, enacting comprehensive legislation within ten years of the first emergence of a problem of race relations. Secondly, British legislation is more comprehensive than American, for American laws do not cover the sale and rental of business premises, do not cover all commercial transactions and do not ban discriminatory advertisements.

On the other hand, British legislation makes less use of criminal sanctions and does not give the person discriminated against the same right of redress that he enjoys under some American laws. An American employer who can be shown to have rejected a job applicant on grounds of race can be forced to employ the person by court order. In Britain the position until 1976 was that the courts could order an employer to abstain from discriminatory activities in the future, but could not give any direct help to the person discriminated against. In 1976, in view of evidence that discrimination in employment was widespread, complainants were given the right to appeal to an industrial tribunal, which had the power to award compensation. However, discrimination is hard to establish and the majority of appeals have been unsuccessful.

A final difference between British and American practice is that there is no legal equivalent in Britain of the positive discrimination that has become common in some field of American life since the 1960s, with some employers and public institutions (including universities) being compelled by the courts to give preferential treatment to members of ethnic minorities when filling vacancies. This kind of policy would be contrary to the strong British tradition that all individuals should be treated as equal by courts and government authorities. There is clearly a case for further efforts to improve employment opportunities for members of racial minorities, but it is difficult to envisage the American type of legal control being acceptable in Britain.

The European Convention on Human Rights

In the immediate postwar years representatives of a number of European states, reacting to the barbarities of fascism, drew up a document entitled the European Convention for the Protection of Human Rights and Fundamental Freedoms. This was ratified by the British Parliament in 1950. However, Britain has not followed the example of the other states that ratified the convention, which have added its provisions to their own domestic law.

The European Commission of Human Rights was established to monitor the situation and this was joined by the European Court of Human Rights, to investigate cases of alleged violation brought by citizens of those countries that permitted their citizens to take cases to the court. Some of the signatories to the convention were reluctant to grant this permission, and Britain was one of these – because it is contrary to British constitutional traditions to empower a court to pass judgement, on the basis of abstract principles, on actions that do not violate British Statute or Common Law. However, in 1966, with some misgivings, it was agreed that British residents could take cases directly to the European Court if they so wished.

In practice few British residents have taken advantage of this right, but there have been four significant cases in which the court found that British practice was in violation of the European Convention. The first of these involved the interrogation of suspected terrorists by the British Army in Northern Ireland. It was found that certain methods, which had been discontinued by the time the case was heard, had violated the rights of the suspects. This judgement made it certain that the Army would not use such methods again.

The second case was brought by the parents of a boy who had been subjected to corporal punishment in school, on the ground that their rights as parents had been infringed by the infliction of this punishment without parental permission. The court upheld this view, which created a slight dilemma for the British government. Educational authorities and teachers' unions in Britain were strongly in favour of the retention of corporal punishment as a sanction of last resort, maintaining that discipline could not be maintained without it. The decisions of the European Court are not legally binding, but national governments affected by them are clearly under a strong moral and political obligation to rectify the situation that gave rise to the adverse judgement. In the end it was proposed that all parents of children at school should be asked to sign a statement indicating whether they did or did not wish their children to be exposed to the possibility of corporal punishment. However, the House of Lords rejected this proposal in favour of an outright ban on corporal punishment in state schools.

The third case involved British immigration law. As it was, until 1985, the law provided that a non-British man resident in Britain could import a non-British wife from overseas whereas a non-British woman resident in Britain was not entitled to import a non-British husband. The basis of this distinction was the principle that the head of a household could import a dependant, combined with the traditional assumption that in a married couple the man would always be head of the household. The European Court decided that the British were guilty of sexual discrimination by implementing this law. The Home Secretary immediately announced that the law would be modified so as to avoid this kind of discrimination.

The fourth case has already been mentioned. In 1988 the European Court concluded that the Prevention of Terrorism Act violated human rights because it permitted the police to detain suspects for up to seven days without bringing them before a court. The British government's view is that this judgement takes insufficient account of the threat to British lives posed by the activities of the IRA, so it has been decided not to comply with the judgement of the European Court in this case.

These cases indicate that, to a limited extent, British adherence to the European Convention has extended the rights and liberties of British residents.

Further Reading

For the legal basis of British civil liberties see Robertson (1989), *Freedom, the Individual and the Law*; for a practical guide see Hurwitt and Thornton (1989),

Civil Liberty: The NCCL Guide; for an essay on maladministration see Wheare (1973), *Maladministration and its Remedies*; for the position of the Parliamentary Commissioner for Administration see Stacey (1971), *The British Ombudsman*; for a discussion of the rights of ethnic minorities see Claiborne (1979), *Race and Law in Britain and the United States*; for a discussion of the problems of ethnic minorities see Smith (1977), *Racial Disadvantage in Britain*.

◇ 17 ◇

The Police and Political Violence

The police can be regarded as the sharp end of the machinery of government. In all societies there are some people who will not comply with the law unless forced to do so, and it is the task of the police to exercise coercive power over this minority. Britain is fortunate in that the police enjoy the support of most citizens. However, since the late 1960s there has been a sharp increase in the incidence of violence, much of it political in character. This has both put a strain on the police and led to political controversies about their role, the way in which they are controlled and the extent to which they are accountable for their behaviour. In view of these developments it is proposed in this chapter to outline the character of the British system of policing, to discuss the growth and nature of political violence and to provide a brief guide to recent controversies.

The British System of Policing

In Chapter 14 it was observed that the British system of local government lies somewhere between that of France, which is highly centralized, and that of the United States, which is highly decentralized. The same observation can be made about the British system of policing. France has thirteen national police forces, each specialized in function and all ultimately controlled by the Minister of the Interior. There are no local police forces as such, and local branches of the national forces are supervised by the departmental prefects, who are ministry officials. In contrast, the United States has a fairly small national force, the Federal Bureau of Investigation, which deals with only a limited category of offences. The great bulk of police work in America is handled by fifty state forces and about 40,000 city, town and county forces, each of them controlled by the representative civil authorities of the area concerned, such as the city or town council.

Britain, on the other hand, has no national police force but fifty-one regional forces. One of these covers the financial district of the City of London, one covers Greater London and the other forty-nine cover regions of the country that are in some but not all cases coterminous with the areas covered for local government purposes by local authorities. Operational control of each force is in the hands of the Chief Constable (or Commissioner of Police in Greater London), though there is also an area police authority that has certain administrative powers. In Greater London the Home Secretary is the police authority.

The organization of each force has to comply with national regulations, drawn up by the Home Secretary in consultation with the Police Council (a body composed of representatives of the police authorities and the police themselves). Expensive pieces of equipment, such as a national computerized records system, are provided by the Home Office.

Each police authority is made up partly of people nominated by the local authorities in the region (who comprise two-thirds of the authority's members) and partly of local magistrates (who comprise the remaining third). The powers of the authority are to appoint the Chief Constable and his immediate deputies (subject to the approval of the Home Office); to approve the budget submitted by the Chief Constable; to provide buildings and equipment for the force; to call on the Chief Constable to submit reports on policing in the area (subject to his right to refuse a report if he thinks it unnecessary for the proper use of the authority's supervisory powers); and to request the retirement of a Chief Constable on grounds of inefficiency (subject to the agreement of the Home Secretary).

These powers are strictly limited, as the underlying principle of police organization is that the Chief Constable in each area should be autonomous in all operational matters. The function of the police, it is constantly asserted, is to enforce the law and maintain the Queen's peace, not to serve the interests of local politicians or the national government. The fact that area police authorities have some control over the budget does not permit them to acquire a degree of operational control through this means. Staffing and salary levels are effectively controlled by the Home Office, and negotiations between Chief Constables and police authorities over budgetary matters relate to more marginal questions, such as expenditure on vehicles, office equipment and uniforms.

This autonomy of the police is fiercely defended by senior police officers, who believe it to be one of the great strengths of the system that the police are both independent of political control and known by the public to have this independence. An interesting example occurred in Manchester in 1981. Following extensive riots in the city, the police authority asked the Chief Constable to attend a meeting of the authority to explain the actions of the police in dealing with the riots and to answer questions. The Chief Constable refused, on the ground that this would compromise his autonomy in operational matters. He submitted a written report instead.

How do the police use the very considerable discretion that their autonomy gives them? According to Sir Robert Mark, Commissioner of the Metropolitan Police from 1972 to 1977, the police 'reflect society as a whole' and 'discharge the communal will, not that of any government minister, mayor or the public official' (Mark, 1977, p. 12). It is to be presumed that they understand the communal will through their experience and intuition. A better way of putting this might be to say that the police try to reflect current social values, partly because they regard this as their duty and partly because they wish to maintain what is commonly called 'the British police advantage', namely that they enjoy the sympathy and support of the majority of the population.

Certainly the police reflect social values, which are probably those of the majority, in the priority that they give to dealing with differing types of offence. For instance, they give high priority to dealing with cases of blackmail, personal violence, robbery and the distribution of hard drugs; low priority to sexual offences, the sale of pornographic literature, under-age drinking and motoring offences other than those leading to personal injury. Being anxious not to alienate the motoring public, they rarely prosecute people for speeding. When radar traps are set, they are often preceded by a sign at the side of the road giving advance notice of them to watchful drivers. Breathalyser tests are conducted, but motorists are not stopped unless some other offence (such as driving without due care) is suspected. Illegal parking has to be punished to avoid congestion, but the main responsibility for this has been hived off to a separate body of officials known as traffic wardens, who are notably less popular than the police.

The police are also careful not to intervene in disputes that can be categorized as private. They are extremely reluctant to intervene in family disputes. Unlike the police in many other countries, they refuse to clear university campuses of students engaged in sit-ins and other demonstrations. They do not keep order at sporting events unless hired to do so (at so much an hour) by the sports club involved. They try not to become involved in industrial disputes, and have been reluctant to deal with mass picketing except when it is likely to provoke personal violence.

By exercising their discretion in these and similar ways, the British police have been remarkably successful in maintaining public trust and support. An international survey conducted in 1959 and 1960 showed that 74 per cent of British people expected that the police would give serious consideration to their point of view in an encounter, compared with 59 per cent in West Germany, 56 per cent in the United States, 35 per cent in Italy and 12 per cent in Mexico. Moreover, Britain was the only one of these countries in which the expectations were just as favourable among people who had left school at 14 or 15 as they were among the better educated (Almond and Verba, 1965, p. 66). In 1972–5 an elaborate study sponsored by the London School of Economics included extended interviews with 1,200 adults and 500 teenagers in London, and yielded the attitudes summarized in Table 17.1.

Since 1975 the police have been involved in various controversies, and there is scattered evidence that, although they are still highly respected, they are not trusted to quite the same degree that they were. In 1984 a national survey revealed that only 61 per cent of people 'generally trusted' the police to tell the

Table 17.1 *Public Attitudes to the Police in London*

Attitude	Adults %	Teenagers %
Police are respected	98	94
Police are liked	93	85
Police are trusted	90	83

Source: Belson, 1975, p. 7.

truth. As the question, the sampling frame and the type of interview (in this survey a brief interview) were all different from those of the earlier survey, it is impossible to be certain that this shows a decline of trust, but it seems likely. In 1984 the police came out as less well trusted (in respect of veracity) than doctors (82 per cent) or judges (77 per cent), but much more highly trusted than civil servants (25 per cent), trade union officials (18 per cent), or government ministers (16 per cent) (Mori survey, reported in *Sunday Times*, 8 January 1984).

In recent years the police have been put under pressure by an increase in crime, an increase in the incidence of violence in society and an increase in political violence. The increase in crime is common to all advanced countries in the non-communist world with the exception of Japan, and the recent increase is dramatic, as is shown by Table 17.2. The figures in this table refer to England and Wales only because offences in Scotland are classified and recorded differently.

It will be noted that the increases in crimes of personal violence are higher than the increases in non-violent crimes like burglary and fraud. Cases of personal violence include murder, assault, mugging, social violence such as that committed by hooligans at football matches, and various types of political violence. It is this last category that is important in the context of this book.

Table 17.2 *Notifiable Offences Recorded by the Police in England and Wales*

Type of offence	1960	1970	1982	Percentage increase 1960–82
	000s	000s	000s	
Violence against the person	15.8	41.1	108.7	588
Sexual offences	19.9	24.2	19.7	*nil*
Criminal damage	4.8	17.9	233.7	*
Burglary, theft, fraud, etc.	750.7	1,480.0	2,712.4	261
Other offences	6.2	5.4	3.8	*nil*
	797.4	1,568.6	3,078.3	

*Increase is misleading because minimum damage recorded has not been adjusted for inflation.
Sources: Whitaker, 1979, p. 82 and Central Statistical Office, *Social Trends*, 1984, p. 165.

Political Violence

Political violence may be defined as violent behaviour engaged in during activities with one or more of the following objectives:

(1) to challenge the personnel or the system of government;
(2) to undermine the authority of the government;
(3) to challenge or influence government policy in a particular field.

In addition, riots, looting and arson have to be counted as political activities if they amount to a demonstration against the police or are engaged in with the knowledge that they will involve a confrontation with the police. If an individual takes advantage of a broken shop window to steal a radio set, or sets fire to a building to claim the insurance on it, the activity is criminal but not political. If several hundred people set out to loot and/or destroy a row of shops, knowing that this will bring them into violent conflict with the police, this is a breach of public order and a challenge to civil authority, which has to be categorized as a political activity.

Political violence of the first kind listed – that is, violence with revolutionary intentions – is rarely engaged in by British people. Members of the Irish Republican Army have been active in Britain in recent years, killing about 100 people by bombs or guns between 1970 and 1989. Their aim is to induce the British to terminate Northern Ireland's inclusion in the United Kingdom, so that it may be united with the Irish Republic. This may fairly be categorized as a revolutionary aim. A small number of people, mostly aliens, have also been killed by Palestinian and Libyan terrorists in the same period, in pursuit of objectives that have little or nothing to do with Britain. However, since the First World War only one British group has used firearms for revolutionary objectives. This was the so-called Angry Brigade, a small group who exploded twenty-five bombs in the London area in a few months in 1971, without actually killing anyone. The activists were what Clutterbuck calls 'educated anarchists', the four who were arrested and imprisoned all being sociology graduates (Clutterbuck, 1977, p. 7).

The forms of political violence that have caused most trouble to the police, and also most political controversy, are violent demonstrations, violent strikes called for political purposes and urban riots. It is important to note that the people engaged in these three types of event are very different in character. The people who participate in demonstrations are political radicals, usually well educated, mainly students or white-collar workers. They have little in common with miners' pickets or with the unemployed young people who engaged in the urban riots of 1981. There has been in recent years not so much a general growth in political violence as a growth in three distinct kinds of political violence, and they will be discussed separately in the following sections.

Violent Demonstrations

The great majority of political demonstrations leading to violence have been related either to defence and international issues or to immigration policy and race relations. Demonstrations regarding defence and international issues have been mounted by radicals motivated by a sense of moral outrage. Most of the participants have been well-educated people, who also vote, join political parties and generally reveal feelings of political competence. The first violent demonstration of this kind occurred outside the US Embassy in London in 1968, when many thousands of people protested about the Vietnam war and attacked police who were controlling the crowd and protecting the embassy. More than one hundred policemen were injured on this occasion. Other violent demonstrations were mounted by anti-apartheid groups in their efforts, which were ultimately successful, to prevent South African teams playing cricket or rugby matches in Britain.

Another motive for political demonstrations has been opposition to nuclear arms. From the late 1950s to the present day numerous meetings and marches have been held to protest about the British possession of nuclear weapons or the stationing of American weapons on British territory. The overwhelming majority of these demonstrations have been peaceful, though some groups have practised a form of 'non-violent resistance' that involves breaking the law. In 1984, for instance, a contingent of women camped for months on end outside the US base for Cruise missiles at Greenham Common, ignoring all orders to leave and eventually forcing the police to drag them away bodily and destroy their makeshift encampment. To avoid a repetition of this, the police barred entry to the area surrounding the second Cruise missile base, issuing identity cards to local residents so that they, but not others, could travel freely in and out of the area. This action caused controversy on the ground that it infringed the right of all citizens to use the Queen's highways as they wished.

There is another type of political demonstration that has caused more violence than those so far mentioned. The National Front organized a number of meetings and marches in the 1960s and 1970s that were explicitly racist in their motivation, the object being to protest about the number of people of Asian or West Indian descent living in Britain and to make the cruel and impracticable proposal that the government should adopt a policy of forcible repatriation. These meetings and marches were commonly attacked by counter-demonstrators of the radical left, with motives that are best described as mixed, leading to violent conflicts with fists, boots, sticks and other improvised weapons.

The common pattern of these clashes was that the National Front secured prior permission from the police for their demonstrations, while the counter-demonstrators took care not to reveal their tactics. The consequence was that the police were obliged to protect the National Front supporters from their opponents, so that much of the fighting was between the police and the radicals.

On at least one occasion, in Red Lion Square, London, in 1972, the radicals launched their onslaught on the police rather than on the National Front demonstrators. It is difficult to see any motive for this behaviour other than that of provoking the police into a violent response that could be photographed and subsequently described as an example of police brutality. Happily, the National Front disintegrated in 1979.

Under the terms of an Act passed in 1985, it is necessary for all organizers of demonstrations and counter-demonstrations to submit their plans to the police a week in advance of the event. The Chief Constable of the area is then empowered to ban the demonstration if he thinks it likely to lead to a breach of the peace. This is an infringement of a traditional British liberty and whether it is justified or not is a matter of opinion. Much is clearly to be gained by banning demonstrations likely to stir up racial hatred or to inflame the fears of ethnic minorities, and it would probably have been better for society if such demonstrations had been banned in the 1960s and 1970s. If the right to ban is used with customary police discretion, it will not result in the prohibition of more than a small minority of other demonstrations, for more than four hundred peaceful protests and marches are held in London alone every year (see Mark, 1977, p. 87). However, the 1985 Act opens the possibility that demonstrations will be held in defiance of police orders, so that the police might find themselves obliged to take the initiative in dispersing demonstrators instead of waiting until they (or those they are protecting) are attacked.

The attitudes of the public to this kind of development are not entirely predictable. In the 1984 survey mentioned above, 62 per cent of respondents agreed with the proposition that the police should 'use plastic bullets, water cannon and tear gas to disperse potentially violent demonstrators' (*Sunday Times*, 8 January 1984). However, this does not indicate what the public reaction would be if the police broke up a demonstration that did not appear to be potentially violent, even though the Chief Constable had previously banned it in the belief that it would be.

Political Strikes Leading to Violence

In a democracy strikes are accepted as a legitimate adjunct to bargaining about pay or working conditions, and are normally without political significance. They become political, or partially political, if one of their objects is to change government policy or to render existing policies or laws unworkable.

Britain has been free of political strikes throughout the twentieth century until the 1970s, but has experienced several in recent years. In 1971–2 there were sporadic strikes by dockers and other groups that had as one of their intentions making the 1971 Industrial Relations Act unworkable. In 1972 the National Union of Mineworkers (NUM) called a strike that challenged (and defeated) the government's policy of restricting wage and salary increases to 8 per cent. In

January 1974 the NUM called another strike, this time in defiance of the government's elaborate statutory incomes policy, which had been accepted by other unions. In 1984 the NUM organized a third strike, the issue on this occasion being the decision of the National Coal Board, in pursuance of a national policy, encouraged and endorsed (and probably insisted upon) by the government, of closing old uneconomic pits in order to concentrate production in newer pits with a much higher yield of coal.

The first three of these campaigns were entirely successful: the government had to abandon its attempts to enforce the Industrial Relations Act; the miners got a pay rise of 27 per cent (instead of the norm of 8 per cent) in 1972; and the miners received further increases of about 30 per cent in 1974 and 31 per cent in 1975 as a result of their 1974 strike. However, the strike of 1984–5 was defeated after twelve months of bitter struggle. In terms of violence, the first campaign was non-violent, the second involved a violent confrontation between mass pickets and the police, the third was relatively peaceful, and the fourth involved violent daily conflicts between pickets on the one hand, working miners and police on the other. Three men were killed and many hundreds on both sides were injured.

The cause of the violence in the 1972 strike was the use by the NUM of 'flying pickets', who moved round the country in chartered buses to block access to ports, power stations and coal depots. In many places this led to scuffles and other minor physical conflicts. The major scene of confrontation, however, was the Saltley coke depot near Birmingham, owned by the Gas Board, from which trucks were collecting coke for use in power stations at the rate of 600 or more truckloads each day. The NUM determined to stop this and sent contingents of pickets to Saltley with the intention of blocking access to the depot and swamping the police. For three days there were struggles between about 2,000 pickets and 800 policemen, with only a few trucks able to get through. On the fourth day the NUM massed 15,000 pickets at the gates, and after a violent struggle in which thirty people were injured the police capitulated (see Clutterbuck, 1981, pp. 20–6). It was the first occasion in British industrial history on which a large-scale mass picket had been deployed, and the complete success of the tactic presaged the repeated use of mass pickets in 1984–5.

In the 1974 strike the miners also made extensive use of flying pickets, but on this occasion they had the support of other unions so mass pickets were not needed to prevent supplies getting through. The use of flying pickets, which came to be known as secondary picketing, was not at that time illegal, though it was subsequently banned by the Thatcher government in 1982. In this whole area Britain suffered somewhat in the 1970s from the dependence on Common Law to regulate delicate questions of behaviour during a strike. There was no legal definition of picketing and no statute setting out the permissible limits of it. Strikers who acted as pickets were guilty of obstructing the highway if they physically prevented workers or trucks from passing, but not guilty of any legal offence if their presence simply intimidated other workers. This kind of legal tolerance did not cause serious problems in the past, because secondary picketing was rare, mass picketing was unknown, and local pickets and police normally came to an amicable understanding about what was acceptable outside factory gates. However, when the NUM organized its picketing on the lines of a military operation, as it did in 1972, the law was exposed as inadequate and violence was an almost inevitable outcome.

There was a further escalation of violence in connection with a strike in 1977, when pickets and police fought outside the Grunwick factory in north-west London. This was not a political strike but a normal industrial dispute magnified by the fact that several thousand political extremists, organized by a Trotskyite group called the Socialist Workers' Party, turned a normal picket into a mass picket. On the most violent day of this dispute, when 243 policemen were injured, there were fights between 18,000 pickets and 3,500 police officers (Clutterbuck, 1981, p. 27). On this occasion, however, the police succeeded in their daily aim of permitting the non-striking workers (actually the majority of the labour force) to get into the plant, and shortly afterwards the strike was abandoned and the strikers lost their jobs. This strike, though of little importance in itself, was significant in two ways; it showed that avowed revolutionaries had seized on the possibilities mass picketing provided for discrediting the police and undermining civil authority; and it also showed that the police were aware of this and able to contain the threat. A price was paid, however, in the visual message, transmitted every evening on television for two weeks, that one of the requirements for a career in the police force was to be good in unarmed combat. It is not surprising if the police in London and other large cities show certain signs of getting rougher and tougher.

The miners' strike of 1984–5, which lasted for exactly twelve months, was the occasion of daily struggles between flying pickets and police. The strike was called by regional councils of the NUM, it being feared that a national ballot of members would not have produced the majority prescribed by union rules. All regions but one agreed to strike, but 35,000 miners in Nottinghamshire (working the most productive pits in the country) continued to work. The NUM sent thousands of pickets into Nottinghamshire to prevent the local miners getting to work, while the police sent thousands of officers into Nottinghamshire to enable miners to get through the picket lines. Violence occurred daily, with pickets using sticks, stones, bricks, poles and other objects as weapons.

A novel feature of the conflict was that the police developed a system of national planning to deal with the pickets. A National Reporting Centre was established under the control of the President of the Association of Chief Police Officers. Several thousand London policemen, as well as contingents from other areas, were sent to Nottinghamshire to deal with the pickets, living for months on end in army barracks. The police set up road blocks round the Nottinghamshire coalfield and turned away miners from other areas. Spot checks were instituted on roads in other parts of the country, including some over 150 miles away, with police turning back motorists who seemed to be prospective pickets.

(The task was facilitated by the habit of displaying NUM badges on the front of miners' cars.) Inevitably, this drew protests from defenders of civil liberties, but the courts upheld the tactic as legal.

As the violence grew worse, the police repeatedly used batons. They also arrested over 6,000 pickets, and the National Coal Board announced that those found guilty of assault would never again be employed in the coal industry. The strike became a national struggle, with the police and government well aware that their authority was under attack. In the end they won, leaving the NUM leaders bruised and embittered. They had got no concessions on the issues of the strike; had received little support from other trade unions; and had (according to the polls) alienated the majority of the general public. However, as will be explained below, police behaviour during the strike, coming on top of the 1981 riots, made police accountability a political issue between the two main parties.

Urban Riots

In the summer of 1981 British cities were swept by a wave of riots and looting, unprecedented since 1932. In 1919–21 there had been sporadic riots in many areas caused by the anger of ex-servicemen, promised 'a land fit for heroes' but finding themselves facing prolonged unemployment. The 1926 general strike, though mainly peaceful, was the occasion of a violent confrontation between miners and police. In 1930–2 there were riots by unemployed workers in several industrial cities.

The widespread disturbances of 1981 were caused by three factors: the alienation of young black people; aggressive policing in two areas (Brixton in London and Toxteth in Liverpool) with concentrations of black citizens; and cynicism on the part of unemployed white teenagers. Race was a factor in all the riots, which occurred in twenty-seven urban areas (including several areas of London), but only one of the riots could accurately be described as a race riot. This took place in Southall, west London, where white 'skinheads' fought with Asians; the police tried vainly to separate the two sides, and the police themselves – eighty-seven of whom were injured – were attacked by the Asians. This was the only disturbance in which Asians were prominent. The Brixton riot (which was the first of the series) was a conflict between black youths and the police; the Toxteth riot (which was the most prolonged) started in the same way, but the black youths were joined by whites; the twenty-four other riots, sometimes described as 'copycat riots', had looting as their main motive, with blacks taking the lead but whites quickly joining in and sometimes outnumbering the blacks.

The Brixton riot was the subject of an official report and is better documented than the events in other areas. Brixton is an area of West Indian settlement with high unemployment. The unemployment rate in 1981 was higher among young people than among older people and higher among blacks than among whites. Among blacks aged 16–18 the rate was 55 per cent. It is reported that young blacks felt socially and politically insecure, as well as being economically disadvantaged. They spent much of their time on the streets and the area suffered from a very high incidence of street crime, mainly mugging and purse-snatching. The police response to this was to stop and search people in the street, which led blacks to complain of harassment. A few days before the riot broke out, police from other areas had been drafted into the district in an operation known as 'Operation Swamp'. The scene was thus set for trouble. The riot itself lasted for two days, with young blacks setting fire to shops owned by whites and attacking the police with stones and fire-bombs. Four hundred and one policemen were injured, 204 vehicles and 145 shops and offices were destroyed or damaged (Scarman, 1982). No figures are available for the number of rioters injured.

The situation in Toxteth was essentially similar but somewhat worse. The area is more run-down than Brixton and has had a high crime rate for many years. Whereas in Brixton the police had only recently started to stop and search people in the street, in Toxteth this was a long-established practice. Whites joined with blacks in attacking the police; the disturbances lasted for six days; the destruction of property was greater; tear gas was used, and one man was killed.

The riots in other areas were less serious, but many thousands of people were engaged in them and they made it dramatically clear that the high opinion of the police held by the majority of the public was not shared by members of ethnic minorities or by unemployed young people in inner-city areas. The figures presented in Table 1.2 on page 17 indicate the existence of a high degree of cynicism among inner-city teenagers, and their behaviour in 1981 confirmed this.

The events of 1981 are significant for students of politics. Government in a liberal democracy has to be based on consent, with coercion applied only at the margin. After the 1981 riots many commentators (including some social scientists) alleged that consent was no longer forthcoming from ethnic minorities or from people suffering from long-term unemployment. As there are 2.4 million citizens in the first category and nearly 2 million in the second, that would have disturbing implications if it were true. The riots therefore called for a political response from those in authority.

Responses to the Growth of Violence

As noted, the government's eventual response to violent demonstrations has been to give the police power to ban demonstrations thought likely to lead to violence. The response to violent strikes has been to improve police techniques for dealing with secondary picketing. The response to the urban riots has taken two forms: to provide technical training for unemployed teenagers and to encourage the police to modify their methods of social control.

The provision of technical training takes the form of the Youth Training Scheme, under the terms of which all teenagers who neither find work nor take up further education are required to spend two years in technical training, given partly at technical colleges and partly in industrial plants where the trainees are given temporary work. During the training the trainees are paid an allowance. This scheme is not without its critics, partly because its duration is insufficient to provide highly specialized training. However, the scheme provides teenagers with basic transferable skills, which may be appropriate for an age in which rapid technological progress is likely to require people to change their jobs several times during the course of their careers. The scheme also has the undoubted political advantage of keeping teenagers off the streets and offering a means of improving their morale.

The reactions of the police to the urban riots have taken two forms. First, there have been moves by the Home Office and by the police forces to increase efficiency in coping with violent situations, and with nipping troubles in the bud wherever possible. Secondly, there has been a movement for the improvement of relations between the police and local communities, both by increasing liaison work and by instituting more foot patrols.

The ability of the police to cope with violent situations has been improved since 1981 by more intensive training, the issue of more riot-shields and protective clothing and an increase in the number of Special Patrol Groups. These are groups of specially trained police officers who can be rushed to the scene of trouble by van and have techniques (first developed in Northern Ireland) for snatching trouble-makers out of a hostile crowd. The Home Office has also held discussions with Chief Constables on the possible use of more aggressive equipment, such as tear gas, water cannons and plastic bullets. Chief Constables are mostly reluctant to use such equipment for fear that its use would damage the relations between police and public. However, another set of riots might change their attitude.

The period since 1981 has also been marked by a great deal of discussion on ways of softening the impact of the police on the community in difficult urban areas. Lord Scarman (one of the Lords of Appeal) said in his report on the Brixton riots that the duty of maintaining 'public tranquillity' should be given priority over the duty of enforcing the law in such areas (Scarman, 1982, pp. 102–4). In tense situations the maintenance of law and justice 'can lead a policeman into tactics disruptive of the very fabric of society' (ibid., p. 103). Scarman also recommended that the police should make strenuous efforts to increase the recruitment of members of ethnic minorities, that more extensive training should be provided for recruits and that efforts should be made to extend what is known as 'community policing'.

This last concept involves greater use of foot patrols and fuller liaison between the police and representatives of local communities. Both tactics have been adopted successfully in some areas, notably in Devon and Cornwall. Both are more difficult to use in tense urban areas. Foot patrols are welcome in principle, but objected to if they are seen as constituting an oppressive police presence. Liaison arrangements work only if there is goodwill on both sides. In Brixton the liaison between the police and the local council for community relations had been broken off by the latter body in 1979. In Tottenham (north London) community policing suffered a severe setback in 1985, when one policeman was hacked to death with a West Indian machete and two others were injured by gunshot wounds during a riot. However, the Commissioner of the Metropolitan Police has spoken of the implied contract between the police and the public, and it is clear that efforts are being made to ensure that the object of 'policing by consent' is achieved in disadvantaged areas as well as elsewhere.

Finally, there has been a political development of potential importance. Since 1981 the Labour Party has become critical of the autonomy enjoyed by the police and has committed itself to a policy of extending the control of local police authorities over the operations of police forces. This is fiercely opposed by the police and by the Conservative Party, so that, for the first time, there is now a difference between the main parties on police matters. The Greater London Council, which had no powers whatever over the police, nevertheless established a Police Committee, which functioned as a platform for ideological criticisms of police tactics and behaviour. In the mining area of South Yorkshire members of the Police Authority criticized the police for their behaviour during the miners' strike, and appeared to regret that the only practical action they could take was to cut financial support for the police band. The radical left is concerned about the extent of police powers and advocates control of the police by elected local officials.

It is not at all certain that a future Labour government would make drastic changes in this field. Labour governments have often ignored resolutions passed by the Labour Annual Conference, and the present parliamentary leaders have disowned some of the commitments made in Labour's 1983 election manifesto, notably two of the commitments about the sale of council housing. However, it is significant that control of the police, like control of local government expenditure, has been thrown into the arena of partisan political controversy.

Further Reading

There are numerous books on the police, many of them somewhat biased. For two balanced accounts see Baldwin and Kinsey (1982), *Police Powers and Politics*, and Whitaker (1979), *The Police in Society*; for a police viewpoint, succinctly expressed, see Mark (1977), *Policing a Perplexed Society*; for an account of the legal and constitutional status of the police see Marshall (1984), *Constitutional Conventions*, ch. 8; on political violence before the 1981 riots see

Clutterbuck (1981), *The Media and Political Violence*; on the riots see Scarman (1982), *The Brixton Disorders, 10–12 April 1981*; for insights into the behaviour of a group whose relations with the police are poor see Cashmore and Troyna (1982), *Black Youth in Crisis*.

◇ 18 ◇

Assessing British Government

Any realistic assessment of British government in the 1980s must focus on the fact that the country has gone through a very difficult period. After a long postwar era of political stability, full employment and steady (even though slow) economic growth, Britain declined in the 1970s into a period of economic recession, mass unemployment and challenges to political authority. Class and sectional conflicts became sharper, while the social services failed to prevent the growth of serious social problems. The British public moved in two decades from being highly complacent about their governors to being somewhat sceptical. The political culture of the country became fragmented, and clear signs of alienation emerged among some disadvantaged groups in the community. It is appropriate to begin this assessment by asking whether the regime has some basic defect or is approaching a state of crisis.

Questions about the Regime

Questions about the regime are posed mainly by Marxists, who are the only ideological group opposed to it in principle. It is therefore appropriate to outline their approach to the matter. Marxists believe that the British system of government is dominated by its relationship to the economic system and the class system. In Marx's original formulation, the government of any society was said to be the instrument of the economically dominant class, which in the modern British case is the capitalist class. Modern Marxists have a more sophisticated view, acknowledging that the government may have a degree of autonomy from the dominant class and also acknowledging that there are apt at any given time to be significant differences of interest between sections of the dominant class. The precise way in which these relationships should be defined has been the subject of much debate, but all Marxists would agree that in a capitalist society the most important conflict is that between classes (defined in economic terms rather than in terms of social status); that the institutions of government cannot be neutral in this conflict but must be biased towards the capitalist class; and that the policies pursued by the government must inevitably be dominated by the interests and needs of the capitalist system.

The basic issue on which Marxists object to the analysis of liberal theorists is the assumption of the latter that in a system of representative democracy the governmental machine is essentially neutral, to be captured temporarily by whichever party does best in the electoral process. On the contrary, it is said, the institutions of government and administration are dominated by members of the dominant class, and much effort has been devoted to showing that most senior civil servants, judges, army officers and so on are drawn from privileged strata of society (see, for instance, Miliband, 1969; Griffith, 1981; Leys, 1983).

If contemporary Britain is analysed in Marxist terms the picture that emerges is of an industrial capitalist system that has been steadily losing its competitive international position throughout the twentieth century, and that has entered a stage of crisis since the mid-1970s. The role of government in this system has been to contain the legitimate pressures of the working class for a greater share of the fruits of production during periods of relative economic success, and to depress working-class living standards in the present period of crisis so as to make resources available for capital accumulation. The Conservative Party has taken the lead in this process, the Labour Party has co-operated in it, and the organs of justice and administration have ensured that popular resistance to it has been firmly controlled.

This analysis cannot be refuted. For several reasons, however, it is possible to doubt the extent of its explanatory value. For instance, it is noticeable that radical analyses that focus on the social composition of élite groups invariably ignore the police. Virtually all senior British police officers, including Chief Constables, are of working-class origins, but this does not make their behaviour noticeably different from that of senior civil servants, judges and so on. If Marxist explanations that emphasize personnel are replaced by those that emphasize structural position, it is of course true that the Civil Service, the judiciary and the police are not neutral as between the preservation of the existing social order and the advocacy or construction of some alternative social order. These institutions are part of the existing social order. They are clearly unlikely to work towards their own replacement or collapse. However, liberal analysts do not (if they are sensible) claim that the institutions are neutral in this rather far-reaching sense, only that they are substantially neutral as between the major parties represented in Parliament.

This raises the question of whether the capitalist system can really be considered a variable in studying British government. Communist and Trotskyite parties, which are the only ones committed to the overthrow of capitalism, have no parliamentary representatives and have difficulty in securing even 1 per cent of the votes in those constituencies in which they nominate candidates. These several parties, and the student groups associated with them, have slightly less than 50,000 members in total. They have not grown appreciably (if at all) during the recent years of economic recession and mass unemployment. There is no possibility of them bringing about a crisis of the regime.

There are of course radical socialists within the Labour Party who would like to modify the capitalist system. As noted in Chapter 5, the political centre of gravity of the Labour Party has shifted to the left in recent years. However, it has not shifted far enough to put the militants or the 'hard left' in control. If Labour returns to power in the next four years, it could be expected to institute a programme of public works, to raise taxes and possibly to reimpose exchange controls. Such policies would cause alarm in financial and business circles, but they would not amount to an economic or social revolution. As Miliband says, 'the men and women in effective charge of the Labour Party . . . do not want a social revolution on any terms, and conceive it to be their duty, as did their predecessors, to block the path of those who do' (Miliband, 1982, p. 159).

Many Marxists would say that this state of affairs reveals the extent to which the British working class has been brainwashed out of perceiving its own true interest by the mass media, which reflect only the dominant values of society. This is a proposition that can be neither proved nor disproved. Whatever the ultimate causes, the undoubted facts are that the capitalist system in Britain is not in danger of collapse and that there is no probability of a substantial political challenge to it in the foreseeable future.

It may further be noted that the capitalist system of production, which dominates most of the world in the last decades of the twentieth century, is compatible with a great variety of political structures. These include liberal democracies, military dictatorships, systems dominated by a single tribe (as in various African states) and theocratic systems (as in Iran). Britain has both a capitalist economic system and a liberal-democratic political system, but the relationship between these is not a deterministic one. What Marxist analysis offers, then, is not so much an explanation of the structure of British government as a way of explaining the character of policy outputs. The particular economic problems of the current stage of capitalist development in Britain help to explain the economic and social policies followed by the government. This is undoubtedly true, and will be taken up again later.

Apart from Marxists and neo-Marxists, there are no substantial critics of the structure of government. The monarchy, the Cabinet system, the House of Commons, the Civil Service, the judicial system and the police all operate with reasonable efficiency and enjoy the respect and support of the major parties and most citizens. The House of Lords has critics, and may be transformed or abolished if the Labour Party returns to power. But then again it may only suffer a slight reduction in its powers, as it clearly performs useful functions and a Labour government might give priority to more urgent and critical issues. The electoral system might be reformed if the centrist parties came to hold the balance of power in Parliament, but the odds are against this. The local government system has been going through a difficult period, with radical changes in central–local relationships. However, those who work in local government have had so much experience of coping with legislative changes that they are well equipped to survive the latest instalments. All in all, it seems possible to conclude that British governing institutions are stable and likely to continue for the indefinite future without major change. There is no sign of a crisis of the regime.

There are, however, serious problems of policy-making, which is rather a different matter. Since 1945, the central problems facing all British governments have been economic problems, defined variously as the problem of deficits in the balance of payments, the problem of inflation, the problem of low productivity and the problem of irreversible decline in several basic industries. The overall consequence of these problems is that Britain has failed to keep up with its international competitors and has fallen from being the third richest country in Europe to being the twelfth. A critical assessment of British government has to tackle the question of how far governmental weaknesses may have contributed to this state of affairs. There are various theories about the matter, which will now be examined in turn.

Ideological Factors

The view that central policy-making has been adversely affected by ideological factors comes in two versions, one Liberal and the other Conservative. The Liberal view, first advanced in 1975 by Finer and several colleagues, is that oscillations between Labour and Conservative governments in the postwar period have created a harmful kind of instability in the policy-making process (Finer, 1975). The main parliamentary parties are said to be 'far more partisan then the electorate' (ibid., p. 15) and the adversary system whereby they take turns to enjoy supreme political power is said to have produced repeated reversals and re-reversals of policy. Monetary policies, incomes policies and regional policies are all cited as examples of policies that have had unfortunate economic effects because governments have failed to display a constancy of purpose.

The trouble with this line of argument is that, as indicated briefly in Chapter 13, the history of postway government does not really bear it out. The parties have certainly differed in many areas, and there have been examples of policy reversals. But in general, as Rose has shown, the economic, administrative and electoral restraints that exist have pushed the parties towards the adoption of consensual policies when in power (Rose, 1980b). Finer's argument was used to bolster the case for electoral reform, but there is little strength in it as an explanation of the apparent failures of British economic policy.

The Conservative argument, advanced by Sir Keith Joseph in the late 1970s, is that Britain has suffered from 'creeping socialism' because there has been too much continuity in policy between governments. There has been, he said in numerous speeches, a 'ratchet-like' process whereby Labour governments have extended the boundaries of state intervention in economic affairs and subsequent Conservative governments have simply accepted the changes without any attempt to reverse them. This is what the Thatcher government, of which he has been a leading member, has been determined to stop.

In terms of values, this argument was put forward to help justify a controversial set of policies. In factual terms, the assertions made about post-war history appear to be nearer the truth than the assertions made to support the Liberal argument mentioned above. The Labour governments of 1945–51, 1964–70 and 1974–9 all extended the boundaries of state intervention (even though to a decreasing extent) while Conservative governments before 1979 did little to roll these boundaries back. Before Thatcher, the only Conservative Prime Minister to announce a clear intention to proceed in this way was Edward Heath, who declared in 1970: 'We were returned to office to change the course and the history of this nation, nothing else.' However, within two years the Heath government had taken Rolls-Royce into public ownership to prevent it from banckruptcy and taken Upper Clyde Shipbuilders under the government's wing to save jobs. Joseph's argument therefore rests on a fairly secure factual foundation, though whether the mixed economy and the welfare state have had an adverse effect on Britain's economic performance is of course an open question.

Administrative Incapacity

The main burden of the arguments that fall into this category is that British civil servants in the policy-making grades, though good enough at carrying out the traditional tasks of government, are inadequately prepared for their relatively new task of administering economic and social policies in a period of extended governmental intervention in these spheres. The attack has been launched on four overlapping fronts. First, it has been said that the social background of most senior civil servants, combined with the fact that they were mostly educated at boarding schools in rural areas, means that they were brought up in total ignorance of the conditions of life in industrial areas. Secondly, the fact that most entrants to the administrative grades studied arts subjects at university, rather than science, law, or the social sciences, is alleged to have given them an imappropriate training for administering the affairs of a modern industrial state. Statistics about the background and education of senior civil servants have been given in Chapter 10.

A further criticism is that the post-entry training of senior civil servants is inadequate. The efforts of the Fulton Committee to establish a thorough system of post-entry training and the limited success that attended these efforts have been detailed in Chapter 10. A student of continental administration has suggested that the trouble lies less with the education of civil servants than with their insulation from the worlds of industry and commerce and their relative ignorance of life outside the confines of London and Edinburgh. Brian Chapman has pointed out that officials who have served in the French prefectoral corps, or its equivalents in West Germany and other European states, have practical experience of dealing at the local level with problems of planning, economic expansion or decline, transport, policing and so forth. They constitute a pool of people from among whom the top administrators can be selected. Compared with such officials, he suggests, 'senior British civil servants are sheltered spinsters' (B. Chapman, 1963, p. 24).

Another line of criticism is directed at the deep reluctance of the central administration to be concerned with the way that industry and commerce are conducted on the ground. Budge and his colleagues have said that governments and administrators have displayed a consistent 'distaste for detailed intervention' (Budge *et al.*, 1983, p. 214). This is a perceptive and correct comment, and perhaps 'distaste' is too weak a word. Higher civil servants have a concept of their role that appears to exclude discrimination between firms or between areas except on the basis of some generalized national rule that can be universally applied.

Regional policy provides a good example. For some years the benefits of this policy were bestowed upon all areas that had an unemployment rate of 4.5 per cent or more, without any attempt to distinguish between areas that were doomed to decline and areas that might become centres of growth. An attraction of the policy, from the Whitehall point of view, was that it provided a simple rule that could be applied from London without any necessity for senior officials to get to know the problems and potentialities of particular cities. It also insulated the department concerned from lobbying and special pleading by representatives of local areas, and made the department invulnerable to allegations of bias, unfairness, or corruption in connection with the implementation of the policy. This particular policy was changed after a few years, but it illustrates the way in which government departments like to run the country's affairs.

Budge *et al.* have suggested that this kind of preference – which has, it may be said, been built into a tradition of behaviour – also helps to account for the reliance of successive governments on central financial policies for the management of the British economy. Such policies, whether Keynesian or monetarist, can be applied across the board by pulling levers in Whitehall. They do not involve central administrators in making discriminatory judgements, as micro-economic policies would (see Budge *et al.*, 1983, pp. 213–6). As the basic problems of the British economy are to be found at the microeconomic level, in low productivity in manufacturing industry above all else, it can well be argued that this administrative tradition has been a handicap in Britain's postwar economic development.

Taken together, these criticisms of the administrative machine amount to a serious indictment. Some of the criticisms are less important than others, and the weight to be given to them is largely a matter of judgement. But at the very least it can be said the British central administration has significant limitations.

Pluralistic Stagnation

This term has been used by Samuel Beer to describe one central aspect of British government during the postwar period, namely the extent to which spokesmen for sectional interests have been able to prevent cohesive policies being followed to deal with the country's economic problems. Beer followed other writers in pointing out that increased intervention by government in economic and social affairs makes the government increasingly dependent on the co-operation of private groups and non-governmental organizations for the design and implementation of its policies. Governments need specialist advice in framing legislation and they need the support of the relevant groups to ensure that laws and regulations are complied with. As one very senior civil servant has said: 'as the scope of the government's involvement in the life of the country gets wider and wider, the more the government has to rely on the willingness of people who are not its employees to do what it wants done' (Richard Wilding, quoted in Beer, 1982, p. 14).

In Britain there has not been any shortage of advice. Pressure groups are highly organized and they have many opportunities, as outlined in Chapter 7 above, to put their views to civil servants and ministers. Postwar governments have followed the practice of consulting them at every turn. This gives them the opportunity to press sectional claims and makes it often difficult for departments to discriminate between them, for a favour to one group will be noticed by the others. There are a multitude of such groups; when the Royal Commission on the Health Service submitted its report in 1979 it listed 1,224 organizations connected with the health services that had given evidence to the commission (Beer, 1982, p. 36). In the social field this situation led in the late 1950s and the 1960s to what Beer calls 'a scramble for benefits' (ibid., 1982, ch. 1), with a consequent rapid expansion of public expenditure.

In the economic field a similar situation has obtained. Britain has a large number of trade unions (421 in 1981), all of which are to some extent rivals in securing pay rises. If one union gets a rise, others with members in the same industry feel obliged to demand a similar rise to protect their relative positions. The 1970s, in particular, were marked by what Beer Calls a 'pay scramble' (ibid., 1982, pp. 48–62). This was collectively self-defeating, since it caused an inflation of prices that left the real incomes of workers no higher than they had been before, while leaving British industry in a weaker competitive position in international trade.

This problem has also been remarked upon by Olson, in his elaborate comparative study of the reasons for economic growth or decline (Olson, 1982). One of the few overall conclusions he was able to draw from this study was that a major factor in economic success is the existence of 'encompassing organizations' that co-ordinate the activities of trade unions, business associations and similar groups. West Germany is a good example, having only seventeen trade unions, all organized on an industry-wide basis, of which sixteen belong to a powerful federation. This federation is able to take a long-term view of the economic situation and to regulate wage claims (and claims for other benefits and privileges) in a way that minimizes the need for strike action while giving West German workers wages and conditions of work that are the envy of workers in most other industrial societies. Britain is at the opposite extreme, having numerous trade unions and a national federation (the Trades Union Congress) that has very little authority over its members. The prevalence of demarcation disputes and leap-frogging wage claims is a consequence of this organizational situation.

The position is not entirely different on the other side of industry. The Confederation of British Industry has little or no authority over its members, and there has never been any realistic possibility that it might negotiate with the Trades Union Congress and the government to produce a meaningful strategy for industrial investment, wages policy, or workers' consultation in industry. There are numerous trade associations, some large and some very small, all negotiating with government departments and engaged in what Beer calls a 'scramble for subsidies' (Beer, 1982, pp. 63–76). Their success in this scramble was helped by the reluctance or inability of civil servants to discriminate between claimants. Thus, when grants were made available in the 1970s to help firms in the woollen textile industry that had promising schemes of modernization, 370 of the 400 or so firms in the industry made successful applications. The overall consequence of government policies, from 1945 through to 1979, was the diffusion of government aid to industry in an astonishing variety of tax concessions, investment allowances, investment grants, subsidized buildings, share purchases and direct subsidies. Variety is not necessarily a bad thing, but the unfortunate fact is that these policies failed to prevent the absolute decline of some vital sectors of industry, such as the car industry, and the relative decline of the entire British economy.

Similar themes have been explored by several other scholars. Thus, Berrington has discussed what he calls 'the paradox of strength' of the British government, suggesting that the inability of ministers to point to any institutional obstacle to doing whatever they decide to do has made it peculiarly difficult for them to resist the demands of pressure groups (Berrington, 1984, pp. 34–5). Hayward has contrasted British inertia in the field of economic policy-making and administration with French efficiency and drive, pointing out that in France a strong and well-informed bureaucratic élite has had the ability to impose its priorities on the entire nation (Hayward, 1976).

All this adds up to a lament over certain aspects of the British situation, which are not entirely, or even mainly, the fault of postwar governments. Ministers do not have the power to knock trade union leaders' heads together, to take one example, and induce them to amalgamate. The policy of the Thatcher government has been to move in a different direction. On the one hand, it has tried to reduce the dependence of business firms on government help, letting the disciplines of the market take their toll in the hope that the survivors will be leaner, fitter and more competitive. On the other hand, the government has deliberately reduced the amount of consultation it participates in with group spokesmen, thereby incurring much displeasure, in the hope of liberating the ministers from at least a small proportion of the pressures with which they have to cope.

The reduction in the extent of consultation with group spokesmen has been highly unpopular with trade unions, somewhat unpopular with trade associations, and sporadically unpopular with professional associations representing doctors, teachers, university lecturers and barristers. It has, however, enabled the government to push ahead with modernization plans and to free British society from a variety of restrictive practices.

The reduction in the spread of government subsidies to industry has proved highly controversial. British industry has certainly become leaner under the Thatcher government, at the cost of numerous factory closures and considerable unemployment. Many sectors of industry have also become more efficient, and the economy as a whole has become (at least since 1982) more dynamic. However, while a number of high technology sectors, such as aircraft manufacturing, have been very successful, in several more humdrum areas British industry is still outstripped by its competitors. Most domestic appliances sold in Britain are made in Italy while much kitchen equipment is made in France or Germany. The automobile industry became more efficient between 1979 and 1989, but Britain still imports about half its cars although for the first twenty postwar years it was a major exporter of them. Britain does well with specialized vehicles, but in the highly competitive market for medium-sized, medium-priced family saloons British firms do not seem able to produce cars that are quite as attractive as their French equivalents or quite as reliable as similar cars made in Japan, Germany and Sweden.

The result of failures like this is that Britain is entering the 1990s with a deficit in the balance of trade that is barely covered by the large surplus in 'invisible' items like banking, insurance, tourism and profits on overseas investments. There is little that any British government can do to overcome this problem apart from a retreat into protectionism, which would mean leaving the European Community and exposing the country to drastic retaliatory action by its trading partners. It follows that the Thatcher government's efforts to free the country from pluralistic stagnation, though successful in their immediate objectives, have been only partially successful in their larger object of restoring the national economy to health and competitive vigour. It is probable that in the later 1990s, as North Sea oil production declines, the country will again be wrestling, as in the 1960s and 1970s, with a deficit in the balance of payments on current account.

Overload and Delegitimation

In recent years theorists in several countries have drawn attention to the fact that the responsibilities expected of modern democratic governments are so extensive that the government machine is in danger of being overloaded. Popular expectations about the benefits to be provided by governments have risen rapidly; more rapidly, perhaps, than the ability of governments to provide these benefits. In consequence people have become disappointed, and there has been a decline in confidence in government. Anthony King summarized this development in an aphorism: 'Once upon a time man looked to God to order the world. Then he looked to the market. Now he looks to government. And when thing go wrong people blame not "Him" or "it" but "them"' (King, 1975, p. 288). It was suggested by King that this had made Britain more difficult to govern, and other writers made the same comment about the United States.

Since King wrote, the development of mass unemployment has sharpened the argument, for the maintenance of full employment is a commitment that the major British parties entered into gladly at the end of the war. Moreover, this development has put a strain on public finances that has made it difficult for the government to improve social services in response to public demand. There is clearly a problem, which is not confined to Britain but appears in a rather sharp form in Britain because the country is now appreciably poorer than most of the other advanced democracies.

Two German neo-Marxists have put this issue into a much broader perspective by describing it as an inevitable problem of a certain late stage of capitalist development. The argument, reduced to bare bones, is that in Western industrial societies the capitalist system is (for a time) legitimized in the eyes of workers by the liberal-democratic state, which gives the impression of pursuing common social interests and being responsive to the demands of the community. In order to protect its legitimacy, and therefore the legitimacy of the whole social order, the state develops welfare services to protect disadvantaged individuals and groups from the inevitable hardships that result from the operations of the capitalist system. As time goes by, political and social pressures lead to the extension of social benefits, in one form or another, to virtually the whole population – a process that costs so much that it eventually creates a fiscal crisis by overloading the national budget.

At this point governments face an insoluble dilemma. If they continue to provide generous, and increasingly expensive, social services they will have to pay for them either by levying higher taxes, which will create difficulties for business enterprise, or by deficit financing, which will cause inflation. In either case, the operation of the capitalist economy will be harmed and further economic difficulties will ensue. The other alternative is to cut public services, which will lead to disenchantment with the political system and an increasing feeling of alienation among workers. In that case, the democratic system will gradually cease to perform its legitimizing function and society will face what Habermas has called a 'legitimation crisis' (Habermas, 1975).

The theories of Habermas and Claus Offe, the other important writer of this school, include many ramifications and interesting sidelights in addition to the basic argument outlined briefly in the preceding paragraphs. However, the main argument is clearly challenging in view of the recent developments in Britain. The Thatcher government has chosen to curtail public expenditure rather than to raise taxes or run budgetary deficits of an inflationary kind. That implies that it has accepted the risk of causing alienation and delegitimation (and the certainty of distress for the unemployed) in preference to accepting the economic costs that would be involved if public expenditures were increased in response to social demands by disadvantaged groups. The question is whether this choice will lead, or has already led, to a condition that could reasonably be described as a crisis of legitimacy.

The answer to this question depends partly on how such a crisis is defined. There is survey and other evidence to show that the British political culture is now, at least in part, fragmented, with a sizeable minority of citizens not sharing traditional political values, not having much respect for the governmental system and being willing to support various forms of direct action, some of them illegal, to press their demands. This evidence has been discussed in Chapters 1 and 17. The urban riots of 1981 showed that thousands of unemployed young people in British cities were ready to take to the streets and fight with the police, for no perceptible prospect of personal gain beyond the possible acquisition of a looted stereo amplifier or television set. By some standards, these riots could in themselves be regarded as evidence of a crisis of legitimacy.

For my part, I incline towards a more relaxed view. The British system of government has shown remarkable powers of endurance over the years. There has not been a revolution since 1688, despite numerous radical movements, riots and threatening situations. In the Gordon Riots of 1780, 285 people were killed in London and 25 of the participants were eventually executed, but the subsequent course of British history was scarcely affected by these events. There have been troubled periods and smooth periods, but the parliamentary system and all that goes with it has survived without serious challenge. In the jargon of political science, the British system has demonstrated a very high capacity for system maintenance.

This capacity has been revealed on several occasions in the twentieth century. The system has coped successfully with a prolonged campaign of direct action by the suffragettes before the First World War; with an armed insurrection in Ireland in 1919–21; with rioting in British cities during the same period; with the general strike of 1926; and with prolonged mass unemployment in the 1930s. From 1939 until the end of the 1960s the system benefited from the feelings of national unity created by the Second World War and the long period of economic growth that followed it. We all tend to base historical judgements on a rather short period of the immediate past, and this period of social and political tranquillity has made the turmoil of the 1970s and 1980s seem particularly distressing. Viewed in terms of a longer historical perspective, it does not seem so bad. It may perhaps be fair to conclude that the British system of government is still in good order, despite the testing times in which we live.

Further Reading

There are numerous commentaries on British government from a Marxist perspective, of which Miliband (1982), *Capitalist Democracy in Britain*, and Gamble (1981), *Britain in Decline*, are particularly pertinent; for a sharp critical assessment of central administration, written years before criticism became fashionable, see B. Chapman (1963), *British Government Observed*; for a fuller account of the 'pluralistic stagnation' thesis see Beer (1982), *Britain against Itself*; for a good general summation see Budge *et al.* (1983). *The New British Political system*, ch. 9; for a guide to the arguments about overload and delegitimation see Birch (1984), 'Overload, ungovernability and delegitimation: the theories and the British case'.

◇　◇

Appendix: Notes on the Politics of Northern Ireland

(1)   The character of politics in Northern Ireland differs sharply from the character of politics in the remainder of the United Kingdom. While in Britain power alternates between the two main parties, in Northern Ireland the Ulster Unionist Party enjoyed power continuously from 1922 to 1972. In Britain religion is of little political significance whereas in Northern Ireland it dominates the political scene. In Britain the main opposition parties are completely loyal to the constitutional system whereas in Northern Ireland their aim is to transform or overthrow it. Above all, British politics has been largely free from violence whereas Northern Ireland has been the scene of violent protests, political assassinations and intermittent guerrilla warfare for the past seventy years.

(2)   The extraordinary character of Irish politics can be explained only in historical terms. While political attitudes in other countries are influenced by history, political attitudes in Ireland seem to be imprisoned by it. For this reason some of the main events in Irish political history will be outlined in the following paragraphs. For reasons of space, the treatment will be sketchy, and paragraphs will be numbered to emphasize this.

(3)   Ireland was dominated by England from the twelfth century to the twentieth century. There was never an independent Irish state until 1921. There were local communities and local rulers, provinces and provincial governors, but the sovereign of Ireland – in so far as it could be said to have a sovereign – was the King of England. The Roman Catholic religion of the Irish people was not affected by the Reformation, but in the late sixteenth and seventeenth centuries a substantial number of Protestant settlers migrated to Ireland from Britain, settling mainly in the northern part of the country.

(4)   In 1641 the 'Ulster Rising' occurred. This was a revolt of the native Irish against British government and against the Protestant settlers in the northern counties (nine of which constituted the Province of Ulster). It was a bloody affair, and troops had to be sent from England to suppress it. The Catholic King Charles was weakened doubly by this episode. In the first place the rebellion increased anti-Catholic feelings in England. Secondly, the need to finance a military expedition forced Charles to convene Parliament, which set in train the events leading to the English Civil War.

(5)   After the Civil War Cromwell's army took their revenge against the Irish. In particular, they attacked the Catholic Church, killing priests and despoiling the churches. However, after the Restoration in 1660 there was a reversal of fortunes. Ireland became a Roman Catholic country once more, an Irish army was recruited that was almost entirely Catholic in composition, and all Protestant judges, officials and aldermen were thrown out of office.

(6)   In the bloodless revolution of 1688 James II fled from England without putting up a fight against William of Orange, his invading army and his English supporters. However, in Ireland only the Protestants recognized William and Mary as legitimate rulers. In March 1689 James landed in Ireland from France and took command of the Irish army, and what was in effect a war for the English throne was then fought out on Irish soil. An attack on Londonderry was frustrated by the courage of the Protestant minority in the city – an event that has been celebrated annually ever since by the 'Apprentice Boys' March' – and on 1 July 1690 James came face to face with William in the Battle of the Boyne. In this famous encounter James's Irish and French troops were defeated by a mixed force of Ulster Protestants, Scots, Englishmen, Dutchmen and Danes and this victory ensured the supremacy of the Protestant religion in Britain.

(7)   From 1690 to 1800 Ireland was ruled by its Protestant minority through a Parliament in Dublin. This Parliament was notable for the 'Penal Laws' with which it discriminated against Roman Catholics. Under these laws, Catholics were not allowed to bear arms, Catholic priests were forbidden to celebrate mass, and Catholics were not permitted to send children abroad to be educated (to stop them going to continental seminaries). In an attempt to help Protestant landowners extend their estates, Catholics were not permitted to buy land, except on a lease of up to thirty-one years, and were not permitted to bequeath their land by will. When a Catholic landowner died his land was divided equally between all his sons, which in a country of large families ensured the fragmentation of Catholic estates. And, as a final twist of the knife, it was decreed that if the eldest son of a Catholic landowner joined the Protestant Church he would immediately be given ownership of the whole estate, with his father remaining simply as tenant for life and his brothers disinherited.

Edmund Burke said that this period degraded the character of the Irish Catholic peasant, and an Irish historian has elaborated the same view:

> His religion made him an outlaw . . . and whatever was inflicted on him he must bear, for where could he look for redress? To his landlord? Almost invariably an alien conqueror. To the law? Not when every person connected with the law, from the jailer to the judge, was a Protestant . . .
>
> In these conditions suspicion of the law, of the ministers of the law and of all established authority worked into the very nerves and blood of the Irish peasant, and since the law did not give him justice he set up his own law. The secret societies which have been the curse of Ireland became widespread . . . dissimulation became a moral necessity and evasion of the law the duty of every God-fearing Catholic.   (Woodham-Smith, 1962, pp. 27–8)

(8)   In 1800 Ireland was made an integral part of the United Kingdom and a sizeable contingent of Irish MPs arrived at Westminster. The Penal Laws were gradually abolished and Catholics achieved equality of status with Protestants. The last decade of the nineteenth century saw the growth of the Irish nationalist movement, and the question of Irish Home Rule became a lively issue in British politics.

(9)   In 1912 Asquith's Liberal government introduced a Home Rule Bill that was designed to give a substantial measure of internal self-government to the whole of Ireland, under the control of an Irish government and Parliament in Dublin. The Ulster Protestants objected passionately to this proposal, being totally unwilling to accept the rule of what would inevitably be a Roman Catholic regime. As loyal subjects of the crown they claimed that the United Kingdom government had no right to place them at the mercy of their historic enemies. In this they had the support of British Conservative leaders and large sections of British public opinion. An armed fighting force, under the title of the Ulster Volunteers, was established to resist the proposed change by force and it is possible that a civil war would have developed had not the outbreak of war with Germany given the British government the opportunity to put the whole reform into cold storage.

(10)   Frustrated by these events, the Irish nationalists turned from moderate leaders to extremists. In 1916 a group of the latter staged the 'Easter Rising' in Dublin, seized the main Post Office, and proclaimed an Irish Republic. The rebellion was quickly put down by British troops, and sixteen of its leaders were executed for treason. The executions were, however, a gift to the nationalist cause, for the dead men were regarded as martyrs, their role was commemorated by Irish poets, and the nationalist movement gained immensely in strength. In 1918 the nationalists successfully sabotaged a British attempt to impose conscription on Ireland and in 1919 they launched a general insurrection.

(11)   In 1921, after nearly two years of fighting, a treaty was concluded between the British government and the nationalist leaders whereby the twenty-six mainly Catholic counties of Ireland were granted political independence as the Irish Free State, while the six predominantly Protestant counties of the north-east remained as part of the United Kingdom, though with their own Parliament in Belfast to legislate on domestic affairs. In view of the militant determination of the Protestants this partition of the country was almost inevitable; the British government could hardly expel a million loyal citizens from the United Kingdom against their wishes, and any attempt to do so would have led to a continuing civil war in Ireland between Protestants and Catholics.

(12)   Unfortunately, the Province of Northern Ireland was (and is) by no means homogeneous in its population. Thirty-four per cent of the inhabitants were Catholics in 1921 and (despite rumours to the contrary) this proportion has remained virtually static ever since. The two communities are highly segregated. For the most part, they are served by different schools, which are equally supported by government funds. The schools teach history in different

ways, so that children tend to be socialized into conflict. They play different games, so that Catholic and Protestant children rarely meet on the sports field. There is considerable segregation in areas of residence and in clubs and pubs visited. There is little intermarriage, which is condemned by both communities. Looked at in a sociological perspective, Northern Ireland is more like a bi-tribal society than a society divided between two branches of the Christian religion. Like tribes, each community in Northern Ireland has its own myths and heroes, its own songs and its own symbols – the orange and green sashes, the Union Jack and the Irish tricolour. Each community also has its own ritual marches, which by celebrating past victories are designed to rub salt in the wounds of the other side.

(13)   In an open society (i.e. one not governed on totalitarian lines) that contains more than one religious or ethnic community there are only three possible patterns of political behaviour. One pattern may be called the politics of integration, in which the differences between religious and other groups have no direct bearing on the competition for political power. A good example is England, where there are only a handful of parliamentary constituencies in which a candidate's religion has any perceptible effect on his electoral support (these all being constituencies with a considerable number of Irish electors). A second pattern is best called the politics of accommodation. In this kind of system a deliberate and conscious attempt is made to ensure that each community or group has a reasonable share of political power. In Canada, for instance, there is a firm convention that, no matter which party holds office, the federal cabinet should contain so many French-speaking Catholics, at least one English-speaking Catholic and representatives from each province of the country. The third pattern is the politics of group dominance, in which each community or group is associated with its own political party and a policy of 'winner takes all' is adopted.

(14)   From the beginning, politics in Northern Ireland followed the pattern of group dominance. The Ulster Unionist Party, which has close relations with a Protestant society called the Orange Order, won every general election and made no attempt to share any of its power with Catholics. At the same time, Catholic politicians made no attempt to win the support of Protestant voters and deepened the antagonism of the Unionists by refusing to recognize the legitimacy of the Belfast regime. For fifty years Northern Ireland had a political system in which a permanent majority nursed their power and a permanent minority nursed their grievances.

Until 1973 the Protestants were always more united than their opponents. The Ulster Unionist Party was well organized and well financed, benefited from the fruits of office and had the advantage of a clear objective: to maintain the constitutional position. This was advantageous to Northern Ireland in some ways, for over a whole range of social affairs the Belfast Parliament had the option of either adopting British legislation or introducing its own variations. By normally adopting British legislation on social and economic affairs the Unionists not only deprived their opponents of the possibility of appealing to the voters with a programme of progressive social policies but also ensured a very heavy concealed subsidy from the British taxpayer.

The Catholics, in contrast, have always been somewhat divided. It is demoralizing to be in a permanent minority and not surprising that Catholics have differed among themselves over tactics. Should they, for instance: (*a*) fight elections and if successful put up a vigorous opposition in Parliament; (*b*) fight elections but if successful boycott Parliament; (*c*) boycott elections; (*d*) offer passive resistance to the Stormont regime; (*e*) take every step, including violence and terrorism, to erode the authority of Stormont; (*f*) engage in guerrilla warfare with the hope of internationalizing the conflict and securing the intervention of the Irish Republic? All six tactics have had their supporters and these differences of view have fragmented the political activities of the Catholics. This has been reflected in the multiplicity of political organizations supported by the Catholic community, which in the past thirty years alone have included the Nationalist Party, the Republican Party, the Social Democratic and Labour Party (SDLP) the Civil Rights Association and both the Official and Provisional wings of Sinn Fein.

(15)   On the most important issue, all the Catholic parties have been united; they have all committed themselves to the unity of Ireland as the only proper solution to the problems of their community. However, on this matter they have not represented the views of the majority of Catholic electors, as revealed by public opinion surveys. The Catholics of Northern Ireland, though on average slightly poorer than their Protestant neighbours, are nevertheless better off in material terms than they would be in the Irish Republic. Whereas the gross domestic product per head in the Republic was only 58 per cent of the United Kingdom figure in 1980 (Chubb, 1982, p. 345), in Northern Ireland the equivalent proportion was 78 per cent. Northern incomes are swollen by large British subsidies to industry and the social services. It is probably for this reason that only a minority of Catholic electors favour an end to partition. A 1979 survey by the Economic and Social Research Institute of Dublin showed that 39 per cent of Catholics in Northern Ireland favoured unification while 49 per cent preferred to stay in the United Kingdom (O'Brien, 1980, p. 81). The knowledge that Catholic political leaders misrepresent the views of the Catholic community on this vital issue increases the contempt with which these leaders are regarded by Protestant leaders and strengthens the resolve of the latter not to share political power with the former.

(16)   In 1969 Northern Ireland was plunged into political violence. This was started by conflict between Catholic demonstrators and Protestant mobs and has been continued since 1970 by a campaign of terror waged by the provisional wing of the Irish Republican Army (IRA). This underground army, with seventy years of intermittent violence and guerrilla warfare to its credit, is the most experienced revolutionary group now operating in the world. Its objects are to induce the British to abandon Northern Ireland, to secure the unification of that

province with the Republic, and then to overthrow the government of the Republic. It has been an illegal organization in the Republic since 1931, but it has commanded such a mixture of sympathy and fear among the public that successful prosecutions have been rare and in practice it is tolerated by the Dublin government. It is well financed from a variety of sources and is well supplied with modern arms from overseas, its chief recent supplier being the government of Libya.

Since 1969 political violence in Northern Ireland, though consisting mainly of bombings and shootings committed by the IRA, has also involved the assassination of numerous Catholics by Protestant paramilitary forces. Although the British army has stationed between 10,000 and 15,000 troops there to help the police maintain security, the casualties between 1969 and 1989 amounted to almost 2,800 deaths and many thousands of people injured. In terms of the ratio of deaths to population, this is equivalent to approximately 428,000 deaths in the United States.

(17) Because the British government felt that it had to take charge of policy in Northern Ireland once the army was heavily engaged there, and also because it was dissatisfied with the advice on security issues emanating from the Northern Ireland government, that government and the Northern Ireland Parliament were abruptly suspended in 1972. Since then the province has been governed directly from London, apart from the period between January and May 1974 when there was a power-sharing executive in Belfast. Policy is mainly controlled by the Secretary of State for Northern Ireland, who is a member of the British Cabinet and commutes between London and Belfast. The policies adopted by the British government can be summarized under four headings, as follows:

(i)   An attempt to remedy the legitimate grievances of the Catholic minority.

(ii)   An attempt to minimize violence and pacify the province.

(iii) An attempt to persuade Protestant and Catholic politicians in the province to share executive power in a Belfast administration responsible for local issues.

(iv) An attempt to secure the co-operation of the government of the Irish Republic in fighting terrorism and improving the political atmosphere in the North.

(18) British efforts to remedy Catholic grievances began in 1969. The local government franchise was extended to all adult citizens, instead of being dependent on a property qualification. The municipal government of Londonderry, which had been controlled by Protestants as a result of electoral gerrymandering, was transferred to a bipartisan commission. The control of public housing was taken out of the hands of municipalities, which had engaged in sectarian favouritism in allocating tenancies, and given to a non-sectarian province-wide Housing Executive. The Royal Ulster Constabulary was put

under the control of an English chief constable and turned gradually into a much more professional force than it had been. The police reserve force, greatly distrusted by Catholics because of its Protestant bias, was disbanded.

The response to these reforms was very discouraging. In London the reforms were regarded as sweeping, rapid and a clear demonstration of the government's fairness. Many Catholic leaders, on the other hand, regarded the reforms as belated concessions made in response to violence, and drew the conclusion that militancy paid dividends. New grievances were quickly discovered. The Catholic members of the Londonderry Development Commission refused to take part in administration. The army, at first welcomed by Catholics as a protection against Protestant mobs, was soon being denounced as an instrument of British oppression. The attempt to remedy Catholic grievances did little or nothing to improve relationships.

(19)   The attempt to pacify the province met with an early reversal. In 1971 the British decided (at the suggestion of the Northern Ireland government) that IRA suspects should be interned without trial, as an answer to IRA intimidation of juries that made successful prosecutions difficult to achieve. This measure infuriated the Catholic community and proved to be a sad mistake. Although several hundred IRA members were interned, they were quickly replaced by new recruits and IRA violence became more widespread and indiscriminate as the months went by. The death rate from political violence increased to 467 in 1972. However, the security forces learned from this blunder and by careful intelligence and improved techniques they were able to reduce the violence to more acceptable levels by 1976. In the 1980s the death rate has been reduced further, to under 100 a year. Whereas Belfast was in a stage of siege in the early 1970s, with barricades and body searches every few yards in the city centre, daily life in the city has now returned to a more normal condition.

However, it is not possible to defeat the IRA completely, so long as it can attract recruits and provide its members with training, weapons, money and safe houses. As underground armies go, it is a very professional outfit, now organised on a cellular basis to frustrate the efforts of British intelligence. Every defeat produces martyrs who can be compared with the original martyrs of the Easter Rising and serve as an incentive for new recruits to join. Having committed itself to two quite unattainable objectives in the unification of Ireland followed by a revolution in Dublin, the IRA will always have a cause to go on fighting for. It would be foolish to regard it as other than a permanent actor in Northern Irish politics.

(20)   Several attempts have been made to persuade Protestant and Catholic politicians to share executive power, so far with only transitory success. In 1973 the Heath government, through the Northern Ireland Secretary, William Whitelaw, persuaded the Ulster Unionist leader of the time, Brian Faulkner, to form a government of both Protestant and Catholic ministers to take charge of domestic affairs in the province and to answer to a newly elected Northern Ireland Assembly. Faulkner was denounced by many of his senior Unionist

colleagues and his action split the Ulster Unionist Party. Nevertheless, the new government took office in January 1974 and ran the internal affairs of the province, apart from security issues which remained under London control, until May 1974. In that month the province was crippled by a general strike called by the Ulster Workers' Council in protest against the power-sharing arrangement. After electricity and water supplies had been interrupted, and when the sewerage workers threatened to block the sewerage system, Faulkner resigned and the whole government collapsed. The Assembly was then suspended and the militant Protestant groups celebrated their victory.

In 1975–6 the British Labour government sponsored a Constitutional Convention to discuss the possibilities of political change, but the elected Unionist majority blocked any agreement on reform. In 1982 the Thatcher government proposed a scheme for 'rolling devolution' to establish a power-sharing executive in stages, but Protestant intransigence blocked this initiative also. In 1985, as will be explained, the Anglo-Irish Agreement set up some incentives for the Protestant leaders to accept power-sharing, but so far there is no sign of these producing results. It is transparently clear that the British preference for a system of political accommodation in Northern Ireland will make no headway so long as the present generation of Protestant leaders dominate the Unionist movement. These leaders regard the Catholic politicians as disloyal and unrepresentative, an attitude for which there is certainly some factual basis, and they would rather see Northern Ireland governed from London than share responsibility with politicians they despise.

(21)   The government of the Irish Republic is another actor in the ongoing drama of Northern Irish politics. On the one hand, the Republic is a bad neighbour, providing a sanctuary for terrorists and repeatedly refusing to extradite persons wanted for terrorist offences, even if these include murder. It is rather as if Canada refused to extradite persons wanted for murder or terrorism in the United States. The Irish border is even more open than the Canadian/US border and the distances are smaller, so that it would be possible for a terrorist to set a bomb in Belfast and be safely over the border an hour later. On the other hand, the Catholic minority in the North tend to look to Dublin for assistance and the British government needs the help of the Dublin government in dealing with the North.

Various negotiations between London and Dublin produced results that were either negligible or short-lived, until in 1985 the Anglo-Irish Agreement was signed by Margaret Thatcher and the Irish Prime Minister, Garret Fitzgerald. This Agreement has two main provisions, one of symbolic importance and the other of practical value. The first of these provisions is a declaration by the British government that Northern Ireland could be united with the Republic if a majority of its citizens voted for this course of action, together with a declaration by the Irish government that it would only want unity with the North if this were desired by a majority of northerners. As there is no prospect of more than a quarter of northerners voting for unity, this provision it is not going to produce any constitutional change, but it has the great merit of making clear that the question is entirely one for the citizens of the province to settle and is not an issue between the British and Irish governments.

The other main provision of the Anglo-Irish Agreement was the establishment of an Intergovernmental Conference, composed of senior members of the British and Irish governments, to meet regularly in Northern Ireland to discuss ways of improving the political situation there. The Conference makes recommendations to the British government that the latter may accept or reject. In practice this liaison body serves as a valuable channel through which proposals emanating from the Catholic minority in the North can be supported by representatives of the Republic and passed to London for consideration. Some of these proposals have been rejected, but others have been acted upon. In consequence, Catholics are now permitted to fly the Irish tricolour and to display other flags and emblems as they wish; there are improved procedures for dealing with complaints about police behaviour; and new measures have been adopted to reduce or eliminate religious discrimination in employment. The Conference is an imaginative way of ensuring that Catholic grievances do not go unheard.

The Anglo-Irish Agreement is highly unpopular with Unionist politicians, who resent the fact that it gives the Republic a legitimate way of influencing government policies in the North. There is, however, a way by which this influence can be reduced or even eliminated. If Unionist and Catholic politicians can agree to share executive power in respect of a particular field of policy – say education or public health – then that field can be excluded from the deliberations of the Intergovernmental Conference. This provision is essentially an incentive to Protestant leaders to move towards a form of political accommodation for the government of the province, as successive British governments have wanted from 1973 onwards. So far there is no sign of the incentive producing results.

(22) What does the future hold for Northern Ireland? This question is best broken down into three separate questions, one relating to constitutional arrangements, one on security and terrorism, and one on social relationships.

In terms of constitutional arrangements, there is no prospect of early change. The province has to be governed from Belfast, London, or Dublin. As rule from Dublin is inconceivable and the British government refuses to devolve power to Belfast unless Northern Irish politicians agree to power-sharing, which they show no signs of doing, the province has to be ruled from London. Though this is not the first preference of any sizeable group in the North, it is an acceptable alternative to all except the Republican extremists. It gives the citizens of the province the same political rights as other British citizens, except in two respects. One is that prosecutions for terrorist offences may be conducted without a jury. The other is that the minister responsible for Northern Irish affairs, being always a member of the Conservative Party or the Labour Party, can never be a member of a party for which Northern Irish citizens vote. It has been suggested that the British parties might organize and compete in Northern Ireland, but there is no present likelihood of that.

The situation regarding security is also unlikely to change much. The IRA cannot win but cannot be completely defeated, so it is likely to continue its campaign of terrorism. Its tactics vary from time to time. In the early years of the Thatcher government its attention was almost entirely confined to Northern Ireland and the British government's policy was one of 'Ulsterization', with the army leaving the police to take the initiative on security issues. In the late 1980s the IRA made the British army its main target, not only in Ulster but also in Britain, West Germany, the Netherlands and Gibraltar. In response to this, the army has employed its crack specialized regiment, the SAS, to fight the IRA. Tactics may change again, but political violence in some form is likely to be a continuing reality.

In this author's view, the best hope of improving the political situation is to try to change the attitudes of the next generation. The way to bring about a reduction in communal tensions, I believe, is to establish integrated non-sectarian schools in place of the denominational schools that now socialize children into segregation and mutual hostility. This would be controversial but not necessarily unpopular, except with some of the churches. A 1978 survey showed that 82 per cent of Protestants and 84 per cent of Catholics were willing to agree that it is not a bad idea (Moxon-Browne, 1983, p. 134). The British authorities have encouraged the establishment of non-denominational schools (though not, it would seem, with any particular energy or sense of urgency) and by 1989 eight of them were operating in the province. In all cases these were working successfully, without the problems that had sometimes been predicted. It remains to be seen whether they will become common and how far they will affect public attitudes. Quick changes are not to be expected, for three hundred years of communal strife cannot easily be overcome. But integrated education may offer some hope for the future in an otherwise depressing situation.

Further Reading

A brief guide to the history of Anglo-Irish relations will be found in Birch (1977), *Political Integration and Disintegration in the British Isles*, chs. 4, 5; the best analysis of politics in Northern Ireland up to the violence of 1969 is that in Rose (1971), *Governing Without Consensus*; a shorter analysis, excellent on the period since 1969, is that in Arthur (1984), *Government and Politics of Northern Ireland*; a fascinating essay on the triangular relationship between the peoples of Ireland, Ulster and Britain is to be found in O'Brien (1980), *Neighbours*.

Bibliography

This bibliography includes only the books, articles, reports and papers that have been mentioned in the text or in the lists of further reading.

Alderman, G. (1984), *Pressure Groups and Government in Great Britain* (New York: Longman).

Alexander, A. (1982), *Local Government in Britain since Reorganization* (London: Allen and Unwin).

Allen, D. (1988), 'Britain and Western Europe', in M. Smith, S. Smith and B. White (eds.), *British Foreign Policy* (London: Unwin Hyman), pp. 168–92.

Almond, G., and Verba, S. (1965), *The Civic Culture* (Boston, Mass.: Little, Brown).

Arthur, P. (1984), *Government and Politics of Northern Ireland*, 2nd edn (London: Longman).

Baldwin, R., and Kinsey, R. (1982), *Police Powers and Politics* (London: Quartet).

Beer, S. H. (1982), *Britain against Itself* (New York: Norton).

Belson, W. A. (1975), *The Public and the Police* (London: Harper & Row).

Benewick, R. J., Birch, A. H., Blumler, J. G. and Ewbank, A. (1969), 'The floating voter and the liberal theory of representation', *Political Studies*, vol. 17, pp. 177–95.

Berrington, H. (1984), 'British government: the paradox of strength', in D. Kavanagh and G. Peele (eds.), *Comparative Government and Politics* (London: Heinemann).

Bevins, R. (1965), *The Greasy Pole* (London: Hodder & Stoughton).

Birch, A. H. (1959), *Small-Town Politics* (Oxford: Oxford University Press).

(1964), *Representative and Responsible Government* (London: Allen & Unwin).

(1977), *Political Integration and Disintegration in the British Isles* (London: Allen & Unwin).

(1984), 'Overload, ungovernability and delegitimation: the theories and the British case', *British Journal of Political Science*, vol. 14, pp. 135–60.

Blackstone, W. (1809), *Commentary on the Laws of England* [1765] 15th edn (Oxford: Clarendon Press).

Blondel, J. (1963), *Voters, Parties and Leaders* (Harmondsworth: Penguin).

Bogdanor, V. (ed.) (1983), *Liberal Party Politics* (Oxford: Clarendon Press).

Bonham, J. (1954), *The Middle Class Vote* (London: Faber).

Borthwick, R. (1979), 'Questions and debates', in S. A. Walkland (ed.), *The House of Commons in the Twentieth Century* (Oxford: Oxford University Press).

Brown, R. G. S., and Steel, D. R. (1979), *The Administrative Process in Britain*, 2nd edn (London: Methuen).

Buchanan, C. (1981), *No Way to the Airport* (London: Longman).

Buck, P. W. (1963), *Amateurs and Professionals in British Politics* (Chicago: Chicago University Press).

Budge, I., McKay, D., Marsh, D., Page, E., Rhodes, R., Robertson, D., Slater, M. and Wilson, G. (1983), *The New British Political System* (London: Longman).

Bulpitt, J. (1983), *Territory and Power in the United Kingdom* (Manchester: Manchester University Press).

Burch, M., and Moran, M. (1985), 'The changing British political élite, 1945–1983', *Parliamentary Affairs*, vol. 38, pp. 1–15.

Butler, D. (1983), *Governing Without a Majority* (London: Collins).

Butler, D., and Kavanagh, D. (1984), *The British General Election of 1983* (London: Macmillan).

Butler, D., and Kavanagh, D. (1988), *The British General Election of 1987* (London: Macmillan).

Butler, D., and Stokes, D. (1974), *Political Change in Britain*, 2nd edn (London: Macmillan).

Carrington, Lord (1988), *Reflect on Things Past* (London: Collins).

Cashmore, E., and Troyna, B. (1982), *Black Youth in Crisis* (London: Allen & Unwin).

Central Office of Information (1975), *The Monarchy in Britain* (London: HMSO).

Chapman, B. (1963), *British Government Observed* (London: Allen & Unwin).

Chapman, R. (1970), *The Higher Civil Service in Britain* (London: Constable).

Chubb, B. (1982), *The Government and Politics of Ireland*, 2nd edn (Stanford: Stanford University Press).

Claiborne, L. (1979). *Race And Law in Britain and the United States* (London: Minority Rights Group).

Clarke, M. (1988), 'The policy-making process', in M. Smith, S. Smith and B. White (eds.), *British Foreign Policy* (London: Unwin Hyman), pp. 71–95.

Clutterbuck, R. (1977), 'Threats to public order in Britain', unpublished paper presented to the annual conference of the Political Studies Association.

(1981), *The Media and Political Violence* (London: Macmillan).

Crick, B. (1970), *The Reform of Parliament*, 2nd edn (London: Weidenfeld & Nicolson).

Crouch, C. (1979), *The Politics of Industrial Relations* (Glasgow: Fontana).

(1982), 'The peculiar relationship: the party and the unions', in D. Kavanagh, *The Politics of the Labour Party* (London: Allen & Unwin), pp. 171–90.

Dale, H. E. (1941), *The Higher Civil Service of Great Britain* (Oxford: Oxford University Press).

Dearlove, J. (1979), *The Reorganization of British Local Government* (Cambridge: Cambridge University Press).

Drewry, G. (ed.) (1985), *The New Select Committees* (Oxford: Clarendon Press).

Drewry, G. and Butcher, T. (1988), *The Civil Service Today* (Oxford: Blackwell).

Drucker, H. (1979), *Doctrine and Ethos in the Labour Party* (London: Allen & Unwin).

Dunleavy, P., and Husbands, C. T. (1984), 'The social basis of British electoral alignments in 1983', unpublished paper presented to the annual conference of the UK Political Studies Association.

Dunleavy, P., and Husbands, C. T. (1985), *British Democracy at the Crossroads* (London: Allen & Unwin).

Dunleavy, P., and Rhodes, R. A. W. (1983), 'Beyond Whitehall', in H. Drucker, P. Dunleavy, A. Gamble and G. Peele (eds.), *Developments in British Politics* (London: Macmillan).

Elcock, H. J. (1982), *Local Government* (London: Methuen).

Ewing, K. (1987), *The Funding of Political Parties in Britain* (Cambridge: Cambridge University Press).

Finer, S. E. (1956), 'The individual responsibility of ministers', *Public Administration*, vol. 34, pp. 377–96.

(1966), *Anonymous Empire*, 2nd edn (London: Pall Mall Press).

(ed.) (1975), *Adversary Politics and Electoral Reform* (London: Anthony Wigram).

Fry, G. K. (1984), 'The attack on the Civil Service and the response of the insiders', *Parliamentary Affairs*, vol. 37, pp. 353–63.

Fulton Committee (1968), *Report of the Committee on the Civil Service* (London: HMSO, Cmnd 3638).

Gamble, A. (1981), *Britain in Decline* (London: Macmillan).

Garrett, J. (1980), *Managing the Civil Service* (London: Heinemann).

Gladstone, W. E. (1879), *Gleanings from Past Years* (London: John Murray).

Grant, W. (1981), *The Political Economy of Industrial Policy* (London: Butterworth).

Griffith, J. A. G. (1966), *Central Departments and Local Authorities* (London: Allen & Unwin).

(1981), *The Politics of the Judiciary*, 2nd edn (London: Fontana).

Grove, J. W. (1962), *Government and Industry in Britain* (London: Longman).

Habermas, J. (1975), *Legitimation Crisis* (Boston, Mass.: Beacon Press).

Halsey, A. H. (1987), 'Social trends since World War II', in *Social Trends 17* (London: HMSO).

Hart, V. (1978), *Distrust and Democracy* (Cambridge: Cambridge University Press).

Hastings, M. and Jenkins, S. (1983), *The Battle for the Falklands* (London: Michael Joseph).

Hayward, J. E. S. (1976), 'Institutional inertia and political impetus in France and Britain', *European Journal of Political Research*, vol. 4, pp. 341–59.

Heath, A., Jowell, R., and Curtice, J. (1985), *How Britain Votes* (Oxford: Pergamon Press).

Heclo, H., and Wildavsky, A. (1974), *The Private Government of Public Money* (London: Macmillan).

Hennessy, P. (1986), *Cabinet* (Oxford: Blackwell).

Himmelweit, H. T., Humphreys, P., Jaeger, M., and Katz, M. (1981), *How Voters Decide* (London: Academic Press).

Hoskyns, Sir John (1983), 'Whitehall and Westminster: an outsider's view', *Parliamentary Affairs*, vol. 36, pp. 137–47.

Hunt, N. (ed.) (1964), *Whitehall and Beyond* (London: BBC Publications).

Hurwitt, M., and Thornton, P. (1989), *Civil Liberty: The NCCL Guide* (Harmondsworth: Penguin).

Ingle, S. (1987), *The British Party System* (Oxford: Blackwell).

Jenkins, R. (1959), 'Obscenity, censorship and the law', *Encounter*, October.

(1967), *Asquith* (Glasgow: Fontana).

Jones, G., and Stewart, J. (1983), *The Case for Local Government* (London: Allen & Unwin).

Jowell, J., and Oliver, D. (1985), *The Changing Constitution* (Oxford: Oxford University Press).

Jowell, R., and Airey, C. (eds.) (1984), *British Social Attitudes: The 1984 Report* (Aldershot: Gower).

Judge, D. (ed.) (1983), *The Politics of Parliamentary Reform* (London: Heinemann).

Kavanagh, D. (1980), 'Political culture in Great Britain: the decline of the civic culture', in G. A. Almond and S. Verba (eds.), *The Civic Culture Revisited* (Boston, Mass.: Little, Brown).

(ed.) (1982), *The Politics of the Labour Party* (London: Allen & Unwin).

Kennet, W. (ed.) (1982), *The Rebirth of Britain* (London: Weidenfeld & Nicolson).

King, A. (1975), 'Overload: problems of governing in the 1970s', *Political Studies*, vol. 23, pp. 284–96.

(ed.) (1985), *The British Prime Minister* (London: Macmillan).

Kogan, M. (1975), *Educational Policy-Making* (London: Allen & Unwin).

Layton-Henry, Z. (ed.) (1980), *Conservative Party Politics* (London: Macmillan).

Lees, J. D., and Kimber, R. (eds.) (1972), *Political Parties in Modern Britain* (London: Routledge & Kegan Paul).

Lees, J. D., and Shaw, M. (eds.) (1979), *Committees in Legislatures: A Comparative Analysis* (Durham, NC: Duke University Press).

Leys, C. (1983), *Politics in Britain* (Toronto: Toronto University Press).

McGrew, T. (1988), 'Security and order: the economic dimension', in M. Smith, S. Smith and B. White (eds.), *British Foreign Policy* (London: Unwin Hyman), pp. 99–123.

Mackenzie, W. J. M., and Grove, J. W. (1957), *Central Administration in Britain* (London: Longman, Green).

Mackintosh, J. P. (1977a), *The British Cabinet*, 3rd edn (London: Stevens).

(1977b), *The Government and Politics of Britain*, 4th edn (London: Hutchinson).

Madgwick, P. J. (1977), 'Linguistic conflict in Wales: a problem in the design of government', in G. Williams (ed.), *Social and Cultural Changes in Contemporary Wales* (London: Routledge & Kegan Paul).

Mansergh, N. (1975), *The Irish Question, 1840–1921*, 3rd edn (London: Allen & Unwin).

Mark, Sir Robert (1977), *Policing a Perplexed Society* (London: Allen & Unwin).

Marsh, A. (1977), *Protest and Political Consciousness* (Beverly Hills, Calif.: Sage).

Marsh, D., and Chambers, J. (1981), *Abortion Politics* (London: Junction Books).

Marshall, G. (1984), *Constitutional Conventions* (Oxford: Clarendon Press).

Marshall, G. (ed.) (1989), *Ministerial Responsibility* (Oxford: Oxford University Press).

May, Timothy (1984), 'The businessman's burden: rates and the CBJ', *Politics*, vol. 4, pp. 34–8.

Mellors, C. (1978), *The British MP* (Farnborough: Saxon House).

Miliband, R. (1969), *The State in Capitalist Society* (London: Weidenfeld & Nicolson).

(1982), *Capitalist Democracy in Britain* (Oxford: Oxford University Press).

Moran, M. (1985), *Politics and Society in Britain* (London: Macmillan).

Morrison, H. (1954), *Government and Parliament* (Oxford: Oxford University Press).

Moxon-Browne, E. (1983), Nation, Class and Creed in Northern Ireland (Aldershot: Gower).

Newton, K. (1976), *Second-City Politics* (Oxford: Clarendon Press).

Northedge, F. S. (1974), *Descent From Power* (London: Allen & Unwin).

Norton, P. (1980), 'The Changing Face of the British House of Commons in the 1970s', *Legislative Studies Quarterly*, vol. 5, pp. 333–55.

(1981), *The Commons in Perspective* (Oxford: Martin Robertson).

(1982), *The Constitution in Flux* (Oxford: Martin Robertson).

(1984), *The British Polity* (New York: Longman).

(1985), 'Behavioural changes: backbench independence in the 1980s', in P. Norton (ed.), *Parliament in the 1980s* (Oxford, Blackwell).

Norton, P., and Aughey, A. (1981), *Conservatives and Conservatism* (London: Temple Smith).

O'Brien, C. C. (1972), *States of Ireland* (London: Hutchinson).

(1980), *Neighbours* (London: Faber).

Olson, M. (1982), *The Rise and Decline of Nations* (New Haven, Conn.: Yale University Press).

Pinto-Duschinsky, M. (1985), 'Trends in British political funding 1979–83', *Parliamentary Affairs*, vol. 38, pp. 328–47.

Potter, A. M. (1961), *Organized Groups in British National Politics* (London: Faber).

Ranney, A. (1965), *Pathways to Parliament* (London: Macmillan).

Richards, P. G. (1959), *Honourable Members* (London: Faber).

(1970), *Parliament and Conscience* (London: Allen & Unwin).

(1972), *The Backbenchers* (London: Faber).

Richardson, J. J., and Jordan, A. G. (1979), *Governing under Pressure* (Oxford: Martin Robertson).

Richardson, J. J., and Moon, J. (1985), *Unemployment in the UK: Politics and Policies* (London: Heinemann).

Ridley, F. F. (1983), 'The British Civil Service and politics: principles in question and traditions in flux', *Parliamentary Affairs*, vol. 36, pp. 28–48.

Ridley, N. (1988), *The Local Right: Enabling not Providing* (London: Centre for Policy Studies).

Robertson, G. (1989), *Freedom, the Individual and the Law* (Harmondsworth: Penguin).

Robson, W. A. (ed.) (1956), *The Civil Service in Britain and France* (London: Hogarth Press).
Rodgers, W. (1983), 'The SDP and Liberal Party in alliance', *Political Quarterly*, vol. 54, pp. 354–62.
Rose, R. (1971), *Governing without Consensus* (London: Faber).
(1974), *The Problem of Party Government* (London: Macmillan).
(1980a) *Politics in England*, 3rd edn (London: Faber).
(1980b) *Do Parties Make a Difference?* (Chatham, NJ: Chatham House).
(1983), 'Still the era of party government', *Parliamentary Affairs*, vol. 36, pp. 282–99.
Rose, R., and McAllister, I. (1986), *Voters Begin to Choose* (London: Sage).
Rosebery, L. (1899), *Sir Robert Peel* (London: Cassell).
Sarlvik, B., and Crewe, I. (1983), *Decade of Dealignment* (Cambridge: Cambridge University Press).
Scarman, Lord (1982), *The Brixton Disorders: 10–12 April 1981* (Harmondsworth: Penguin; first published London: HMSO, 1981).
Shackleton, M. (1984), 'Britain and the EEC', in R. L. Borthwick and J. E. Spence (eds.), *British Politics in Perspective* (Leicester: Leicester University Press).
Shell, D. R. (1985), 'The House of Lords and the Thatcher government', *Parliamentary Affairs*, vol. 38, pp. 16–32.
Sisson, C. H. (1959), *The Spirit of British Administration* (London: Faber).
Smith, D. J. (1977), *Racial Disadvantage in Britain* (Harmondsworth: Penguin).
Smith, M., Smith, S., and White, B. (eds.) (1988), *British Foreign Policy* (London: Unwin Hyman).
Stacey, F. (1971), *The British Ombudsman* (Oxford: Oxford University Press).
Stephenson, H. (1982), *Claret and Chips: The Rise of the SDP* (London: Michael Joseph).
Street, H. (1963), *Freedom, the Individual and the Law* (Harmondsworth: Penguin).
Thompson, G. (1984), 'Economic intervention in the postwar economy', in G. McLennan, D. Held and S. Hall (eds.), *State and Society in Contemporary Britain* (Cambridge: Polity Press), pp. 77–118.
Utley, T. E. (1975), *Lessons of Ulster* (London: Dent).
Vital, D. (1968), *The Making of British Foreign Policy* (London: Allen & Unwin).
Walkland, S. A. (1968), *The Legislative Process in Great Britain* (London: Allen & Unwin).
(ed.) (1979), *The House of Commons in the Twentieth Century* (Oxford: Clarendon Press).
Wallace, W. (1977), *The Foreign Policy Process in Britain* (London: Allen & Unwin).
Wheare, K. C. (1955), *Government by Committee* (Oxford: Clarendon Press).
(1973), *Maladministration and Its Remedies* (London: Stevens).
Whitaker, B. (1979), *The Police in Society* (London: Eyre Methuen).
Williams, F. (1961), *A Prime Minister Remembers* (London: Heinemann).
Williams, R. (1980), *The Nuclear Power Decisions: British Policies, 1953–78* (London: Croom Helm).
Wilson, F. M. G. (1959), 'The roots of entry of new members of the British Cabinet, 1868–1958', *Political Studies*, vol. 7, pp. 222–32.
Woodham-Smith, C. (1962), *The Great Hunger* (London: Hamish Hamilton).
Wootton, G. (1978), *Pressure Politics in Contemporary Britain* (Lexington, Mass.: D. C. Heath).
Zentner, P. (1982), *Social Democracy in Britain* (London: John Martin).

Index

DATE DUE

GAYLORD   PRINTED IN U.S.A.